Pakistan 2005

Pakistan 2005

EDITED BY
CHARLES H. KENNEDY
AND CYNTHIA BOTTERON

OXFORD
UNIVERSITY PRESS

OXFORD

UNIVERSITY PRESS

Great Clarendon Street, Oxford OX2 6DP

Oxford University Press is a department of the University of Oxford.
It furthers the University's objective of excellence in research, scholarship,
and education by publishing worldwide in

Oxford New York

Auckland Cape Town Dar es Salaam Hong Kong Karachi
Kuala Lumpur Madrid Melbourne Mexico City Nairobi
New Delhi Shanghai Taipei Toronto

with offices in

Argentina Austria Brazil Chile Czech Republic France Greece
Guatemala Hungary Italy Japan South Korea Poland Portugal
Singapore Switzerland Thailand Turkey Ukraine Vietnam

ISBN-13: 978-0-19-547120-5
ISBN-10: 0-19-547120-2

Typeset in Calisto MT
Printed in Pakistan by
Print Vision, Karachi.
Published by
Ameena Saiyid, Oxford University Press
No. 38, Sector 15, Korangi Industrial Area, PO Box 8214
Karachi-74900, Pakistan.

Contents

Preface

This is the fifth volume in the Pakistan Briefing Series initiated in 1992 originally with Westview Press and in affiliation with the American Institute of Pakistan Studies. The earlier volumes in this series were: Charles H. Kennedy, ed., *Pakistan: 1992* (Westview Press, 1993); Charles H. Kennedy and Rasul B. Rais, eds., *Pakistan: 1995* (Westview Press, 1995); Craig Baxter and Charles H. Kennedy, eds., *Pakistan: 1997* (Westview Press, 1998); and Charles H. Kennedy and Craig Baxter, eds., *Pakistan: 2000* (Lexington Books; Oxford University Press, 2001). In general, this series covers issues relevant to Pakistan's domestic politics, foreign policy and economy. As in earlier volumes each of the contributors to this volume is a specialist on Pakistan, and each has had recent research experience in the state relevant to their respective contribution.

In Chapter 1, Charles H. Kennedy presents a brief overview of recent political issues that have dominated politics in Pakistan and serves as an introduction to the volume.

Faisal Bari provides a detailed analysis of Pakistan's macroeconomic performance (2003–2005) in Chapter 2. Bari argues that Pakistan's recent economic successes are fragile and are largely hostage to international events over which Pakistani decision-makers have little control. This chapter serves as a sequel to his very useful contribution to *Pakistan: 2000*.

Indo-Pakistan relations are discussed in Chapters 3 and 4, authored respectively by Rasul B. Rais and Robert G. Wirsing. Rais' analysis paints a fairly dismal picture for the prospects of meaningful and long-term improvement in such relations unless and until the core issue of Kashmir is resolved to the satisfaction of both parties—an unlikely scenario. Wirsing is more optimistic concerning an improvement in Indo-Pak relations. Although like Rais, he cautions that the recent and noteworthy improvement of relations will only result in long-term improvement if there is a well intentioned and concerted effort made by decision-makers in both states—again, an unlikely scenario.

Chapter 5 authored by Aqil Shah presents a very creative and perceptive analysis of the interplay of international donor interests and domestic policy responses to such interests which ultimately resulted in Pakistan's much-heralded and discussed local government devolution. The Local Government Plan is perhaps the most important domestic initiative of Musharraf's government and aspects of the Plan are also discussed in chapters six and eight.

In Chapter 6, authored by Charles H. Kennedy, an attempt is made to define a 'military governance paradigm' which encompasses the experience of Pakistan's three military regimes: Ayub, Zia, and Musharraf. In this chapter Kennedy delineates ten sequential steps which each of Pakistan's military rulers have followed throughout the course of their respective tenures—one of these steps is to 're-invent local government.'

Cynthia Botteron (Shippensburg University) in Chapter 7 presents a detailed analysis of the Supreme Court's role in validating Musharraf's (self-serving?) revisions to the electoral process which established educational qualifications for holding political office. Her analysis of the Pakistan Muslim League (Q) decision explores both the logic and political consequences of the revision.

In Chapter 8, Saeed Shafqat and Saeed Wahlah return to the discussion of the effects of the Local Government devolution plan on the civilian bureaucracy. They argue that the Plan has had the effect of significantly restructuring local administration and, as a consequence, has wholly altered the district administration system of governance as well as directly targeting the lineal descendent of the Civil Service of Pakistan—the District Management Group.

In Chapter 9, Christopher Candland explores the *madrassa* system of education in Pakistan. He concludes, *inter alia*, that Pakistan's *madrassas* have flourished in recent years largely owing to the desperate and growing need for affordable primary and secondary education in the state; and that the stereotypical portrayal of *madrassas* as 'training grounds for Islamic terrorists' is largely misguided.

Finally, Kathleen McNeil has prepared an exhaustive Chronology of Events in Pakistan since Musharraf's assumption of power. This chronology continues the chronologies presented in earlier volumes in the series.

This volume is the collective responsibility of the two editors as well as Oxford University Press, Karachi. We would like to thank Ameena Saiyid, Managing Director, Oxford University Press Pakistan for her continued support. The co-editors are particularly grateful that Oxford University Press has offered a permanent home for the Pakistan Briefing series and continues to tolerate with good humour the co-editors' procrastinating tendencies. Closer to home Hank Kennedy would like to express his particular gratitude to Carolyn and Kipp Kramer who provided him with a place to work, their beach cottage at Nags Head.

We also gratefully acknowledge the help of our respective universities—Wake Forest and Shippensburg; and the continuing support of our spouses—Patricia Poe and David Nash.

Charles H. Kennedy   Cynthia Botteron
Winston-Salem, NC   Shippensburg, Pa

This book is dedicated in memory of our fathers-in-law C. Horton Poe and Donald J. Nash

About the Authors

Faisal Bari (Ph.D., McGill) is an associate professor of economics at the Lahore University of Management Sciences. Currently on leave from LUMS he is the Executive Director of the Mahbub ul-Haq Development Centre in Islamabad. Professor Bari has published extensively in fields relevant to his expertise—his research interests include the areas of applied microeconomics and game theory, development theory, and industrial organization.

Cynthia Botteron (Ph.D., Texas) is an assistant professor of political science at Shippensburg University. Her primary research interest is the impact of global norms on the formulation of domestic policy and state capacity building. She has conducted field research in Pakistan and India where she was sponsored by the National Science Foundation and the American Institute of Pakistan Studies.

Christopher Candland (Ph.D., Columbia) is an assistant professor of political science at Wellesley College. His research focuses on the politics of human development in South and Southeast Asia—particularly in the fields of labour, health and education. He has conducted research in Pakistan with the support of the American Institute of Pakistan Studies and the Guggenheim Foundation.

Charles H. Kennedy (Ph.D., Duke) is a professor of political science at Wake Forest University. He has published extensively on various topics relating to Pakistan including politics, law, administration and ethnonationalism. He was the second and last Director of the American Institute of Pakistan Studies, serving in that capacity from 1988–2002. He has conducted extensive research in South Asia (particularly Pakistan and Bangladesh) since 1975.

Kathleen Mc Neil (MA Wake Forest University) is a specialist on women's issues in the Muslim world. She has been affiliated with the Women Living Under Muslim Law project and was co-editor of *Pakistan at the Millennium*. She conducted field research in Pakistan with the support of the American Institute of Pakistan Studies.

Rasul B. Rais (Ph.D., UC Santa Barbara) is a professor of political science at the Lahore University of Management Sciences. Before coming to LUMS Professor Rais was Director of the Area Studies Centre at Quaid-i-Azam University. Professor Rais has held numerous international fellowships, including the Fulbright, and during his long and distinguished career has taught and/or been affiliated with Columbia, Stanford, Harvard and Wake Forest universities. At Columbia he held the Quaid-i-Azam chair. He is the author of numerous publications which deal with Pakistan's foreign policy

Saeed Shafqat (Ph.D., Pennsylvania) is the Director of the National Institute of Pakistan Studies in Islamabad. Before coming to NIPS he held the Quaid-i-Azam Chair at Columbia University on leave from his permanent position as Chief Instructor of the Civil Services Academy, a position he has held since 1988. He has held numerous international fellowships including the Fulbright. Professor Shafqat has published extensively on domestic political and policy issues related to Pakistan.

Aqil Shah (M.Phil., Oxford) is a doctoral student in political science at Columbia University. At Oxford he was a Rhodes Scholar. His research interests include the comparative politics of democratization and authoritarianism in South Asia and especially in Pakistan.

Saeed Wahlah (MPA Rutgers) is a career civil servant with the Government of Pakistan who currently serves as Additional Secretary, Finance (Local Government Finance Wing) with the Government of the Punjab. He is a former Hubert Humphrey Fellow. His research focuses on local government issues and he is a frequent contributor to relevant journals in Pakistan.

Robert G. Wirsing (Ph.D., Denver) is a professor in the Asia-Pacific Center for Security Studies. Prior to joining the APCSS he was a professor of international studies at the University of South Carolina. His primary research interests focus on the contemporary politics, international relations, and defense and security issues of South Asia. He is perhaps most-widely known for his well-regarded work on Kashmir. He has conducted extensive field work in South Asia (particularly Pakistan and India) since the late 1960s.

1

Political Issues in 2004*
Charles H. Kennedy

The Seventeenth Amendment and Short-Term Promises

The deadlock over the validity of the Legal Framework Order (LFO) which dominated politics in Pakistan following President Musharraf's promulgation of the Order on 21 August 2002 was 'officially resolved' on 31 December 2003 by the passage of the Seventeenth Amendment to Pakistan's Constitution. However, to gain the necessary two-thirds majority for passage of the amendment in the bicameral Pakistani parliament required that the government of then Prime Minister Zafarullah Jamali and President Musharraf make a deal with the Islamist Muttahida Majlis-i-Amal (MMA—the largest opposition political party). The terms of the deal were that MMA parliamentarians would abstain from relevant votes in the Senate and the National Assembly in exchange for three concessions from the government:

1) The government would drop the provision in the LFO which had extended the mandatory retirement age of superior court judges from sixty-five to sixty-eight years;
2) The government would drop the provisions in the LFO which mandated the establishment of a National Security Council; and
3) Musharraf would be obliged to relinquish his position as Chief of Army Staff (COAS) by 31 December 2004.[1]

---

* This is an expanded version of Charles H. Kennedy, 'Pakistan 2005: Running Very Fast to Stay in the Same Place', *Asian Survey* Vol. 45, no. 1 (January 2005).

With this deal in place the Seventeenth Amendment gained passage and accordingly several contentious provisions of the LFO were legally validated including:

1) The reintroduction of the power of the president (Article 58) and the governors (Article 112) to respectively dismiss the national and provincial assemblies.;
2) The confirmation of validity of the 2002 referendum which had elected Musharraf president for a five year term; and
3) The confirmation of the validity of the general election of 2002 and the creation of the Jamali government.

But, the crowning achievement of the 'deal' was the blanket legal validation of Musharraf's actions taken since assuming office in October 1999 (Article 270AA).[2]

The first 'promise' that the mandatory retirement age of superior court judges would revert to the pre-LFO age of sixty-five was automatically fulfilled consequent with the passage of the Seventeenth Amendment. Accordingly, on 31 December 2003 ten superior court judges including the Chief Justice and two other judges of the Supreme Court stood retired having exceeded the age of sixty-five. Justice Nazim Hussain Siddiqui became the new Chief Justice.[3] The second promise was fulfilled in that the NSC was disestablished by the Seventeenth Amendment. Nonetheless, the institutional role and functions of the NSC have largely been replicated by the newly-created National Command Authority (NCA).

At the time of writing of this chapter, General President Musharraf is still vigorously attempting to renege on the third promise he made with the MMA—the promise to relinquish his position as COAS by 31 December 2004. However, it is proving to be a hard promise to break. The opposition contends that the constitution disallows the president from holding two positions in the government simultaneously—a proposition which was accepted and recognized in the Seventeenth Amendment. Specifically, Article 41(2) of the constitution provides that a president must be a person eligible to become a member of the national assembly; and Article 63(1)(d) states that a person would not be eligible to become a member of the national assembly if 'he is holding a properly paid post in the service of Pakistan'. The LFO suspended Article 63(1)(d) but the Seventeenth Amendment inserted a clause in Article 41(7)(b) that 'Article 63(1)(d) will come into force from 31 December 2004'.[4] The government countered by introducing a bill before the National Assembly: 'President to Hold Another Office Act, 2004' in October. The bill would allow the President of Pakistan to hold another government service post but it would be valid 'only for the present holder of the office of the President'. After several stormy sessions which included walkouts by the opposition, the National Assembly passed the bill on 13 October.[5] But, this issue is far from being resolved. The MMA has refused to recognize the validity of the 'Another Office Act' and has threatened to disrupt the political system if Musharraf remains COAS past 31 December. It is also very likely that the bill will be challenged before the courts on the seemingly unassailable legal grounds that a provision of the constitution can only be revised through a formal amendment to the constitution. This option is unavailable to the government as it does not have enough support in parliament to pass a constitutional amendment against a recalcitrant opposition.

Also, during the year President Musharraf found occasion to informally utilize his newly-validated constitutional powers to 'dismiss' two governments. On 26 June, Prime Minister Jamali resigned his position amidst chronic rumors that he was being strongly encouraged, if not forced, to resign by Musharraf. In his resignation speech he curiously nominated his successor, Chaudhry Shujaat Hussain (the President of the Pakistan Muslim League [PML]), and even more curiously also stated that the latter nominee would only serve until Shaukat Aziz (the Finance Minister) could become eligible to hold the post. Pakistan's constitution mandates that a Prime Minister must be an elected member of the National Assembly. During the next several months Jamali's scenario was played out. On 29 June, Shujaat Hussain was elected Prime Minister securing a majority of 190 votes in the 342 seat house. When vacancies became available in two constituencies in July (Attock and Tharparkar), Shaukat Aziz duly filed his nomination papers and campaigned. In the subsequent by-elections held on 18 August,

Aziz won both seats making him a member of the National Assembly. Nine days later he was duly elected Prime Minister, securing 191 votes in the National Assembly.[6]

Although no formal explanation has been given by any of the principles for why Jamali offered his resignation, or why the government decided to pursue the unusually untidy process of electing a stand-in prime minister until Shaukat Aziz could secure the necessary credentials to assume the post, it is apparent that Musharraf orchestrated the process of government change. From this it is safe to assume that Musharraf is firmly in control of the government and that Musharraf is planning to remain in charge of the government for the foreseeable future—at least until the end of his five-year term (2007). It is important to note in this regard that Shaukat Aziz is not a professional politician but rather a technocrat—an economist and banker. Before Musharraf named him Finance Minister in 1999, he was a senior executive in Citibank. Musharraf is not looking to Shaukat Aziz to help him politically; rather he is hoping that Aziz will help him to govern in spite of politics.

During 2004 Musharraf made significant progress in validating the legal basis of his claim to govern. The passage of the Seventeenth Amendment formally legitimized his regime; and insulated him from prospective juridical challenge. Also, Musharraf was able to flex his newfound political muscle by orchestrating a change of government, and installing the hand-picked Shaukat Aziz to the office of prime minister. These are no small feats. But, during 2004, little if any progress was made with respect to democratizing the political process and opposition to Musharraf and to his regime hardened during the year. This was due in part to Musharraf's decision to renege on the promises that he made to the MMA to gain passage of the Seventeenth Amendment. And also because of the seemingly cavalier way that he manipulated the National Assembly regarding the appointment of Shaukat Aziz. Pakistan's parliament remained largely dysfunctional (its sessions chaotic; its accomplishments few) since its re-composition in 2002. The main cause of this dysfunction was originally the festering legacy of military rule and the profoundly undemocratic manner of regime change associated with the 1999 coup, and the subsequent promulgation of the LFO. Following the passage of the Seventeenth Amendment there was a glimmer of hope, albeit short-lived, that the 'deal' with the opposition would lead to enhancing the power of the politicians and of weakening the authority of the military. Unfortunately, President Musharraf's actions and political style during 2004 have dashed such hopes.

The Abdul Qadeer Khan Affair

During January 2004, evidence began to accumulate that Dr Abdul Qadeer Khan, the former head of Khan Research Laboratories (KRL); the 'father of Pakistan's nuclear weapons program', and accordingly the recipient of numerous state awards for services to the nation; a *bona fide* 'national hero' had transferred nuclear weapons secrets to several non-nuclear states including Libya, North Korea, and Iran. In early February, as evidence continued to mount in the international press implicating Khan's involvement and that of the KRL, A.Q. Khan submitted a 'mercy petition' to President Musharraf seeking clemency for his actions in 'view of his services to national security'. In an official statement, the government reported that in a meeting with President Musharraf 'Dr A.Q. Khan reconfirmed to the president the details of the proliferation activities that he had committed in the past and had admitted in earlier interviews with the investigative team appointed by the government'. The statement went on to say that Khan 'accepted full responsibility for the proliferation activities' and that he recognized that such activities 'were in clear violation of different Pakistani laws, could have seriously jeopardized Pakistan's nuclear capability and put the nation at risk'. On 5 February, President Musharraf pardoned A.Q. Khan; calling him a 'hero'.[7] But, subsequently he has been kept under house arrest and some of his property (ostensibly bought with the ill-gotten proceeds from selling nuclear secrets) has been reportedly confiscated by the government.

Although the details of Khan's misdeeds are beyond the scope of this chapter, it is important to note that the scale of his activities was quite significant consisting of dozens of transactions with several states and involving the transfer of tens of millions of dollars over a period of more than a decade. Virtually all narratives of the event claim that A.Q. Khan's primary, or perhaps sole motive, was to make money—personal gain.

This event was a public relations and diplomatic nightmare for the Pakistani government; and an implicit strategy was quickly formulated to deal with the problem, a strategy which has been rigorously followed since. First, the government claimed that the illegal transactions were entirely the work of Dr Khan and one other associate, Dr Mohammad Farooq, both employed by the KRL. No one in the current Pakistani government knew anything about the transfer, including the military and the ISI. Moreover, no one in previous governments, including former COASs, had any knowledge of Dr Khan's activities. Second, the disclosure of the affair came as a 'complete surprise' to the government—they found out about it at the same time and in the same way as the world community; through press reports. Third, the activities of Dr Khan have been completely halted and Pakistan's nuclear weapons system is under stable and responsible control. Fourth, steps have been taken to prevent any such event from happening in the future. And, fifth (and perhaps most importantly) Dr A.Q. Khan has been kept isolated from international officials and the press. During the year Pakistan has rejected numerous requests for interviews with him and has firmly resisted any attempts at extradition.

Of course, some of the above claims of the Pakistani government stretch the limits of credulity. Particularly hard to believe are the claims that Dr Khan acted alone and/or that no one in Pakistan's efficient and relatively intrusive military-security community would not have known something about Dr Khan's extensive activities. However, the international community wants to believe or perhaps needs to believe Pakistan's story. The United States has been particularly eager to express its support for the official Pakistani version of events; and even India, usually very skeptical of Pakistani government claims, has been relatively silent about the issue. Nevertheless, the A.Q. Khan affair is a ticking time bomb. President Musharraf lectured members of Pakistan's media at the 5 February news conference in which he announced the decision to pardon A.Q. Khan, by speculating that if the government, the army or both were implicated in nuclear proliferation 'the UN Security Council will immediately impose sanctions against us, next we will be asked to sign the NPT (Non-Proliferation Treaty) and the CTBT (Comprehensive Test Ban Treaty) and roll back, then we will be declared a rogue state and finally our vital interests would come under imminent physical danger'.[8]

Anti-Terrorism: International and Domestic Implications

The Musharraf administration was confronted with both a threat and an opportunity as a consequence of the horrific acts of 11 September 2001 and the resultant US response. Pakistan was 'asked' to comply with the US interpretation of the causes of, and remedies against international terrorism. In exchange, Pakistan would be 'cut a break' with respect to its lingering 'issues'. To be more precise, Pakistan was asked to:

1) Cut its ties with the Taliban government in Afghanistan;
2) Be helpful to US and coalition plans to attack and occupy Afghanistan;
3) Counter the anticipated extremist (anti-American) fallout likely to occur from the above within Pakistan;
4) Reduce sectarian violence within Pakistan; and
5) Curb alleged Pakistani state support for *jihadi* and/or terrorist activities related to the Kashmir issue.

In exchange, the US would be supportive of Pakistani attempts to improve its standing in the international community (particularly with respect to international financial institutions), and the US would not put too much official pressure on the military regime to 'democratize'. The US also held out the 'promise' that it would at least look with fresh eyes with regard to the Kashmir issue. Of course, underlying this implicit arrangement, the United States 'promised' not to target Pakistan, as a facilitator or harbour for international terror, if it complied with the US global war against terrorism.[9]

Musharraf promptly accepted the US 'offer' (perhaps it was an offer Pakistan could not refuse) and ever since both the US and Pakistan have complied with the terms of the implicit agreement. From the Pakistan side Musharraf moved quickly to beef up the largely dysfunctional Anti-Terrorism Courts, institutions which had been introduced by the predecessor civilian regime of Nawaz Sharif. Musharraf also banned several militant ('terrorist') sectarian and Kashmir *jihadi* groups, arrested many of their members and disrupted their financial bases. Pakistan also dropped its erstwhile support for the Taliban and became a front-line state in the war against terrorism—crucial to the US-led war and later coalition occupation of Afghanistan. Pakistan has also provided lukewarm official support for the US-led war in Iraq. The US has largely made good on its promises as well. Generally speaking, Pakistan's anti-terrorism regime has been officially typified as pro-active and in accord with the US' interest in the region and Pakistan has benefited from this perception. Most importantly, Pakistan has rarely been mentioned as one of the states that should undergo regime change (cf. Iraq, Iran, Syria etc.) as a result of changed international realities. Indeed, Pakistan (and particularly the Musharraf government) is most often typified, at least by US decision-makers, as part of the solution, not part of the problem. Similarly, Pakistan has largely been 'forgiven' for its past transgressions (nuclear testing, the Kargil Operation, the 1999 military coup, the Legal Framework Order, etc.). Indeed, the US and to a more limited extent the G-8 have normalized relations with Pakistan. Pakistan has resumed its long-standing security relationship with the US, and Pakistan is once again privy to international assistance from the G-8, especially the US.[10]

But, this arrangement is fragile. In December 2003 two unsuccessful assassination attempts were made against Musharraf—both targeted Musharraf's heavily guarded military convoy as it made its twice daily trip between Rawalpindi and Islamabad.[11] Suspects were subsequently arrested, and the attempts have been characterized by the government as related to Musharraf's crackdown against international terrorism. Whether this explanation is wholly accurate or not, Musharraf's anti-terrorism and pro-American policies have clearly sparked opposition to his regime.

Also highly controversial has been the Pakistan military's ongoing South Waziristan Operation. Starting in February 2004 and sharply escalating in the late summer and early fall, Pakistani military and para-military units have been fighting a small scale, yet bloody war, against tribal *lashkars* mostly from the Mahsud tribe in the Pushto-speaking Federally Administered Tribal Area of Waziristan. The ostensible purpose of this operation is to root out and capture or kill remnants of the Taliban and foreign mercenaries ('terrorists', '*jihadis*', 'Al-Qaeda') who have allegedly found shelter in the forbidding terrain of the region.[12] The fiercely independent Pushtuns, who inhabit the tribal areas, have given protection to such strangers, and deeply resent the Pakistani government's interference in what they consider to be their own sovereign affairs. The FATA is only peripherally integrated into the Pakistani state; many of the tribal militants consider Pakistan to be a foreign state and the presence of its military to be a foreign occupation. Accordingly, previous governments in Pakistan, including Musharraf's, prior to 2004, have been exceedingly reluctant to interfere in the affairs of the tribal agencies. However, the US government has long been concerned about the sanctuary provided to the Taliban and foreign mercenaries in Pakistan's tribal areas and has encouraged Pakistan to close this escape route. Until 2004, Musharraf was able to stave off such pressure. But, perhaps owing to fallout from the A.Q. Khan affair, Pakistan's cooperation in this venture became a litmus test of Pakistan's continued participation in the global war against terrorism.

Although the Pakistan government has kept tight control over the media's coverage of the Waziristan Operation, a consensus narrative has emerged that the Operation has cost the lives of well over a hundred Pakistani soldiers; as well as occasioning considerable 'collateral' damage to tribal militants and civilians. Thousands of villagers have sought refuge in surrounding districts of Pakistan. Few foreign militants have been captured or killed by Pakistan military (of the handful captured or killed, most have been

Chechens), and no major leader of the Taliban or Al-Qaeda, let
alone Osama bin Laden or Mullah Omar have been located. There
is widespread domestic opposition to Pakistan's involvement in the
Operation and a common belief that Musharraf's actions have been
orchestrated by Washington and that Pakistan's national security is
actually being harmed by the military's involvement in the
Operation. Both the Human Rights Commission of Pakistan and
the Peshawar Bar Association have condemned the operation on
the grounds of human rights violations. The MMA has also typified
the Operation as a form of racism—targeting Pushtun nationals.

From the American side there is also increasing evidence that
the US is re-thinking its implicit bargain with Pakistan. The A.Q.
Khan affair has seriously weakened the carefully nurtured
proposition that Pakistan (and the Musharraf regime) is crucial to
the success of the US' global strategy against terrorism. Perhaps
most ominous is the introduction of the 'Black Market Elimination
Act' sponsored by Reps. Tom Lantos and Gary Ackerman before
the House's Committee on International Relations in August.
Reminiscent of the infamous Pressler Amendment, the Act would
place restrictions on US economic and military assistance to
Pakistan unless the President of the US certifies to Congress that
there is a 'rollback of the Khan nuclear network'.[13] Regardless of
fate of this legislation, it is apparent that the US-Pakistan anti-
terrorism entente is a temporary instrumental arrangement—one
that is not likely to survive the decade.

Notes

1. For details see Charles H. Kennedy, 'A User's Guide to Guided Democracy: Musharraf and the Pakistani Military Governance Paradigm' (chapter six) in this volume.
2. 'Text of 17th Amendment Bill' *Dawn* (30 December 2003); I.A. Rehman, 'Grand Deal 2003', *Dawn* (5 January 2004). The text of Article 270 AA is found in chapter six in this volume.
3. 'New Chief Justice Takes Oath: 10 Judges Retire', *Dawn* (1 January 2004).
4. Ghafoor Ahmed, 'Constitution, Oath and the Uniform', *Dawn* (28 September 2004).

5. 'Bill on President in Uniform Moved in NA' *Dawn* (9 October 2004); Raja Asghar and Ahmed Hassan, 'Dual Office Bill Passed Amid Protests', *Dawn* (15 October 2004).
6. Numerous news articles and editorials found in *Dawn* (27 June–5 September 2004). Particularly useful were: Irfan Hussain, 'Musharraf's Dilemma' *Dawn* (3 July 2004); Ardeshir Cowasjee, 'The Jokers in the Pack', *Dawn* (5 September 2004); and Raja Asghar, 'Aziz Elected as Opposition Boycotts Vote' *Dawn* (28 August).
7. For text of A.Q. Khan's statement see: Rafaqat Ali, 'Dr Khan Seeks Pardon', *Dawn* (5 February 2004). Also see, Peter LaVoy and Feroz Hassan Khan, 'Rogue or Responsible Nuclear Power? Making Sense of Pakistan's Nuclear Practices', *Strategic Insights*, Vol. 3, no. 2 (February 2004).
8. M. Ziauddin, 'Dr A.Q. Khan Pardoned', *Dawn* (6 February 2004).
9. For background see Charles H. Kennedy, 'The Creation and Development of Pakistan's Anti-Terrorism Regime, 1997-2002', in Satu Limaye, Robert Wirsing, and Mohan Malik eds., *Religious Radicalism and Security in South Asia* (Honolulu: Asia-Pacific Center for Security Studies, 2004), pp. 387-411.
10. For instance the US introduced an economic aid package in 2003 which would provide Pakistan $3 billion in economic aid over a period of five years. Similarly, the US conferred the status of a 'major non-NATO ally' on Pakistan in June 2004.
11. Najmuddin Shaikh, 'The Assassination Attempts', *Dawn* (31 December 2003).
12. Ishmail Khan, 'Operation in S. Waziristan', *Dawn* (19 February 2004); M. Ilyas Khan, 'Who are These People' *Herald* (April 2004); numerous news articles in *Dawn* (June 2004-October 2004).
13. Nadeem Malik, 'Bill on Pak-Specific Sanctions in US House', *The News International* (7 August 2004); Anwar Iqbal, 'Lawmakers Want More Control Over Pakistan', *The Washington Times* (18 August 2004).

2

Macroeconomic Performance and Prospects
Faisal Bari[1]

Introduction

The President of Pakistan General Pervez Musharraf, the elected Prime Minister Shaukat Aziz, the last Prime Minister Mir Zafarullah Khan Jamali, and numerous ministers and government officials have been claiming, since the start of 2003, that the economy of Pakistan is 'ready for takeoff'.[2] They build their case of revival and bright future prospects on the facts that GDP growth has started to return to the mean, and GNI growth has been very healthy largely due to the large remittance inflows from overseas Pakistanis, more relaxed lending from various multilateral lenders, and aid inflows in the post-September 11 world. These increased inflows have eased pressure from our foreign account and Pakistan has not only been able to manage international debt better, it has also been able to pay off some of the more expensive debt, reschedule most of the rest, and build dollar reserves of more than $12 billion. The favourable foreign account situation has also allowed the State Bank of Pakistan (SBP) to keep the exchange rate stable, bring down inflation, and lower domestic interest rates.

The second argument for 'takeoff' is that the government insists that the structural reforms carried out over the last decade and a half are finally paying off. These reforms, discussed in detail later, consisted of reductions in the budget deficit, rationalization of government role and size, downsizing of government, privatization, liberalization and decentralization, taxation reforms, removal of subsidies, tariff reductions and rationalization, and major reforms in the financial sector of the country. The financial sector, SBP claims,[3] is on much sounder footing. Privatization and downsizing have allowed the budget deficits to come down and taxation reforms, the government claims, are starting to yield benefits in terms of more receipts. The success of these reforms should bring the investors back again.

Thus, the official position is that given macroeconomic stability, with low interest rates and rate of inflation with a stable exchange rate, private investment and economic activity should soon pick up. Stability is now based on sounder structures, hence the recovery should be more permanent which will keep us on the path of rapid growth—we are now ready for 'takeoff' and for assuming a high growth trajectory.[4]

However, some commentators have pointed out another side of the picture: Islamabad, we might have a problem. This side of the picture is presented with the help of Tables 1 and 2.[5]

Table 1 shows that where Pakistan made steady progress in reducing poverty up to the late 1980s,[6] poverty on the whole started to increase since then and the trend is continuing. Though urban poverty has increased in the last few years only, rural poverty has increased through the decade of the 1990s. In 2003 we are almost at the same place as we were in the 1970s. The poverty trend is reinforced by the analysis of inequality. The Gini Co-efficient has increased significantly in the 1990s, and where the percentage share of top 20 percent of households, in national income, has increased over the 1990s, the share of the poorest 20 per cent of households as well as the middle 60 per cent has decreased substantially. The last column of Table 1(a) shows that over the same period unemployment, even given the government definition which has often been criticized for underestimating the true picture, has increased from 1.4 per cent in the 1980s to 7.8 per cent in 2003; which means every tenth person seeking work cannot find it. One can only guess at the increase in misery that must have accompanied the above changes for the poor, the disabled and the old with no governmental safety 'nets'.

Table 2 shows that almost 50 per cent of the Pakistani population is still illiterate. It also shows that we spend only 1.7 per cent and 0.7 per cent of our GNP on education and health respectively. These are figures for a country with a population of about 150 million people out of whom 32 per cent live below the poverty line. On these dimensions Pakistan lags behind most of its South Asian neighbours and if the majority of the people in Pakistan do not see that the country is ready for a 'takeoff', is this so strange?

In the sections that follow, we will analyze the state of the economy in some detail. We will try to see how we can, if at all, reconcile the contrasting views that have been given above. In the next section we will start our analysis with the macroeconomic picture. In the third we will analyze the agricultural, industrial, financial and infrastructure and social sectors in detail. These constitute the main sectors of the economy. In the fourth section we discuss some of the salient institutional reform efforts that have been attempted by the state in the last few years. We focus on the efforts that could potentially impact the macroeconomic conditions the most. The concluding section will bring the argument together and come back to the reconciliation issue.

Macroeconomic Trends and Performance

An encouraging sign for Pakistanis has been the recent improvements in the GDP growth rate of the country. After a number of years of sluggish performance we have crossed the 5 per cent per annum mark once more. Pakistan has traditionally had a fairly healthy GDP growth rate, on average it has stayed above the 5 per cent per annum mark, but the performance of the 1990s has been a clear deviation. Apart from 1995 and 1996, the GDP growth rate has been below the 5 per cent mark, and in some years, 1997, 1993, and 2001, GDP growth rates have fallen well below even the 3 per cent mark. Table 3 gives the detailed GDP performance.

The slowdown in GDP growth in the 1990s is reflected in the slowdown in both agriculture as well as industry growth rates. These will be studied in detail later in the following sections. Looked at from the angle of either the traditional or new growth theories, the importance of domestic savings and investment cannot be overestimated in determining the growth pattern and economic trajectory of a country. Bari and Cheema (2003) detail the differences between South Asia and individual South Asian countries in contrast with the East Asian countries in this regard.[7] Table 5, from Bari and Cheema (2003), shows the savings-investment gap for selected South Asian and East Asian countries. The gap is consistently negative for South Asia, and larger as well,[8] across both time periods. Bari and Cheema (2003) also show that not only are there large differences in levels of investment and domestic saving in South and East Asia, with East Asia being way ahead, they also show that the rates of growth in these variables also significantly favour East Asia. Within South Asian countries where India has been able to maintain a decent domestic saving rate, Pakistan has lagged behind India in this regard. The negative savings-investment gap has tended to be larger in Pakistan, which has not only slowed down investment and hence growth, but has also increased Pakistan's dependence on inflows of capital to maintain even reasonable levels of investment. If we assume a rate of four to one from investment to increase in output, in order for Pakistan to grow at around 6 per cent, which is the minimum required to make a dent in the massive poverty levels, we need investments of at least 24 per cent per annum. With savings languishing at around 14 per cent, as they have for most of Pakistan's history, the reliance on foreign inflows or borrowing will remain high in order to make the investments needed. However, we are not taking into account that higher sustained investments over a number of years might eventually induce higher saving rates as income grows because, historically this trend has not been seen in Pakistan. Until incomes increase significantly, one might not expect to see this positive impact on savings. Table 3 provides the national saving rate and as has been noted the rates have been consistently low throughout Pakistan's history. The last two years have shown higher numbers, and the government has built their hopes on these numbers, but these might just reflect the large remittance inflows that have been pouring in post-September 11, and might not mean a structural change in the saving ratio at all.

Investment as a percentage of GDP had declined in Pakistan through the 1990s. The peak came in 1993 when Pakistan invested 20.7 per cent of its GDP, but the rate declined to only 14.7 per cent in 2002. There has been a slight revival over the last year, but it hard to know if this is just a blip or the beginning of a trend. What should be clear is that with investment around 15 per cent of GDP, low GDP growth rates of 3-4 per cent are not difficult to explain.

Table 3 shows that the rate of inflation, taken in form of growth in Consumer Price Index (CPI), after being in double-digits for a number of years, started to come down from 1997-8 onwards. This tracks the reductions in the growth of the money supply (M2) in the economy and the connection between them is well documented. The government, throughout the 1990s, was under pressure to not only raise M2 as it had to finance the public sector deficit, but it had to monetize the changes in the exchange rate and also manage the pressure on the foreign currency account. This resulted directly in higher rates of inflation. As GDP growth rate tapered, and the government started cutting its expenditures under the structural adjustment programmes, the economy went into a recession, reducing pressure on the trade deficit side and reducing the need to keep inflating the economy.

Large accumulated external and internal debt (Table 4) had, by start of the 1990s, started to constrain the ability of the government to maintain interest payments, development expenditure and other expenses, while holding fiscal deficits within acceptable bounds, and at the same time not inflate the money supply too much. But the balancing act was hard to achieve and as the government moved to multilateral institution-funded structural adjustment and stabilization programmes, the policy priorities changed accordingly. The government wanted to cut down expenditure, to control fiscal deficits, and to lower inflationary pressures. It also wanted to reduce the debt burden on the country and increase its revenue base.

It did have some success in achieving these objectives by the end of the 1990s. Table 4 shows that from a high of 8.8 per cent in 1993, the budget deficit was systematically brought down to 4.6 per cent by 2003. 1998 was the only year where the deficit went up significantly, but this was an exceptional year. Pakistan exploded nuclear devices in May 1998 and had to face economic sanctions as a consequence. Where there has been some success for the government in raising additional revenue from indirect taxes, such as the General Sales Tax (GST), the government has not been able, despite its best efforts, to increase the net of direct taxes and taxpayers. Hence, the real control over budget deficits has come from reductions in expenditure.

On the expenditure side, as Table 4 shows, interest payments started coming down only after 2000 and the rate of decline in defence expenditure, in percentage terms, has been quite slow. The main cuts have been in development expenditures where from 7.6 per cent of GDP in 1992, it went down to a low of 2.1 per cent in 2001. It has only been in the current budget that development expenditures have been set at 4.1 per cent again. This partly explains the decrease in GDP growth rates over the 1990s, and also provides some explanation for the rise of poverty. The government cut its expenditures on building and maintaining infrastructure, starting new development projects, spending on health and education, agriculture and other subsides, and new initiatives in areas like electricity generation. Literature in economics identifies the 'crowding-in' role of government too. The idea is that government investments in infrastructure and 'enabling environment' increase the returns to investment by the private sector by either reducing the cost of doing business or by raising revenues in some way. The reduction in development expenditures, over the 1990s, not only reduced these crowding-in effects, the lack of investments might have raised the cost of doing business to the extent that it might have reduced investments by the private sector as well. The breakup of investment by private and public sector does show that where public sector investment did go down substantially, private sector investment did not rise enough to compensate for the decrease.

External and domestic debt, as well as interest payments, as a percentage of GDP, continued to rise through the 1990s despite government efforts at structural adjustment. By 2001 the total debt was almost equal to the GDP of the country. Interest payments alone were taking up 8.3 per cent of the GDP (see Table 4 for details). The change in total debt and interest payments started to be seen only after the Paris Club re-negotiations and the willingness of multilateral and bilateral agencies to start dealing with Pakistan again in the aftermath of the 11 September attacks. Though the State Bank of Pakistan (SBP) has, in its various publications, pointed out that debt negotiations had started prior to the September events, it is hard to believe that these events did not increase the willingness of donors and lenders to deal with Pakistan.

A positive externality of the United States' crackdown on money laundering in its efforts to reduce the funding of terrorist organizations, has been the increased inflow of remittances to Pakistan. Though the trade deficit has continued, however at much smaller levels, due to the long recession in the economy, the current account has turned to a surplus due to the significant remittance inflows. This year alone total remittance payments were close to 4.5 billion dollars, while total export earning is about 10 billion dollars. The trade gap is only about 2 billion dollars. Current account, for Pakistan, has finally moved into a surplus.

The macroeconomic story of the decade seems to be as follows. Accumulated debt, current deficits, and the inability of the state to alter expenditure patterns for most significant expenses (debt servicing and defence) meant that the state had very limited fiscal space at the start of the 1990s. This space was further constrained by the unwillingness of multilateral and bilateral agencies to lend to a country that they thought was not seriously concerned about structural reform. The Pakistani state and successive governments, from across the political spectrum, were therefore forced to go for structural reforms and macroeconomic stabilization. These reforms, mentioned above, induced a significant and deep recession in the economy. The success of the reforms will be discussed in the following sections, with reference to particular sectors. But it should be clear that there was little visible evidence of the success of the reforms before the 11 September events changed things. Since then the macro indicators have shown some improvement, especially on the monetary and financial side, but the GDP and investment growth rates still remain relatively low and below trend.[9] To look at the sustainability of the revival we have to study the dynamics of each important sector. This is done in the following sections.

Agriculture

The Pakistani economy still depends significantly on the agricultural sector and will continue to do so for quite some time to come. Almost 25 per cent of the national output comes directly from agriculture. The sector provides employment to more than 50 per cent of our employed workforce and it provides the surpluses needed for export (cotton and rice), including that of our primary industry: cotton textiles. But agriculture has had a very turbulent decade in the 1990s. The average annual growth rate has fallen compared to the 1960s and 1980s, and more importantly, the variation in growth has increased significantly compared to the past. The good years show high positive growth while the bad show high negative growth and the number of years where we have had negative growth has also increased.

As Table 6 shows there are four years, 1993, 1997, 2001 and 2002, since 1991, in which there was strong negative or low positive growth. At the same time there were only two years, 1992 and 1996, in which there was strong positive growth. The variations in agricultural output were largely driven by changes in the output of major crops. It is the output of wheat, rice, sugarcane and cotton that determine how well the agricultural sector performs. Table 6 shows the close connection between the overall agricultural growth rates and the rates of growth for these crops. The minor crops have had a steadier performance. Table 6 also shows that in most years that there has been a strong positive or negative growth, it is usually when the major crops have either done well, which positively impacts growth, or done poorly, which negatively impacts growth for that year. This implies that usually it is not a crop specific factor, but a general one, that has caused the negative shocks.

There are various arguments put forward to explain the increased variation in agricultural output. The new seeds, introduced as a result of the Green Revolution, have reduced bio-diversity in our agriculture. This allows negative or positive shocks to travel across the system more easily. The new seeds also depend much more on timely and appropriate applications of various inputs like water, pesticides, fertilizer, and weeding and any variation in weather also affects the entire crop. Too little or too much rain, a common phenomena, now affects agriculture more than in the past. Given the larger variations possible, Pakistan has to learn to live with, and manage, agriculture more effectively so as to minimize the variations and their impact on the rest of the economy, From the negative performances in the last couple of years, it is clear, that Pakistan has not learnt to manage this as yet.

For the last few years, Pakistan has also had relatively dry summers, leading to almost drought-like conditions in some areas, with significant shortages of water across all agricultural areas. Even where tubewells and other ground-water extraction mechanisms have provided water, the cost of water went up significantly, which of course lowered agriculture profitability. With low investment in infrastructure and low development expenditure, Pakistan was in no position to address irrigation and water issues. The government has recently increased outlays for water management and is planning to invest major resources for creating water reservoirs in the next decade. However, this is long-term planning and for the next few years Pakistan will have to live with, and plan for uncertainties about water availability and therefore, agricultural output. The last column of Table 6 shows annual farm-gate water availability. The figures do not take into account seasonal variation or the mix between ground-water and canal water. Hence it tends to show little general variation from year to year but even small changes or stable supply, when demand is increasing, shows how water availability has become a binding constraint.

A number of commentators have argued that Pakistan's agriculture cannot expand by bringing more land under cultivation[10] but that major gains will have to come from increasing yields through better management of existing levels of land input. Commentators support this argument by noting that yield levels for most crops are well below levels of the major performers, thus, showing significant room for improvement. But this is where there has been almost no progress so far.

As part of structural adjustment programmes and the effort to reduce government expenditure and cut subsidies, the government, over the 1990s, has reduced its involvement in agricultural input and output markets. On the output side, the government has reduced its role in providing price floors for most products and it no longer buys all surplus production. It is reducing its role in providing storage facilities as well which has had a significant impact on agricultural markets. With fragmented, fractured, highly imperfect and incomplete credit markets, the withdrawal of price floors can, and has, hit the small farmer hard. Significant price variations, at the time of reaping, can ruin small farmers who are forced to sell their crops quickly, impacting their ability to sow for the next season. The full impact of this policy was visible two seasons ago, when the government removed the binding price floor and a large number of small wheat farmers became victims to unscrupulous middlemen. Should government plans of withdrawal be carried out, without correcting information asymmetries in the markets, such as credit, cases like the wheat farmers will become more common. A strong case can be made that this will significantly raise uncertainty in the agricultural sector, including product output variation. Since the majority of Pakistan and the majority of Pakistani poor depend on agriculture, these changes have a negative impact on incomes of the rural population and especially for the rural poor.

The reduction in subsidies on agricultural inputs has allowed their prices to rise rapidly. In general, the rise in price of inputs has been greater than the rise in Consumer Price Index (CPI). The most significant increases have come in the price of fertilizers, pesticides, and the provision of electricity, which has reduced the profitability of agriculture. The question of subsidies to agriculture is a complicated one; with the European Union and the United States providing billions of dollars in subsidies to agriculture. If all countries are to compete in the same market, the question of subsidies must be looked at globally and in any case, Pakistan will be ill-advised to act alone.

It is difficult to separate the various factors that have contributed to the poor performance of the agricultural sector in the past decade. The government, in most of its analyses, tends to blame the entire problem on the shortage of water. As we have shown above, where water availability has definitely been a problem, it has not been as significant as the government would have us believe. The cuts in subsidies, the significant increase in the cost of inputs, and the difficulties in markets must also be blamed. We have not yet seen any research rigorous enough to satisfactorily explain the drop in performance. Structural adjustment will continue for the next few years in the form of lower subsidies on inputs, especially electricity, and in the form of lower government involvement in output markets. So, agricultural output will likely continue to vary significantly and until we settle into new institutional structures we should expect several low-growth years.

Industry

The manufacturing sector's rate of growth also faltered in the 1990s. Where the average annual growth rate was 8.2 per cent during the 1980s, it was only 4.0 per cent in the 1990s. Table 7 amply demonstrates that manufacturing, like agriculture, has had a turbulent decade. Part of the explanation for the weak performance in industrial growth comes from the variance in agriculture. Pakistan's major industries, cotton and cotton textiles as well as sugar, depend directly and heavily on agriculture. Agricultural variance, with suitable lags, is transferred to industry.

The last decade has also seen a major structural change in industry. Polices of privatization, de-regulation, liberalization, and decentralization have reduced the role of government in many industries. However, the regulatory structures for the new institutional setups are only now being created. The interim period has seen some major adjustment issues and one particularly significant example has been the price and output issues relating to the cement industry. The cement sector was deregulated in the early to middle 1990s. When state-owned enterprises dominated the sector, allowing government to act as a price leader, the price of cement was about Rs 100 per bag. After privatization and the reduction of state holdings, the price of cement climbed to above Rs 200 per bag. The industry expanded with new entries as well as the expansion of the capacity of existing producers. At the same time, the demand for cement stagnated due to the overall recession in the country, and instead of prices falling and the inefficient units being forced out, there were cuts in capacity utilization on the part of most producers which resulted in prices stabilizing at the higher rate. This was a fairly slam-dunk case of illegal cartelization, but the regulatory structure was not in a position to deal with it. In the medium term, the lack of a regulatory structure at a time when the industrial sector is being liberalized has tended to hurt and discourage new investment by making the investment climate more uncertain.

Through the decade, the government has been reducing tariff and non-tariff barriers to trade. Most export duties and barriers have been phased out, while import duties have been reduced significantly. The maximum tariff rate has been brought down to 25 per cent for most goods and the number of tax slabs have been reduced to four. This is consistent with our commitments to multilateral donors, lenders, and to the WTO. But the reduction in import barriers has also exposed domestic industry, which has traditionally been heavily protected, to foreign competition. Many industries have struggled to compete and many have become untenable, though some will survive after making changes in their structure, others will go under. Until the process is complete, we are unlikely to see major industrial activity or significant investment.

Table 7 shows that there was some recovery in the manufacturing sector in 2002–2003. Large-scale manufacturing grew at 8.65 per cent which boosted the overall manufacturing sector growth to 7.7 per cent, but this growth was largely concentrated in a few industries which were not traditional to Pakistan. The growth came from a 48 per cent increase in the automobile industry and those related to this sector. There has been some positive growth in other consumer durable sectors as well. This growth has been under very heavy tariff protection, in some cases similar to that which has been accorded to the automobile sector. Demand for consumer durables and automobiles have expanded largely due to the opening up of lease/credit markets, larger remittance inflows that have already been mentioned, and a dearth of investment opportunities. Because imports cannot compete in some of these markets, though the increased demand has translated into increases in production, this growth is not sustainable. As soon as the automobile sector is opened up for competition, the local industry will collapse.[11] Sectors that we can compete in internationally, shown in Table 7, have still not picked up production. It is also important to note that each of the significant sectors given in Table 7 has had a few bad years over the last decade where the growth rates have actually turned negative.

Various survey-based studies of the manufacturing and services sector of Pakistan have documented in detail that the cost of doing business is very high in Pakistan compared to its neighbours in South Asia as well as the rest of the world.[12] The electricity tariff is one of the highest in the world and compounding this cost is the problem with the erratic supply of electricity which forces manufacturers to invest in backup power, raising the electricity cost even further. Pakistani ports are among the most expensive in the world and cause significant delays in transportation and Pakistan's rail and road networks are also not very efficient. Other infrastructure like water, access to sewage, telecommunication facilities, and gas are also expensive. Given the higher cumulative infrastructure cost, it becomes harder for Pakistani businesses to compete with countries in East Asia and up-coming giants like India and China.

The second major factor that explains the high price of doing business in Pakistan is the cost that the regulatory structure of the state imposes on businesses. This includes both the cost of compliance as well as the cost of corruption. Dealing with the government requires a good deal of time investment on the part of top management, which could have been better spent on business matters. It is not the case that Pakistan has excessive regulation, the problem is that the regulations are opaque, require more paperwork, and involve longer inter action with officials[13] and the intensive nature of the regulation produces more opportunities for corruption. Transparency International has repeatedly rated Pakistan amongst the more corrupt countries of the world and this certainly affects local business. Nearly all businesses in Pakistan rate almost all government departments as corrupt and that they pose significant impediments to doing business. The Central Board of Revenue

(CBR) and WAPDA, the official electricity provider, usually top the corruption list. Unfortunately, the police and the judiciary are not far behind.

Column 3 of Table 7 also makes for interesting reading. It shows that the growth of small-scale manufacturing has also slowed down in the last decade. From an average growth of 8.4 per cent in the 1980s, the growth rate has slowed to 5.31 per cent. *The Economic Survey 2002-03* shows that the SME sector grew at a constant rate of 5.31 per cent over the last ten years. This hides the fact that the small sector growth rate is actually an imputed growth rate and not a directly calculated one. Surveys for small scale are done infrequently and for the intervening years the government just uses the same growth rate. After showing a growth rate of 8.4 per cent for most of 1980s it was found that the actual rate in 1992 was much lower. From then on the government has given the growth rate as 5.31 per cent. The government has not adjusted earlier figures for the overstatement and it has, even more interestingly, not tried to do regular surveys to check if the same mistake has been made over the last decade as well. Since the economy slowed down in the last decade, for all we know, we could still be overstating the growth rate. Independent estimates, for the same periods, put growth rates at around 3 per cent or less.[14] If these estimates are even close, we are off by quite a bit in the official figures.

Due to the threshold effect, the dual costs of compliance and corruption for the manufacturing sector tend to be still higher for the Small and Medium Enterprises (SMEs). Bribes have a lower bench mark and do not rise proportionately with sales. As a percentage of sales, they create a relatively larger burden for small enterprises. The argument is the same for compliance cost. This threshold effect creates distortions against entering the formal sector as well as against growth for small enterprises. If they keep below the threshold of becoming formal, they can avoid most of the compliance cost and some of the cost of corruption. But this occurs at the cost of lower and distorted growth,[15] and it goes against the objective of encouraging the SMEs to grow into larger enterprises.

The story of the manufacturing sector seems to be as follows: Investment has not picked up as yet and, in fact, financial institutions are finding it very hard to lend to the productive sectors despite significant drops in interest rates. The reasons seem to be related to the high cost of business due to regulatory impediments, market imperfections, corruption, poor infrastructure, and large uncertainties due to political and international factors. The sectors that have seen relatively high growth rates are those receiving heavy protection from the government, thus, their growth is unlikely to be sustainable.

Financial Sector

The financial sector has also undergone significant restructuring during the 1990s. The restructuring included introduction of privately owned domestic banks, fewer restrictions on foreign banks, greater autonomy to banks for policies on lending, fewer sectoral targets, privatization of state owned banks, dismantling of most Development Finance Institutions (DFIs) and their privatization, and the introduction of more effective prudential regulations. The restructuring has also led to major institutional changes in the State Bank of Pakistan (SBP) and has led to the creation of the Securities and Exchange Commission of Pakistan (SECP) for the regulation of the corporate sector, the equity markets, insurance sector, and all Non-Bank Financial Institutions (NBFIs). SECP, in turn, has introduced stricter regulation of the equity markets, including a new Code of Corporate Governance (CG).

By the mid-1990s, it was clear that state owned banks and financial institutions were in a crisis. State owned banks and DFIs had become too bureaucratic, the quality of their service was poor, they were overstaffed, and they had large portfolios of Non-Performing Loans (NPLs) or bad loans. NPLs were largely a result of political interference and state involvement in dispensing patronage through state banks and DFIs. Moral hazard, where state financial institutions had implicit assurance that they would not be allowed to fail, and adverse selection, due to political interference and payoffs, led to poor quality internal monitoring, evaluation and selection on the part of banks. Moreover, the incentive to recover bad loans was almost non-existent.

The government and the SBP decided that the banks and DFIs needed to be restructured to assure their viability and the decision was taken to liberalize the banking sector while most state institutions would be privatized and the rest would be corporatized and private and foreign banks world be allowed freer access to the local market. Over the last decade three state owned banks have been privatized: Allied Bank of Pakistan, the Muslim Commercial Bank, and the United Bank of Pakistan. The government is looking at the possibility of privatizing two more: National Bank of Pakistan and Habib Bank Limited.[16] Table 8 shows the relative shares of private, foreign, and state owned banks in overall banking assets. The shares of private and foreign banks have gone up, while the shares of state owned banks have declined. These figures do not include the privatization of the United Bank Limited and Habib Bank Limited, which occurred in 2002 and 2004 respectively.

The government has also shut down or privatized a number of DFIs. Bankers Equity Limited was initially privatized but was later liquidated under SBP supervision as it went into bankruptcy and other DFIs have been restructured completely. Table 8 column 7 shows that the share of DFIs in NBFI assets has fallen over the last decade.

The last column of Table 8 shows the seriousness of the Non-Performing Loans (NPLs) issue. NPLs stand around 20 per cent of gross advances. Though SBP has, over the last decade, forced banks to make provisions for NPLs on their balance sheets, the process is far from complete. The share of state owned banks and DFIs is much larger in NPLs than for private or foreign banks (columns 8 and 9 of Table 8 give the relevant details). The reasons for this have already been explained in terms of the moral hazard and adverse selection problems that these institutions faced. With the privatization of state banks, the introduction of better prudential regulations and the liberalization of the sector, the incentives for the remaining banks are going to change and they will not be as susceptible to corruption and inefficiency as they once were.

For the last two years national savings has been higher than investment as a percentage of GDP than in prior years. This has largely been due to the increased savings based on remittance inflows and the collapse of investment. At the same time, though interest rates have come down on industrial loans, from 18-20 per cent to as low as 6-8 per cent, banks have not been able to move loans and they consequently possess excess liquidity. Since interest rates on savings have also come down at the same time, and equally steeply, the spread[17] of banks continues to be as high as 5 per cent, and gives an indication of the continued relative inefficiency of the banking system.[18] The percentage of bad loans has started to decrease and lessening of interference by the SBP and government will also have a positive effect on bank efficiency. However, the effects of these reforms are not visible yet and a wait of a few more years will be necessary to see if they pay off.

SBP has also introduced a range of new prudential regulations that are designed to give better information to the regulator while allowing the banks more discretion to run their institutions according to their own priorities. These include a regular and more systematic flow of information from banks to the SBP, the dismantling of the Banking Council of Pakistan and of the structure that gives sectoral lending targets, and also of the regulations that determine interest rates.

SBP has initiated a significant program for capacity building and restructuring within the institution as well. Salary structures have been revised to bring them closer to market rates, inductions from the private sector have been made, and ambitious recruitment and re-training programs have been initiated. Most commentators have already pointed out that there has been a marked improvement in both the output and performance of SBP, as well as its ability to perceive market trends and act on them. For example, the SBP has been able to foresee and manage financial sector crises well and has managed the exchange rate policy quite credibly in the last few years.

The main sources of project finance for the corporate sector in Pakistan have been, and continue to be, personal resources and financing from state owned banks and DFIs. Equity markets have never played a major role for raising capital. The main incentive for enrolling in equity markets were the tax breaks that the government used to provide at one time. In addition, the government also required firms of a particular size and larger to enrol in stock markets. Table 9 shows that even in 2003 average market capitalization for Pakistan's stock markets was only around Rs 600 billion and there are only 700 listed companies. These 700 companies form only about 2 per cent of registered companies in Pakistan.

With the collapse of the DFI model, corporations will have to focus more on equity markets for raising new capital and this had not happened up until the reforms were instituted. In fact, the number of listed companies has declined and there have been few new listings and new issues on the equity markets.

The government, anticipating the need for reform in capital markets, initiated the process with the formation of the SECP in 1997. Since then, SECP has introduced a number of reforms in the capital markets for increasing transparency and fairness. These include measures for more transparent management of the Stock Exchanges, clearer regulations on reporting by the Registrar of Companies, and last but not least, the introduction of a CG code.[19] It is this last action that has been the most contentious and has led to some de-listings from the exchanges. Some of the larger firms on the Pakistani stock exchanges continue to be family owned (majority holding) and managed firms. The CG code has sought to wrest control over these firms from families so that small investors can be adequately protected and a number of these families have chosen to de-list rather than cede control.

Capital market and financial sector reforms are continuing. It will be a few years before we have a well-regulated, transparent, and 'fair' equity market working in Pakistan. Though the banking sector reforms have been successful thus far, again the results of the reforms will only be fully known after a period of consolidation in the domestic market and the resolution of the bad loans issue. The SBP reform has indeed being going well and this partially explains improved management of interest and exchange rate regimes over the last few years.

Infrastructure and the Social Sector

We have already stated that infrastructure is more expensive, less reliable, and of lower quality in Pakistan than in neighbouring countries or comparable developing societies. Electricity charges for industry are one of the highest in the world and its[20] supply tends to be erratic and the quality of service poor. This forces many industries to invest in backup power that might not ever be optimally utilized. Higher tariffs and backup power raise the costs of manufacturing directly, while erratic supply raises costs by making delivery times longer and more uncertain.

Multilateral agencies have identified reforms in the electricity sector as being crucial for sustainable economic revival. Despite the fact that reforms were on the agenda throughout the 1990s and many of them were attempted, WAPDA has been rigidly reform resistant.[21]

What is true of WAPDA is also true of other infrastructure sectors. The telecommunication services, though they have improved significantly with the introduction of mobile telephones and competition in international dialling, are still not on par with other countries at similar levels of income and development and the cost is higher in Pakistan as well. What is true for telecommunication is true of Internet connection charges as well.

The road network has been allowed to deteriorate significantly since the middle of the last decade. Though the government has, in recent years, tried to make some amends, most roads need to be rebuilt and upgraded. The farm to market network also needs to be substantially extended.

Pakistan's sea and dry ports are inefficient and expensive. Hence delivery times are long and there is substantial uncertainty as to when deliveries can be made.[22]

Access to water and sewage is also an issue, even within urban areas. Karachi, the chief industrial centre for Pakistan, faces chronic water shortages. Most industrial units do not have treatment plants and given the poor state of the sewage system, effluence and hazardous waste is usually dumped in the city. Environmental degradation and biohazards resulting from industry's meagre efforts are disproportionately impacting urban areas.[23]

For a country that has low literacy rates, low school enrolment rates, high drop-out rates from even primary education, low access to university education, very poor quality educational institutions, and a large gender bias (favouring boys, of course) in education, spending 1.7 per cent of our GNP on education makes little sense. To make matters worse, Table 2 shows that, as percentage of GNP, the expenditure on education has declined when compared to the 1990s. On the education front, Pakistan's performance has been poorer than its neighbours who have lower per capita income. Sri Lanka and India are good examples of this.

Expenditure patterns reflect and reveal the priorities of a state. Education has never been a priority for any of Pakistan's governments. In fact, the government has increasingly given up its role and duty to provide education, even at the primary level. As the private sector has been allowed to enter the field of education and expand at all levels, the government has increasingly withdrawn and subsequently allowed the quality of public schooling to go down. As more people from the middle and upper economic strata have shifted to private schooling, the pressure on the state to improve educational quality has also decreased. The entry of Non-Governmental Organizations (NGOs) into the educational sector, bolstered by arguments for their superiority in providing quality education, has further weakened government resolve. The conversation in policy circles now is about the extent of government-NGO partnership or private-public partnership, and so on. There are few who any longer press the argument for state responsibility and provision.

This also holds true for the health sector, only more bindingly. Pakistan spends only 0.7 per cent of its GNP on the health sector and expenditure has been holding steady at this low level for a number of years. The state has again allowed private sector entry and the private sector has, as it is supposed to do, created good facilities. But, of course, these come at a price. For the poor, the standard of health facilities is low and consequently Pakistan has high infant and child mortality rates, high pregnancy related death rates, low contraceptive use ratios, high child malnutrition rates, high disease rates, high morbidity rates, and a fairly low life expectancy rate. Health insurance is not very widespread either. The result is that most people in Pakistan have only partial access to poor quality health services and it shows. Tuberculosis has made a come back in Pakistan in recent years and, more disturbingly, the spread of various strains of hepatitis has become very extensive. Heart related ailments, pulmonary diseases, and kidney failure incidents have also significantly increased, especially in the urban areas. The government's response to these trends has been notably non-existent.

Though the new-growth theories, as well as the empirical evidence on growth, have amply demonstrated the importance of investments in human capital, policymakers in Islamabad seem to have missed these studies. More to the point, the failure of government to address the issues of the poor reflects badly on the state and the bureaucracy.

Institutional Reforms

The Musharraf government, when it took over in 1999, justified its move by arguing that the political government had allowed a number of institutions to deteriorate and only a quasi-military government had the ability to properly rejuvenate and reform them. The list of institutions and organizations needing reform included the judicial system, the police, the Central Board of Revenue (CBR), WAPDA, KESC, Pakistan Railways, the SECP, SBP, the overall regulatory framework for most industries, the political system, local governance, and even the 1973 Constitution. Musharraf's government was going to root out corruption and would create permanent bodies, like the National Accountably Bureau (NAB) and the National Reconstruction Bureau (NRB), to ensure that institutional reforms were truly enacted and enshrined in the system of governance. However, apart from partial success in reforming a few organizations, primarily the SECP and SBP, government efforts have not been very successful. This lack of success at institutional, organizational and structural reform is the primary failure of the Musharraf government and is what makes the sustainability of any economic revival suspect as well.

The case of the CBR is the best example. After the takeover General Musharraf identified the CBR as one of the key institutions needing reform. The state required more tax revenue and the CBR was considered to be a very corrupt and inefficient organization. Inefficiency and corruption frustrated the efficient collection of tax revenue. The goal of the reforms was to increase collection efficiency while decreasing complaints from the public and lowering feelings of resentment from individual and corporate tax payers. In the ensuing four years the government has conducted numerous studies on or for the CBR, have paid consultants working on the reforms huge salaries, have had various tax surveys done, undertaken documentation drives and devised tax amnesty schemes.[24] Yet all micro level surveys still find the CBR to be viewed by the public as corrupt and inefficient as before. The bureaucracy at the CBR has successfully resisted all reform efforts and, in fact, has induced such exhaustion in the government that talk of reform has also diminished. The failure of reform efforts is not without cost; not only has the opportunity to reform been lost, much time and money on the effort have been wasted, and the inability of the government to manage institutional reform has been exposed, and in the process, the public is even more skeptical about 'reform rhetoric'. All of these will impose costs on future reform efforts.

The other spectacular reform failure has been WAPDA. WAPDA, the electricity provider, has been in financial trouble for a long time. Lack of market based prices, subsidies to domestic users and agriculture, corruption and colossal inefficiency have led to and exacerbated these problems. From the army taking over the running of WAPDA to privatization, corporatization, downsizing and even stronger legal action for tariff recovery, everything has been tried and failed. WAPDA too continues to head the list of organizations that are thought to be amongst the most corrupt and inefficient organizations in Pakistan. It continues to provide poor service at a very high cost, especially to industry and for commercial usage.

The basic story of failure given above is true for most other reform efforts undertaken by the Musharraf government. The question is why have these efforts failed so consistently? Clearly, this is an important question but beyond the scope of this paper. However, one notable consequence of these failures is that any story of a revival seems premature. The case made by the government that this revival of government and society will be sustainable seems even more exaggerated given the reality of the situation.

Conclusion

Pakistan stands divided today between the government story of the macroeconomic situation that emphasizes the successes on current account, exchange rates, interest rates, inflation rates, and the foreign reserve and the story told by 'others' who emphasize the increases in poverty and inequality, low investment levels, the poor record in infrastructure, the social/human sectors, and the poor record at both managing institutions and managing institutional change. As usual, there is much truth in both versions of the story of Pakistan's macroeconomic performance. However, for the rosy version to sustain itself, the latter story must change in a positive direction. Additionally, there does not appear to be a necessary link moving from the positive to the negative story; that is, if we maintain the positive situation for sometime that the latter will automatically change for the better.

There is no doubt that debt renegotiations, better financial management, and externalities from the changing international scenario in the wake of the 11 September tragedy have allowed Pakistan to improve its financial position and reduce the fiscal pressure on the government. But this has, as yet, not translated into economic revival and high growth. The main hurdles seem to be coming from political and international uncertainty, micro impediments to growth, poor management of institutions and failure to manage institutional change. This interpretation is supported by our sectoral reading across agriculture, industry, financial sector, infrastructure provision, and the social sector. If these constraints remain as binding and are not addressed quickly, the people and government of Pakistan will lose out on the opportunity provided by the current macroeconomic stability and the supportive international conditions. The success that has been achieved with macro stability could easily be eroded in a matter of months if the problems with institutions and organizations are not addressed quickly.

Bibliography

Bari, F. & A. Cheema, (2003), *Towards a Common Investment Strategy For South Asia,* Report submitted to South Asia Center for Policy Studies (SACEPs).

Bari, F., Cheema, A. & E. Haque, (2002), *Regulatory Impediments, Market Imperfections, and Firm Growth: Analyzing the Constraints to SME Growth in Pakistan,* A Study Conducted for the Asian Development Bank.

Cheema, A., Bari, F., and O. Siddique, (2003), Corporate Governance in Pakistan: Ownership, Control and the Law, in Sobhan and Werner (ed.), *A Comparative Analysis of Corporate Governance in South Asia: Charting a Roadmap for Bangladesh,* Bangladesh Enterprise Institute: Dhaka.

Government of Pakistan, (2003), *Economic Survey, 2002-03.* Islamabad: Finance Division, Economic Advisor's Wing.

Government of Pakistan, (2000), *Economic Survey, 1999-2000.* Islamabad: Finance Division, Economic Advisor's Wing.

Government of Pakistan, (1998), *50 Years of Pakistan in Statistics,* Volumes 1, 2, 3, & 4. Islamabad: Federal Bureau of Statistics, Statistics Division.

Gazder, H., (1999), Poverty in Pakistan: A Review, in S.R. Khan (ed.), *Fifty Years of Pakistan's Economy,* Oxford University Press: Karachi.

Hussain, A., (2003), *Pakistan National Human Development Report 2003: Poverty, Growth and Governance,* United Nations Development Programme.

Karachi Stock Exchange, www.kse.net.pk.

Majid, N., (2000), *Pakistan: Employment, Output and Productivity.* Issues in Development, Discussion Paper 33, International Labor Organization, Geneva.

Noman, O., (1988), *The Political Economy of Pakistan,* Routledge and Kegan Paul: London.

Sen Gupta, A., (2003), Presentation at the South Asia Center for Policy Studies (SACEPs) Conference in Lahore, in May. Technical Session 3: Macroeconomic Policy in South Asia.

SPDC (2003) Various Publications.

State Bank of Pakistan, (2002), *Pakistan: Financial Sector Assessment 1990-2000,* Research Department: Karachi.

World Bank, (2002), *Pakistan Poverty Assessment: Poverty in Pakistan: Vulnerabilities, Social Gaps, and Rural Dynamics.* Poverty Reduction and Economic Management Sector Unit: South Asia Region. Report No. 24296-PAK.

Zaidi, S.A., (1999), *Issues in Pakistan's Economy,* Oxford University Press: Karachi.

Notes

1. The author would like to thank Adeel Faheem for his able research assistance in making the tables, the bibliography, as well as in ironing out some of the arguments.

2. Almost all Presidential and Prime Ministerial addresses have claimed this, as had the official pronouncements around the time of the Finance Minister's budget speech.

3. See any recent SBP quarterly or annual report for the argument.

4. For a relatively brief and concise account of Pakistan's politico-economic history see Noman (1988). For a more in-depth analysis of most issues see Zaidi (1998).

5. All statistics in this chapter, unless otherwise specified, are from Government of Pakistan publications.

6. For a detailed discussion of poverty issues in Pakistan see World Bank (2002). And for regional/provincial details see Gazder (1997).

7. See Chapters 1 and 2 of Bari and Cheema (2003) in particular.

8. East Asia saved more than it invested, even when it had higher investment rates.

9. Dr Arjun Sen Gupta, an eminent Indian economist, has made the argument repeatedly that South Asian governments, like many developing countries, need to decide that they will not sacrifice human development, social sector development, and the fight against poverty at the altar of growth and/or stabilization. See Sen Gupta (2003) for details. A number of commentators have argued that Pakistan has chosen stabilization over human development as well. See Social Policy Development Center (SPDC) critiques of government policy for this.

10. See Hussain (2003), Chapter 1 as an example.

11. Currently, there is a Parliamentary committee looking into domestic automobile prices and protection issues. Domestic parts manufacturers and automobile manufacturers are carrying out a very vocal, expensive and extensive campaign to stop the government from liberalizing the sector in any manner.

12. See Bari and Cheema (2003) Chapter 4, and Bari, Cheema and Haque (2003). The argument has been made in studies by the World Bank as well as the Small and Medium Enterprise Development Authority (SMEDA).

13. One expatriate Pakistani entrepreneur mentioned that he had spent more time in government offices in one year of doing business in Pakistan than in 26 years in Singapore, even though Singapore is more heavily regulated.

14. See Majid (2000) for a fairly extensive estimation exercise.

15. A fairly large retail business has chosen to register all retail outlets that it owns as separate businesses to avoid higher taxation and compliance requirements. But this also means that this business cannot access formal credit markets and so its expansion path is likely to be sub-optimal. This is not an uncommon story

amongst small and medium retail chains. See Bari, Cheema and Haque (2002).

16. Habib Bank has also been privatized recently.

17. Spread is the difference between interest rates that a bank gives to depositors and the one it charges on loans. This is from where the bank makes its profits and covers its costs.

18. The large spread cannot indicate monopoly rents as low demand for loans and competition for customers would have squeezed out rents.

19. For a detailed discussion of the consequences of the collapse of the DFI model and the introduction of the CG code in Pakistan, see Cheema, Bari and Siddique (2003).

20. See Bari and Cheema (2003), Chapter 3 for evidence and the relevant comparisons.

21. See next section on institutional reforms as well.

22. In our survey work on investment we found that almost all exporters/importers complained that they could not get international orders as they could not promise on-time delivery. They could ensure that goods reach the port by a certain date, but given the inefficiency and corruption within the Customs Department and the port authorities they could not guarantee a date for shipment.

23. Table 10 gives some details regarding provision of infrastructure facilities in Pakistan.

24. The reform efforts have been an amalgam of local Pakistani initiatives and World Bank/IMF supported and funded efforts.

Tables to Chapter 1

Table1
Poverty, Inequality and Unemployment

Years	Poverty: Head Count			Household Income Distribution (Percentage share of income)				Unemployment Rate (% per annum)
	Total	Rural	Urban	Gini co-efficient	Lowest 20%	Middle 60%	Highest 20%	
1960s	42.37	42.28	42.75	0.35	7.55	49.33	43.13	...
1970s	38.61	40.81	32.35	0.35	7.90	48.93	43.17	...
1980s	27.62	27.79	27.09	0.35	7.70	47.48	44.08	1.4
1991	26.10	25.20	26.60	0.41	5.7	45.00	49.3	6.22
1992	...	...	...	...	...	...	...	5.85
1993	26.80	24.60	28.30	0.41	6.2	46.60	48.2	4.73
1994	28.70	25.40	26.90	0.40	6.5	46.30	47.2	4.84
1995	...	...	...	...	...	...	...	5.41
1996	...	...	...	...	...	...	...	5.41
1997	29.80	33.10	22.60	0.40	7.0	43.60	49.4	6.12
1998	...	...	...	...	...	...	...	6.12
1999	32.60	34.67	20.91	0.41	6.2	44.10	49.7	6.12
2000	...	...	...	...	...	...	...	6.00
2001	32.10	38.99	22.67	...	...	...	...	6.00
2002	...	...	...	...	...	...	...	7.8
2003	31.80	38.65	22.39	...	...	...	...	7.8

... : Not available (not reported)

Source: Economic survey (1999-00, 2002-03)

Table 2
Social indicators

Years	Population (mln)	Education				Health				
		Middle Schools (000 Nos.)	High school (000 Nos.)	Literacy rate (%)	Expenditure as % of GNP	Registered Doctors (000 Nos.)	Hospitals (Nos.)	Dispensaries (000 Nos.)	Rural health Centres (000 Nos.)	Expenditures on health as % of GNP
1960s	...	...	...	...	...	2.00	380	1.70	...	...
1970s	...	...	...	...	...	6.30	521	2.80	0.10	0.60
1980s	96.32	2.70	2.20	29.5	0.80	28.10	651	3.50	0.30	0.80
1991	110.79	8.80	8.20	34.9	2.10	52.90	756	3.80	0.50	0.70
1992	113.61	9.00	8.40	36.00	2.20	56.60	776	3.90	0.50	0.70
1993	116.47	11.80	8.70	37.20	2.20	60.00	778	4.10	0.50	0.70
1994	119.39	12.10	9.20	38.40	2.20	63.00	799	4.20	0.50	0.70
1995	122.36	12.60	9.50	39.60	2.40	66.20	822	4.30	0.50	0.60
1996	125.38	13.30	9.50	40.90	2.40	69.70	827	4.30	0.50	0.80
1997	128.42	14.50	9.90	42.20	2.50	74.20	858	4.50	0.50	0.70
1998	131.51	17.40	11.10	43.60	2.30	78.50	865	4.50	0.50	0.70
1999	134.51	18.00	12.30	45.00	2.20	82.70	872	4.60	0.50	0.70
2000	137.51	18.40	12.60	47.10	2.10	87.10	879	4.60	0.50	0.70
2001	140.47	18.80	12.80	49.00	1.60	91.80	876	4.60	0.50	0.70
2002	145.96	18.80	12.90	50.50	1.90	96.20	907	4.60	0.50	0.70
2003	149.03	...	...	51.60	1.70	101.60	906	4.60	0.60	0.70

... : Data not available
Source: Economic Survey (2002-03)

Table 3

Macro Indicators

Years	GDP (Growth Rate %)	M2 (Growth Rate %)	CPI (Growth Rate %)	Investment (% Of GDP)	National Savings (% Of GDP)
1960s	6.80	16.30	3.20	...	...
1970s	4.80	21.00	12.50	17.10	11.20
1980s	6.50	13.20	7.20	18.70	14.80
1991	5.60	17.40	12.70	19.00	14.20
1992	7.70	26.20	10.60	20.10	17.00
1993	2.10	17.80	9.80	20.70	13.60
1994	4.40	18.10	11.30	19.40	15.70
1995	5.10	17.20	13.00	18.40	14.30
1996	6.60	13.80	10.80	18.80	11.60
1997	1.70	12.20	11.80	17.70	11.60
1998	3.50	14.50	7.80	17.30	14.30
1999	4.20	6.20	5.70	15.60	11.70
2000	3.90	9.40	3.60	16.00	14.10
2001	2.20	9.00	4.40	15.50	14.70
2002	3.40	15.40	3.50	14.70	17.00
2003	5.10	12.50	3.30	15.50	19.50

... : Data not available.

Source: Economic Survey (2002-03)

Table 4
Deficits, Debt, Defence and Development Expenditure (% GDP mp)

Years	Budget Deficits	Trade Deficits	External Debt	Domestic Debt	Interest payments	Defence Expenditure	Development Expenditure
1960's	2.10	…	…	…	…	…	…
1970's	5.30	…	…	…	…	…	…
1980's	7.10	8.90	…	…	3.80	6.50	7.30
1991	8.80	5.50	33.24	44.08	4.90	6.40	6.40
1992	7.50	4.60	35.52	44.10	5.20	6.30	7.60
1993	8.10	6.40	36.62	46.16	5.90	6.60	5.70
1994	5.90	3.90	39.11	45.55	5.80	5.90	4.60
1995	5.60	4.20	36.42	43.29	5.20	5.60	4.40
1996	6.50	5.90	35.92	43.41	6.30	5.60	4.40
1997	6.40	5.00	37.10	43.49	6.60	5.20	3.50
1998	7.70	3.00	37.49	44.80	7.60	5.10	3.90
1999	6.10	3.50	39.70	49.45	7.50	4.90	3.40
2000	6.60	2.30	41.73	52.19	8.30	4.80	3.30
2001	5.20	2.20	43.41	52.56	7.30	3.80	2.10
2002	5.20	0.50	45.65	48.44	7.20	4.10	3.50
2003	4.60	…	41.32	45.10	6.00	3.90	4.10

… : Data not available

Source: Economic survey (1999-00) statistical supplement; Economic Survey (2002-03); <u>Annual Reports of SBP (1991, 1992, 2000)</u>

Table 5
Saving-Investment Gap (as percentage of GDP)

Country	1980-90	1990-2000
South Asian Economies		
Bangladesh	-10.19	-5.78
India	-2.66	-2.47
Nepal	-8.70	-10.11
Pakistan	-10.36	-6.11
Sri Lanka	-13.29	-9.18
NICs		
South Korea	0.28	0.68
Thailand	-2.98	-0.99
Singapore	-0.66	13.12
Malaysia	2.49	4.34
Indonesia	3.34	2.55

Source: Faisal Bari, and Ali Cheema (2003).

Table 6

Agriculture (Growth Rates (%) of major agriculture products):

Years	Agriculture	Major crops	Wheat	Rice	Cotton bales	Minor crops	Water* Availability (MAF)**
1960's	5.10	7.11	7.42	9.87	6.94	4.73	69.65
1970's	2.40	1.99	4.43	3.17	5.51	4.39	82.85
1980's	5.40	3.40	3.30	0.34	11.65	4.06	106.06
1991	5.00	5.69	1.74	1.27	12.48	3.51	119.62
1992	9.50	15.48	7.68	-0.55	33.17	2.37	122.05
1993	-5.30	-15.60	3.02	-3.92	-29.39	3.95	125.12
1994	5.20	1.24	-5.84	28.21	-11.19	12.62	128.01
1995	6.60	8.69	11.76	-13.72	8.16	6.91	129.65
1996	11.70	5.96	-0.56	15.09	21.82	4.89	130.85
1997	0.10	-4.33	-1.51	8.52	-11.52	0.94	132.85
1998	4.50	8.27	12.27	0.65	-2.03	8.13	122.15
1999	1.90	-0.02	-4.47	8.47	-4.29	4.23	134.72
2000	6.10	15.42	17.59	10.64	27.42	-9.10	133.28
2001	-2.70	-10.27	-9.52	-7.69	-4.46	-0.14	134.77
2002	-0.10	-1.83	-4.21	-18.75	-0.93	-1.82	134.39
2003	4.10	5.80	5.49	15.38	-3.77	0.41	...

. At Farm Gate

.. Million acre-feet

Source: Economic Survey (1999-00) Statistical Supplement; Economic Survey (2002-03)

Table 7

Industry (Average growth rates (%) of major industrial items):

Years	Large scale Manufacturing	Small Scale manufacturing	Manufacturing	Cloth	Cotton Yarn	Fertilizer	Cement	Sugar
1960's	13.39	2.91	9.90	3.05	5.60	27.50	10.70	34.30
1970's	4.84	7.63	5.50	-5.24	3.40	13.20	2.50	2.20
1980's	8.16	8.40	8.20	-1.07	10.00	10.70	8.60	14.40
1991	5.42	-0.61	6.3	-0.64	14.14	0.00	4.00	57.89
1992	7.91	5.31	8.1	5.05	12.49	593.33	6.41	-6.67
1993	4.14	5.31	4.4	5.75	4.10	-84.62	3.61	14.29
1993	4.27	5.31	4.5	-3.23	7.47	21.88	-4.65	21.88
1994	1.53	5.31	2.5	2.19	7.10	-2.56	3.66	-2.56
1995	3.14	5.31	3.7	1.62	6.56	10.53	11.76	10.53
1996	-2.14	5.31	-0.1	1.99	1.74	-4.76	0.00	-4.76
1997	7.60	5.31	6.9	2.04	0.79	-2.50	-1.05	-2.50
1998	3.57	5.31	4.1	13.02	0.46	-10.26	2.13	7.69
1999	-0.01	5.31	1.5	13.68	8.57	-31.43	-3.12	4.76
2000	9.46	5.31	8.2	12.12	2.93	20.83	4.30	-13.64
2001	4.87	5.31	5	-15.12	5.11	10.34	-8.25	0.00
2002	8.65	5.31	7.7	1.51	-10.83	3.12	-4.49	2.63

Source: 50 years of Pakistan in Statistics (1998); Economic survey (2002-03)

Table 8

Leading Money Market Indicators:

Years	All Banks' assets growth Rates (%)	Share of Private Banks' assets in Banking Sector's Assets (%)	Share of Foreign Banks' Assets in Banking Sector's Assets (%)	Share of SOBs' in Banking Sector's Assets (%)	*NBFIs' assets growth rate (%)	**DFIs' assets shares in NBFIs assets (%)	Share of ^SOB's NPLs to gross advances (%)	Share of ^^DFIs' NPLs to gross advances (%)	~NPL's to Gross Advances
1960s	17.25	...	...	...	...	...	...	...	...
1970s	25.27	...	...	...	...	...	...	...	...
1980s	17.05	...	...	...	...	...	...	...	...
1991	23.00	...	10.90	89.10	25.30	71.10	19.90	18.30	18.90
1992	23.53	3.8	12.50	83.70	38.20	58.40	18.60	20.30	17.40
1993	19.00	5.2	14.70	80.10	16.30	59.30	22.10	22.00	20.00
1994	23.28	6.3	15.20	78.40	24.30	54.00	25.60	30.00	21.70
1995	17.07	8.5	14.80	76.70	7.40	55.30	23.30	29.00	19.30
1996	15.48	9.7	18.00	72.30	4.70	56.60	23.50	40.00	19.20
1997	11.45	11.3	20.10	68.70	8.80	61.50	26.50	36.90	20.10
1998	-25.43	11.4	18.10	70.50	-10.00	61.30	25.40	44.60	19.50
1999	9.24	11.9	16.3	71.80	-3.50	58.70	27.70	52.20	22.00
2000	3.88	13.6	15.2	70.60	-1.30	57.00	24.40	58.70	19.50
2001	10.12	...	...	...	...	...	...	...	...
2002	15.98	...	...	...	...	...	...	...	...
2003	10.73	...	...	...	...	...	...	...	...

*Non-Bank Financial Institutions   **Development financial institutions   ^ State Owned Banks

^^ Development Finance Institutions   ~ Non-Performing Loans   ... Data not available

Source: 50 years of Pakistan in statistics (1998); Economic survey (2002-03); Pakistan Financial Sector assessment (1990-2000)

Table 9

Capital Market (Leading indicators of Karachi Stock market):

Years	Stock Price Index (Base 1980-81)	Average market Capitalization (Rs. billion)	Total listed companies
1960s	68.94	...	81*
1970s	68.87	5.39	291*
1980s	190.16	25.74	314*
1991	387.67	68.50	528
1992	730.76	218.36	628
1993	626.94	214.43	653
1994	1125.13	404.58	724
1995	724.36	293.30	764
1996	659.78	368.21	782
1997	554.45	469.60	781
1998	385.62	259.28	773
1999	408.02	286.22	765
2000	499.44	391.86	762
2001	460.24	339.25	760
2002	413.80	407.64	711
2003	549.33	602.99	700

* These values are not the averages but the specific no. of companies corresponding to the year (e.g. on 1960 listed companies were 81 etc.)

Source: 50 Years Of Pakistan in Statistics; Economic Survey (2002-03). www.kse.net. pk

Table 10
Physical Infrastructure

Years	Energy		Roads (000 Km)	Communications			Transport	
	Gas (Supply) Bln. CF	Electricity (installed capacity) 000 MW		Internet connections (million)	Telephones (Mln. Nos.)	Post Offices (000 Nos.)	Motor Vehicles on road (mln. Nos.)	Cargo handled at Karachi port (000 tonnes)
1960s	...	...	70.5	...	0.10	7.1	...	8583
1970s	165.4	1.3	74.1	...	0.20	9.0	0.36	8786
1980s	385.2	3.1	123.8	...	0.60	11.8	1.35	8779
1991	518.50	8.70	170.80	...	1.19	13.40	2.12	18709
1992	550.70	9.40	182.70	...	1.46	13.40	2.47	20453
1993	583.50	10.60	189.30	...	1.55	13.20	2.65	22170
1994	642.20	11.30	196.80	...	1.80	13.30	2.83	22569
1995	628.20	12.10	207.70	...	2.13	13.30	3.03	23098
1996	666.60	13.00	218.30	...	2.38	13.40	3.26	23581
1997	697.60	14.70	229.60	...	2.56	13.40	3.50	23475
1998	699.70	15.60	240.90	...	2.75	13.20	3.70	22684
1999	744.90	15.60	247.50	0.01	2.86	12.80	4.00	24053
2000	818.30	17.40	248.30	0.01	3.10	12.80	4.00	23761
2001	857.40	17.60	250.00	0.03	3.30	12.20	4.50	25981
2002	923.80	17.70	251.70	1.3	3.60	12.30	4.60	26692
2003	724.10	17.70	251.80	1.9	4.60	12.30	4.90	19743

... : Data not available

Source: 50 Years of Pakistan in statistics (1998); Economic Survey (2002-03).

3

Aiding Authoritarianism? Donors, Dollars and Dictators

Aqil Shah

The conquest of the earth, which mostly means the taking it away from those who have a different complexion or slightly flatter noses than ourselves, is not a pretty thing when you look into it too much.
— Joseph Conrad, *Heart of Darkness*

Pakistan's development needs are acute. With a low per capita GDP of US$ 408, it ranks 142nd on the UNDP Human Development Index amongst countries with the lowest human development indicators.[1] 32.6 per cent of the population lives below the national income poverty line.[2] The country's accumulated external debt and liabilities of US$ 35.8 billion, while low in comparison to some countries with similar per capita income and population levels, stand at a staggering 37.8 per cent of the GDP.[3] Debt servicing and military expenditures absorb an estimated 70-80 per cent of the budgetary resources available to the government.

Since the late 1980s, chronic balance of payments problems and high debt burdens have left the Pakistani economy dependent on financing from the International Monetary Fund (IMF, hereafter Fund), as well as on its clean bill of health to gain access to other aid agencies and private creditors. Pakistan's overriding need to stay financially solvent has meant that international financial institutions (IFIs) can virtually pre-define terms and conditions on which loans are extended. Given this extreme influence, it is no surprise that World Bank and Fund officials have come to dominate economic policy making in Pakistan. In the 1990s, a caretaker Prime Minister, a Finance Minister and the Governor of the State Bank have all at one time been senior level economists from these Bretton Woods Institutions. As globalization continues to reduce the scope for domestic economic interventions, the level of influence wielded by the IFIs, however, remains quite independent of who is in power in any recipient nation with each government accepting harsh loan conditionality to tide over economic crises. Successive governments in Pakistan, like many other aid dependent countries, have had to tailor their policies and position their reforms in line with the needs and incentives generated by external donors.

External aid interventions have often helped provide military rulers with the semblance of external legitimacy they need for regime survival and consolidation. All three of Pakistan's military dictators—Generals Ayub, Zia and Musharraf—have benefited from favourable external conditions to elicit international support for prolonging their stay in power. For instance, Pakistan's decision to join the American led anti-terror coalition against the Taliban and Al-Qaeda swiftly translated into removal of American sanctions imposed in the 1990s. Generous grants-in-aid, more loans from the international financial institutions and a rescheduling of the country's external debt followed. Even before the events of 11 September 2001, external involvement in General Musharraf's 'good governance' initiatives had reached unprecedented levels. Well aware of the changed international environment (with its unmistakable, albeit rhetorical, emphasis on democracy) in which the military took over power in October 1999, Musharraf swiftly placed devolution of political power at the centre of his purported reforms agenda, enticing the external development community with the rare opportunity to redefine state structures. Not to be left behind, many aid agencies quickly seized the chance to 'reconstruct' Pakistan from 'bottom up'.

This chapter is a qualitative case study of the role of foreign aid in relation to politics and policymaking in Pakistan. First, the terms on which aid is given and its impact on development are briefly analyzed. Second, the historical trajectory of external economic assistance is traced to explore the geo-political determinants of aid. Next, structural adjustment lending is reviewed for its impact on democratic consolidation and legitimation in Pakistan. Lastly, external involvement in critical public policy areas (such as administrative and political reforms), otherwise known as 'Good Governance' assistance, is analyzed in the context of donor support for General Musharrraf's Local Government Plan (LGP) 2000. In doing so, the disproportionate policy influence of foreign donors in setting the parameters of, and designing, institutional reforms in Pakistan is examined against their declared objectives of support to democracy and participatory governance.

External Aid: Composition and Impact

Pakistan relies almost exclusively for external economic assistance on countries that form the Aid-to-Pakistan consortium, now renamed Pakistan Development Forum, which provides 84 per cent of total aid commitments.[4] Japan, by far the largest bilateral donor, disbursed roughly 2.4 billion dollars from 1994 to 1998. The United States, UK, Canada, France and Germany are other prominent members of the Forum. The World Bank, along with the Asian Development Bank (ADB), contributes the bulk of multilateral donor financing. Over the decades, the United Nations development agencies (UNDP, UNICEF, and UNFPA) have also funded extensive technical assistance activities in Pakistan.

External aid, when properly used, is a vital source of finance for low-income countries. Under traditional macroeconomic precepts, aid flows contribute to long-term economic growth and poverty reduction by providing additional resources for investments in countries with low incomes. With a rise in per capita incomes, domestic savings and investment rates are expected to reach levels that make more aid unnecessary. In sharp contrast to this 'self limiting' theory, however, evidence from many low-income countries shows that large aid flows over long periods have created aid dependence, undermining democratic accountability and retarding institutional development.[5] In African countries like Zaire decades of large-scale foreign assistance have 'left not a trace of progress' and have promoted 'incompetence, corruption, and misguided policies'.[6]

The aggregate impact of foreign aid on growth and development in Pakistan has been negative. Empirical evidence shows a strong negative correlation between aid and growth.[7] Besides, a lion's share of aid is tied directly to specific projects and purchase of donor country goods and services. For instance, the share of project related aid during 1999-2000 was 77.7 per cent (see Fig. 1). In addition, 10 per cent of all aid in Pakistan is absorbed by consultancy fees, with the share as high as 50 per cent in some projects.[8] Besides, 'tying' raises procurement project costs by almost 30 per cent.[9]

According to some estimates, untying aid alone could increase the value and impact of development assistance by 10-20 per cent.[10] This is, in part, because of the distortions caused by the impact of tied aid on the import and production structures of the recipient country since donors typically use aid to finance their own investments, employ their nationals as 'experts' or create a market for subsidized imports in the recipient country which can compete, and often displace, national products.[11]

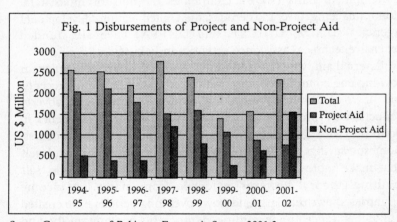

Fig. 1 Disbursements of Project and Non-Project Aid

Source: Government of Pakistan, Economic Survey 2001-2.

Over the decades, the share of grants as a proportion of overall aid has declined considerably. The share of grants, which averaged around 80 per cent during the First Five Year Plan (1955-1960), was down to 13-16 per cent during the 1990s.[12] According to one aid official, this hardening of loans reflects the growing consensus in donor policy circles that 'substantial amounts of aid as grants would threaten the long term prospects of aid flows without enhancing aid effectiveness'.[13] Compared to the 1950s and 1960s, the average rate of interest on external loans and credits has surged, while average maturity periods have been reduced. With stagnant export earnings and domestic revenues, the deteriorating terms of aid meant that the only way for Pakistan to repay loans was to borrow more money, thus driving itself deeper into the debt trap. As shown in Table 1 (and Fig. 1), the net value of foreign aid transfers turned negative in 1996-97, and again in 1999–2000/2000–1 as debt repayment obligations registered a steep rise. Additionally, aid and debt leads to a deleterious 'foreign exchange drag' insofar as debt repayments cause the outflow of scarce, free standing foreign exchange as compared to the tied foreign exchange inflows as part of aid.[14]

Table 1
Debt Servicing and Net Transfers

(US$ million)

Year	Gross Disbursements*	Debt Servicing**	Net Transfers	Net Transfers as % of disbursements
1990-91	2045	1316	729	36
1991-92	2366	1513	853	36
1992-93	2436	1648	788	32
1993-94	2530	1746	784	31
1994-95	2571	2042	529	21
1995-96	2555	2136	419	16
1996-97	2231	2265	(-) 34	(-) 1
1997-98	2800	2353	447	16
1998-99	2440	1530	910	37
1999-00	1426	1512	(-) 86	(-) 6
2000-01	1597	1961	(-) 364	(-) 23
2001-02	2364	981	13831	58

Source: Government of Pakistan, Economic Survey 2001-02
*Excludes relief Assistance for Afghan Refugees
** Excludes interest on short-term loans and IMF charges up to 1998-99.

Figure 1. Net Transfers as % of Gross Disbursements

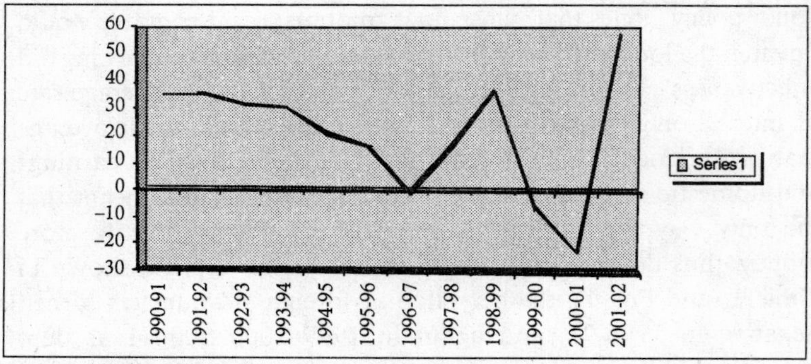

Source: Government of Pakistan, Economic Survey 2001-02

The contours and conduct of development assistance are determined largely in donor capitals. Besides, aid allocations are typically shrouded in secrecy; and even where figures are available, it is often quite difficult to determine the exact priorities or outcomes for which it is disbursed. Instead of fine-tuning development assistance to root it locally, standardized prescriptions, irrespective of the economic needs and institutional constraints of developing countries, are commonly employed by aid agencies in many cases to 'to fulfill the primary motive of timely disbursements'.[15] This 'one size fits all' way in which development assistance is conducted has led to the strange situation in which a diverse range of countries are sold the same medicine for different illnesses.[16] As shown below, aid has traditionally been driven by political and strategic motivations, often allowing corrupt and inefficient bureaucratic practices to survive and flourish. Wastage and corruption in donor funded aid programs is also commonplace.

A significant feature of both bilateral and multilateral aid is the complex range of economic and political conditionality attached to it. In recent decades, conditionality has become much more strict especially in the case of multilateral financing which comes attached with stringent fiscal, trade and exchange rate polices. In the 1990s, new prescriptions of 'good governance' encapsulating administrative reforms, primarily democratization and decentralization, have also been added. The scope of aid conditionality thus has been widened from economic governance to include 'good governance' in a much broader, normative sense. Prescriptions for 'democratic governance' seek to redefine the very relationships between the state, political society, and civil society.[17] In the process, governments, as well as civil society organizations who access donor funding have had to recast their projects and programs to fit the loosely, and often recklessly, defined rubric of 'good governance'.

While a few individuals sporadically voice independent views, the marketplace of ideas with regard to economic policy reform is regulated and shaped in large measure by donor funded research and analysis. Typical of aid dependent states, the chronically low levels of state capacity to analyze and redress Pakistan's development problems means that better equipped external donors are influential actors in the formulation and articulation of development policy. In the virtual absence of quality research institutions or higher centres of learning, donor-driven development prescriptions are rarely ever challenged systematically and locally appropriate structural reforms seldom articulated. A case in point is the salience 'devolution' discussed in the last section, has assumed in the institutional reform domain. While some form of local government has existed in Pakistan since the early years of independence, the growing emphasis and policy attention given to decentralization in donor rhetoric and practice has endowed it with the status of 'must do' reform. Even though governments and civil society organizations might internalize and adopt prevailing developmental fads for their own benefits, wider societal ownership and acceptance is much more elusive.

Geopolitics Still?

While developing strategic alliances with authoritarian regimes was a dominant feature of external cooperation during the cold war, 'strategic' interests more than the nature of the political regime or the policy performance of governments still explain why aid is given. For instance, the European Union admits rather frankly:

Given Pakistan's location in a volatile region, with widespread incidence of drugs and arms trafficking as well as illegal migration, it is important for the EU to engage the country for geo-political reasons.... More recently, there has been a major re-orientation by the donor community towards Pakistan in view of its support to the coalition against terrorism.[18]

Evidence suggests that foreign policy preferences of donor governments (with a few exceptions such as the Nordic countries) continue to dictate aid, with factors such as 'colonial past and political alliances' playing a much more important role than governance and economic efficiency. Rewards for 'good' policies, more notably democratic liberalization and openness, represent only a marginal share of aid over time in a country.[19] There is also no evidence that less corrupt governments receive more aid. On the contrary, more corrupt governments, according to some measures of corruption, receive more aid.[20]

Besides empirical evidence, donor practice in Pakistan shows that the morally charged rhetoric of 'democratic governance' is often deployed to gloss over the minor inconvenience of supporting authoritarian regimes for geo-political reasons. Couching programs and policies in such overused but politically correct buzzwords also helps donors project the normative view of aid to blunt criticism for failure and ineffectiveness from legislators who approve their funding.

Foreign aid was a vital component of Pakistan's cold war military alliance with the United States. Underlining the generous nature of American military and economic assistance was Washington's need to prop up the military as 'a major rallying point in the defence against communist expansion and penetration'.[21] Under the terms of the Mutual Defence Assistance Agreement, Pakistan received about US$ 270 million from 1951 to 1958 through the PL-480 (Public Law 480).[22] While the loan mainly provided for purchase of US wheat, 30 per cent was designated for military sales, 11 per cent for providing loans to U.S. and Pakistani firms engaged in marketing American goods, and 3 per cent for the US for its propaganda activity in Pakistan.[23] General Ayub's October 1958 military coup gave added impetus to the strategic partnership between the two sides. Primarily designed to keep Pakistan in the US camp, aid (measured on a per capita basis) almost doubled between 1960/61 and 1964/65. With more American aid came the influx of American economic advisors. By the early 1960s, the Harvard Advisory Group (HAG) had come to play a dominant role in Pakistan's development policy planning.

The next major injection of American aid into Pakistan also coincided with the assumption of power by the army under General Zia-ul-Haq (1977–1988).[24] In April 1979, President Carter had imposed unilateral military and economic sanctions under the Symington amendment after Pakistan reportedly attempted to enrich weapons grade uranium.[25] When the Soviet Union militarily intervened in Afghanistan in late 1979, however, these sanctions were swiftly waived to rally Pakistan as a bulwark against Soviet expansionism. The Reagan administration provided a US $3.2 billion economic and military aid package, fifty per cent of which was tied to the sale of American military equipment.[26] Another US $4 billion aid package was signed in 1987. Meanwhile, in 1985, the US Congress had passed the Pressler Amendment to the Foreign Assistance Act 1961. The amendment stipulated that US aid and government-to-government military sales would be cut off unless the President could certify annually that Pakistan did not possess a 'nuclear explosive device'. Given the need for continued Pakistani cooperation in the anti-Soviet effort, the US continued to provide such waivers until 1989 even though Pakistan had declared its capability both to enrich uranium for weapons purposes and to assemble an atomic weapon.[27] In 1990, after the Soviet Union withdrew from Afghanistan and the United States lost interest in the region, the American president refused to certify Pakistan's non-nuclear status triggering sanctions under the Pressler amendment.

While Pakistan received some security and humanitarian aid under the Brown Amendment in 1995, Islamabad's decision to conduct atomic tests in response to India's nuclear detonations in May 1998 prompted President Clinton to impose yet another round of sanctions under the Glenn amendment.[28] Economic aid was terminated, foreign military sales were proscribed, new loans from the IMF and World Bank were suspended, and exports of dual-use nuclear or missile items were banned.[29] Japan, Pakistan's largest bilateral donor, also froze aid making its resumption contingent on Pakistan's accession to the Comprehensive Test Ban Treaty (CTBT).

The October 1999 military coup triggered the so-called 'democracy sanctions' under Section 508 of the US Foreign Operations Appropriations Act that bars Washington from providing military or economic assistance to non-elected governments. Once again, the events of 11 September 2001 dramatically changed the situation. In light of Pakistan's decision to align itself with the American-led anti-terror coalition, the Bush administration lifted nuclear-related and democracy sanctions and provided US $1 billion in aid for 2002. Japan resumed bilateral aid, and Norway and Denmark entered into debt rescheduling agreements with Pakistan. The European Commission rushed through trade concessions of over a billion US dollars. In December 2001, the country's bilateral creditors agreed to an unprecedented 're-profiling' of the entire stock of US $12.5 billion bilateral debt by allowing for a 38-year repayment period for ODA assistance (US$8.8 billion) and a 23 year-period for non-ODA assistance (US$3.7 billion). In June 2003, President Bush announced his administration's commitment to seek a five-year US$3 billion aid package from Congress as a further reward for the Musharraf regime's co-operation. Military and security assistance constitutes 50 per cent of this package.[30] A senior White House official asserted at the time that long-term US aid required that the United States be 'satisfied' with Pakistan's progress on non-proliferation, anti-terrorism, and democratization.[31] A stark reminder to many in Pakistan that the US was willing to overlook the military's coercive, anti-democratic actions at home as long as it cooperated in the war on terror.

Adjustment, Authoritarianism and Democracy

While the World Bank has been closely associated with financing development since the 1950s, it was Zia's military regime which initiated the first stabilization program with IMF support. Ever since, IFI assisted stabilization and adjustment programs have become almost a permanent feature of economic policy planning in Pakistan. Typically geared to address macroeconomic imbalances and structural defects through fiscal austerity, liberalization and deregulation of the economy, these loans carry a formidable array of conditions: reduction in budget and trade deficits, liberalization of trade and import controls, stabilization of the exchange rate, removal of tax exemptions, reduction in domestic borrowing for budgetary support, reduction or elimination of subsidies on fertilizers and other agricultural inputs, and imposition of sales tax on critical food items and medicines. Since 1999, the IMF has initiated the Poverty Reduction and Growth Facility (PRGF), a new 'low interest' lending facility but one that comes with a more stringent framework for conditionality enforcement under which both the Fund and Bank align their conditionality with priorities articulated in the recipient country's Poverty Reduction Strategy Paper (PRSP).[32]

Critics say conditionality turns a loan into a policy tool as loan instalments are tied to verifiable steps towards specified policy targets. 'Even when well-intentioned', argues Stiglitz, 'the myriad of conditions—in some cases over a hundred each with its own rigid timetable—detracted from the country's ability to address the central pressing problems'.[33] While recipient governments typically sign on to harsh conditionality to tide over a financial crisis, lapses are quite common during implementation since these adjustment programs are not owned locally and often carry prohibitive political costs. Besides policymakers have less incentive to take the politically difficult steps necessary for IMF prescribed structural reforms when they know that aid flows are truly contingent on geopolitical considerations. Successive governments in Pakistan have hedged their bets on the country's geo-strategic importance and nuclear status in the hope that the international community will not allow a 'nuclear-armed, Islamic country' to go bust. While Fund decisions are less than transparent, press reports suggest that endorsement by the United States has been crucial to IMF bailouts of Pakistan. In early 1999, for instance, new IMF lending worth US$1.56 billion was approved only after the United States decided to ease non-military sanctions in light of a deepening economic crisis triggered by Islamabad's nuclear testing.

Why have successive governments sought IMF financing? To plug chronic fiscal deficits governments had traditionally relied on high levels of deficit financing from the domestic banking system. By the mid-1980s, however, the costs of public borrowing had increased astronomically due to the reduced availability of concessional financing in the aftermath of the 1981-82 debt crisis and the substitution of bank borrowing with non-inflationary but higher interest rate, non-bank financing.[34] By 1986-87, the fiscal situation worsened further due to a sharp decline in worker remittances from the Middle East, the continued rise in public expenditures (public sector wages and high military spending), and a rise in public sector interest payments.[35] The abrupt termination of American aid in 1990 also forced the government to look for alternative sources of external financing. Unable to generate revenues and address the persistent macroeconomic imbalances, government after government sought IMF bailouts. Between 1988 and 2003, successive elected and non-elected governments entered into multiple structural adjustment loan (SAL) agreements with the IFIs.

The IMF blames Pakistan's poor macroeconomic and social sector outlook in the 1990s on 'slippages in reform implementation and relaxation of macroeconomic discipline'.[36] The Fund's tendency to pin the failure of its programs entirely on recipient countries, to underestimate their social and political costs in these countries and the serious flaws in its approach are all well known and do not need repeating here.[37] What is interesting from our perspective is that one of the main reasons cited by military-backed presidents for the dismissal of successive elected governments in the 1990s was also 'economic mismanagement'. While mismanagement and (allegations of) pervasive corruption marked the ostensibly civilian rule of both the PPP and PML-N, a more plausible explanation for their premature dismissals is to be found in the attempts by civilian prime ministers to assert their constitutional authority in ways that the Pakistani military deemed inimical to its influence in the domestic (and foreign policy) arenas. Besides, the country's economic crisis stemmed from deeper political fault lines. In post-Zia Pakistan, political leaders were handed over the unenviable task of balancing the state's strategic imperatives and the economic needs of its populace but without the authority and resources required to achieve these objectives.[38] In 1998–99, for instance, the PML-N government was facing a shortage of Rs 70 billion in meeting just its debt service and defence requirements.[39] Vulnerable to the premature loss of power at the hands of the military and unable to fully meet voter expectations, elected authorities were mainly concerned with short-term political management and survival since 'existing practice represents a politically optimal solution to the problem of staying in power or extracting rents'.[40]

Specific donor demands to follow the 'one size fits all' set of economic policies and 'austerity' measures undermined the process of democratization in a direct way by creating an additional set of constraints on the already limited policy space available to elected governments. In the process, governments became increasingly answerable to external donors rather than to voters. That the IMF could virtually dictate the nature and direction of economic policy to elected governments was also a function of the active collaboration of a powerful authoritarian coalition (comprising technocrats, civilian bureaucrats and the military) contemptuous of consent-driven, partisan politics. In the telling words of the current State Bank governor, Ishrat Hussain, one of the motivations for accessing IMF loans was 'the attempt of reformist economic managers to *restrain and block the pursuit of populist policies by political leaders*'[41] (emphasis added). Once in power, elected officials were allowed limited policy latitude and 'signed on the dotted line'.[42]

The terms and conditions of the three year (1988-1991) Structural Adjustment Facility (SAF) were negotiated and settled in advance of the military's planned transfer of power to an elected government in 1988. Once in office, the newly elected PPP government of Prime Minister Benazir Bhutto had little choice but to 'come to terms with the Fund quickly so that such of its conditions as were acceptable could be implemented while the PPP's popular standing was still high'.[43] In fact, analysts have speculated that acceptance of the IMF program was one of the conditions set by the military for her elevation to the office of the PM.[44] Similarly in 1993, after the PML-N government of Prime Minister Nawaz Sharif was dismissed by President Ghulam Ishaq Khan on corruption charges, a former Pakistani Vice-President of the World Bank, Moeen Qureshi, was appointed as caretaker Prime Minister. One of his earliest actions was to start negotiations with the IMF for a standby loan and announce wide ranging economic policy measures that effectively set the economic policy of the incoming government. Upon getting elected for the second time, the PPP government endorsed the loan, and within four months, it signed another three-year loan under the IMF's Extended Fund Facility (EFF) and the Enhanced Structural Adjustment Facility (ESAF). Reportedly, the elected government merely 'rubber-stamped' these agreements to ensure its political survival.[45]

The PPP government's inability to meet the strict revenue and tariff targets mandated by the 1995-96 budget prompted the IMF to freeze the ESAF.[46] The Bhutto government adopted a 'mini-budget' of increased taxes, expenditure cuts and rupee devaluation to secure the aborted loan. These measures resulted in sharp price increases in essential food items, gasoline and kerosene oil, generating widespread public resentment and demands for their withdrawal. While the IMF approved a standby loan with stricter terms, it was later suspended on the grounds that the government had failed to adequately comply with required conditionality.[47] In November 1996, the President of Pakistan sacked the PPP government on charges of economic mismanagement paving the way for yet another interim government. This time, Shahid Javed Burki, a serving Vice-President of the World Bank, was parachuted in overnight from Washington, D.C. to assume the mantle of the finance ministry. The IMF released the second tranche of the standby loan shortly before the general elections of February 1997 ostensibly after the interim government slashed government expenditures, reduced public borrowings, and raised taxes. The loan tranche had reportedly been withheld to pressure the government to comply with the conditions attached to a US$ 300 million World Bank financial sector reforms loan.

In October 1997, the IMF extended another Enhanced Structural Adjustment Facility (ESAF)/Extended Fund Facility (EFF) loan for three years. After Pakistan decided to test its nuclear devices in May 1998, the state's financial crisis deepened further 'as a result of loss of investor confidence, a decline in private capital inflows, imposition of economic sanctions, and the suspension of new official bilateral and multilateral disbursements for non-humanitarian purposes'.[48] Faced with a serious balance of payments crisis and eager to access the second year ESAF financing, a beleaguered PML-N government responded by raising retail gasoline prices, reducing planned development expenditures, and devaluing the Pakistani rupee vis-à-vis the U.S. dollar, eliminating most import duties, simplifying tariff structures and extending the sales tax net to several areas ahead of the schedule agreed earlier with the Fund.[49]

Relations between Pakistan and the IFIs soured when the Nawaz Sharif government initiated investigations into allegations of kickbacks and overpricing in power purchase agreements signed by the previous PPP government with mostly western private companies. Forecasting energy shortages, the Bhutto government had decided to privatize the energy sector in 1994 with the World Bank's backing which had committed US$ 1.3 billion under a Private Sector Energy Development Fund.[50] A total of nineteen contracts were signed between the government of Pakistan and Independent Power Producers (IPPs), many backed by World Bank financing and guarantees.[51] After the Sharif government cancelled as many as half the contracts on charges of corruption in June 1998, it soon discovered how aid could be used as an arm-twister. The World Bank issued a stern warning to the government of Pakistan to keep its legal actions separate from 'the commercial and contractual issues involving IPPs'.[52] Payments from the IMF were reportedly delayed because of the dispute.[53]

When General Musharraf assumed power in October 1999, both the country's precarious financial situation and the needs of regime legitimacy required that the Pakistani economy be rapidly reintegrated into the international financial system. Pakistan had reached a situation of near default on external payments in the aftermath of the decision to conduct nuclear tests in May 1998 (a policy decision backed and pushed, paradoxically enough, by the military). These urgent imperatives underlined the military's willingness to fully embrace the IMF's economic prescriptions which elected governments had found difficult to implement.

To establish his regime's credibility with the international financial institutions, Musharraf appointed Shaukat Aziz, a senior Citibank executive as Finance Minister and Ishrat Hussain, a World Bank official, as the State Bank governor. The IMF management approved a ten-month standby loan in November 2000 which came with strict criteria such as reduction in the budget deficit from 6.4 to 5.2 per cent, a free float of the rupee, the imposition of agricultural income tax and the extension of GST to the retail trade and services. Since the military-led regime had earlier reported to the IMF the previous government's alleged misreporting of fiscal data in the year 1998-1999, Pakistan was also obliged to get the accounts of all its income and expenditure scrutinized periodically and closely by Fund staff. Following the timely completion of a stabilization program under the stand by arrangement, Pakistan became eligible for a US $ 1.3 billion medium term Poverty Reduction Growth Facility (PRGF) in 2001.

Since the military coup in October 1999, donor concerns about Pakistan's economic 'derailment' under elected governments have gradually given way to upbeat assessments of the military regime's macroeconomic performance: a strong external position, lower public debt burden, access to international capital markets and a revival in economic growth.[54] In December 2004, Pakistan withdrew from the IMF programme as officials claimed that IMF structural support was no longer necessary because the government's macroeconomic discipline and reforms had brought the economy out of the dock.[55]

Critics argue that improved macroeconomic indicators have less to do with the vision of Musharraf's economic managers than the windfall gains from renewed U.S. grants and assistance, external debt rescheduling and increased remittances from overseas Pakistanis in the wake of 9/11.[56] Lending credence to this view is the regime's less than shining overall economic record. Contrary to its claims, macroeconomic gains have so far failed to control or dent income inequality and poverty.[57] Unemployment in the country is at a high level and rising.[58] The military's economic managers, however, continue to underestimate the social and political costs of their polices which, in their view, can be redressed if Pakistan sticks to a steady neo-liberal reform path.[59] This is not surprising in light of their virtual immunity from any personal or political consequences for their actions. Both Aziz (who was elected to the Senate to fulfil procedural requirements) and Hussain retained their posts even after the election of a civilian government in November 2002. In August 2004, the military went so far as to elevate Aziz to the office of Prime Minister in what many see as a bid to further boost the regime's 'hard earned' international credibility.[60] Even though the military resorted to blatant electoral fraud in the process, the IMF welcomed the appointment as auspicious for the 'continuation of reforms'—a common donor euphemism for keeping the economy out of the purview of politicians and political parties.[61] Continuation or not, the real question is when, if ever, will the benefits of macroeconomic stabilization trickle down? It is difficult to imagine how a deeply contested military-authoritarian political order can sustain economic growth and spread its benefits when it is devoid of popular legitimacy and relies primarily on coercion, electoral manipulation schemes and legal chicanery to stay in power. Pakistan's economic difficulties have deep roots in the political economy of national (in)security under which the needs and demands of the military override those of the rest of the polity. Political problems require political solutions, not just deft economic management.

Reconstructing Pakistan 'Bottom Up': Devolution and Donors

Centralization was the master concept in aid policy right up to the late 1970s. In the aftermath of the Second World War, strong, centralized authority was seen in the West as a bulwark against the threat of communism and internal fragmentation in artificially created, post-colonial states.[62] Centralized, technology-led approaches to development were privileged by external donors as they offered the biggest and quickest bang for their bucks. While the earliest attempts to decentralize development management came in the form of 'Integrated Rural Development Programs' initiated by the World Bank in 1974, it was not until the mid 1980s that international lending agencies singled out state failure as the prime suspect preventing sustainable economic growth and poverty reduction in developing countries. Around that time, a new academic and policy consensus on 'Good Governance' which favoured 'bottom-up' or decentralized governance over centralized approaches was also gaining prominence.[63] The end of the Cold War gave this new approach further impetus, as donors no longer faced the rigid geopolitical barriers to interventions in hitherto sensitive areas of state policy. The result: an unmistakable emphasis on decentralization as a key component of the external pressure on developing countries to liberalize. Notwithstanding donor rhetoric on local empowerment and autonomy, decentralization is mainly seen as a means of shifting financial and administrative responsibility away from centralized developing country governments to the local levels for making resource allocations and social service delivery more efficient.

Ironically, in Pakistan as in many other authoritarian states, military dictators have used decentralization, in one form or another, as a substitute for democracy. Contrary to the time tested pretext of building grassroots democratic institutions, the real motivation has been to justify military intervention and ensure regime survival.[64] Like his military predecessors, Musharraf too quickly seized upon the idea of using local government for political legitimation and consolidation. Within a month of the coup, he created the National Reconstruction Bureau (NRB) under a retired general, Tanvir Naqvi, to develop a devolution plan. In May 2000, the NRB prepared its draft Local Government Plan (LGP) 2000.[65] Like previous local bodies schemes, the NRB's plan called for the re-establishment of district and sub-district (*tehsil* and union) governments. Unlike previous devolution schemes, the LGP 2000 proposed the transfer of substantive political and administrative authority to local governments. Notably, the plan recommended the abolition of the office of the Deputy Commissioner (administrative head of the district) to be replaced by an elected district *nazim* (mayor). Ostensibly inspired by the democratic principle of making public officials accountable to elected authorities, this was the first time in Pakistan's history that the district level bureaucracy was subordinated to an elected mayor. On 13 August 2001, the provincial governments issued local government ordinances to operationalize the devolution plan (see chapter by Saeed Shafqat in this volume for details).

In devolving powers, Musharraf was no doubt replicating past attempts at decentralization. But the military faced a different set of constraints in the context of the October 1999 coup. Both Ayub and Zia had taken over when external conditions were conducive to military rule. Having deposed an elected government in a post cold-war environment where electoral democracy has emerged as the preferred form of government, this military regime's need to dispel international apprehensions was far more acute. Three days after the coup, Clare Short, the then British Secretary for International Development, confirming that Britain had frozen all direct development assistance to the Government of Pakistan, had said:

Pakistan needs a democratic government which is transparent and accountable. We are deeply concerned at the situation in Pakistan: widespread corruption, economic mismanagement, increasing poverty and now military rule...obviously, we cannot provide development assistance to the military authorities in Pakistan. No new funds for programmes linked to governmental institutions will be made available and all our specialists who have been advising the Government have stopped work.[66]

Keen to end its external isolation, the military pledged devolution reforms to establish its democratic credentials and confirm its intent eventually to restore civilian rule. Announcing his local bodies plan on the eve of US President Clinton's visit, Musharraf declared, 'Democracy starts here at the district and local governments, from here we will move up step by step to provincial and federal (elections) in due course'.[67]

In its methods and rhetoric, the regime's devolution closely resembled the decentralization reforms favoured by some donor agencies.[68] This was more than coincidental. Both bilateral and multilateral donors had led the debate on the need for decentralization from the front long before the October 1999 coup. For instance, the World Bank's *Framework for Civil Service Reforms in Pakistan* had strongly recommended 'devolution of substantive authority' to lower tiers of government. The Bank had also strongly emphasized the need for 're-examining the roles of District Commissioners and their Deputies' and for placing 'safeguards to prevent their encroachment on local governments and intervention in their affairs.[69] In April 1998, the Local Dialogue Group (LDG), a donor-government coordination body with the UNDP, the World Bank, the Asian Development Bank as its key members, held a key meeting on 'decentralization of development management to the provincial and district levels', with the discussion focusing almost exclusively on local government reforms. In preparation for the LDG meeting, the UNDP had contracted a former deputy chairman of the Planning Commission to prepare a detailed background paper to synthesize the different strands of thinking on decentralization as well its practical experience in Pakistan. In addition, the Swiss Development Corporation (SDC) had arranged for a leading Swiss expert to study the legal aspects of decentralization and local government. In February 1998, four provincial seminars on local government were conducted by the Planning Commission's Good Governance Group (G3) with UNDP assistance. Legislators, civil servants, NGO leaders and aid officials took part in extensive discussions. Lauding this 'consensus building process', the World Bank had urged the government to use these inputs, and draw on another 1996 World Bank report 'Supporting Fiscal Decentralization in Pakistan', to make *early strategic decisions on devolution*.[70]

After Musharraf's coup, donors such as the United Nations Development Program (UNDP), sensing a unique opportunity, approached the military regime with generous offers of technical assistance. With little else to base its external legitimacy on, the military was more than keen to co-opt aid agencies, making calculated overtures to enlist their support for the 'bottom up' reconstruction of the country. The NRB requested UNDP to coordinate support to the 'national reconstruction reform process' from other UN programs, as well as from multilateral and bilateral partners. Accordingly, the regime relocated the Good Governance Group (G3) from the Planning Commission to the NRB, making it the focal point for external assistance for LGP 2000. Soon after, the UNDP re-activated its US$ 1.89 million support to G3 project providing national consultants as well as a senior international governance advisor for NRB's Devolution think tank.[71] UNDP advisors were extended unprecedented access to high-powered NRB policy planning meetings with these advisors drafting background papers, policy briefs and substantial parts of the original devolution plan. Through the Institutional Development Task Force (IDTF), an inter-aid agency coordination body on governance issues (renamed the Governance Group), the UNDP also provided the main platform for donor coordination and discussion on the devolution plan.[72] As General Musharraf consolidated his grip over state authority, initial scepticism in some international lending agencies over support to a military government (and/or about the project's financial viability) gave way to heightened enthusiasm over the rare opportunity to reshape and redefine governmental structures in Pakistan with the UK Department for International Development (DFID), the Canadian International Development Agency (CIDA) and a host of other external donors committing their 'democratic governance programs' to the military's devolution project.[73] In the words of the Asian Development Bank, which approved a US$300 million decentralization support program in November 2002, 'the government's far-reaching Political Devolution and Administrative

Decentralization Plan is among the boldest governance reforms ever undertaken by a developing country'.[74]

As donors re-routed their 'governance' resources to build democracy from below, the military regime took on the task of dismantling it from the top. With General Musharraf simultaneously occupying the offices of the Chief Executive (and later President), Chief of Army Staff, Chairman Joint Chiefs of Staff and Defence Minister, military officers were appointed to top civilian posts in the federal and provincial governments. Political rallies were banned, parliament stood dissolved and the constitution was suspended. On 26 January 2000, the Chief Justice and half the bench of the Supreme Court were arbitrarily removed for refusing to take oath under Musharraf's Provisional Constitutional Order. None of this autocratic centralization made the slightest difference to these donors who continued to support the military's devolution of power even as the regime used coercive tactics to obtain favourable results in the elections for *nazims* held under the LGP 2000 in July 2001. After 11 September 2001, even the token international emphasis on a return to civilian rule was put on the back burner to support General Musharraf in the fight against Al-Qaeda and the Taliban in Afghanistan. Emboldened by his newly found international recognition, Musharraf deployed local government personnel to manipulate the electoral process preparatory to the countrywide polls held in October 2002. *Nazims* were ordered to organize public rallies and mobilize voters in favour of Musharraf's fraudulent presidential referendum held in April 2002. Those who refused were threatened with corruption charges and accountability for their official actions.[75] In the national and provincial assembly elections, *nazims* loyal to the Pakistan Muslim League (Quaid-i-Azam), a pro-military rump of the of the PML-N, openly mobilized support for the party, generously using state resources placed at their disposal.

Despite the extensive 'pre-poll rigging' that led international observers to censure the entire electoral process as 'seriously flawed,[76] the UNDP, DFID, CIDA and the Norwegian Agency for Development Co-operation (NORAD) continued to support a US$ 5 million umbrella project on 'Supporting Democratic Electoral

Processes in Pakistan (SDEPP)' to provide 'the basis for coordinated international donor community support for the preparation of *truly democratic elections*'[77] (emphasis added). Even more alarming is the support of donor agencies like the UNDP for the NRB's proposed constitutional amendments to 'provide constitutional coverage to and ensure stability of the devolution initiatives'.[78] In fact, only a small fraction of the constitutional amendments package, promulgated in August 2002 as the Legal Framework Order (LFO) 2002, relates to constitutional protection for devolution.[79] The main features of that package, now enshrined in the constitution as the Seventeenth Amendment, are widely seen as an attempt to institutionalize military rule. These include, among others, the validation of all laws, ordinances and acts promulgated since October 1999; the restoration of the President's power to dismiss an elected government and dissolve the national assembly (albeit in consultation with the Prime Minister) as also the powers to appoint military services chiefs.

Donors remain undeterred. Applauding the inclusion of devolution in the 1973 constitution, a recent joint study by the World Bank, the ADB and DFID authoritatively argues that devolution has been designed to 'inject new blood into a political system' dominated by 'historically entrenched interests', 'to provide positive measures enabling marginalized citizens to access formal politics', and 'to introduce a measure of stability into a turbulent political scene by creating a stronger line of accountability between new politicians and local electorates'.[80] Are donors ignorant of the politics of devolution? As far as donors are concerned, the prospect of 'efficient service delivery' under devolution overrides democratic criteria. 'We knew that regime security was central to devolution', says one ADB official, '...that the military was circumventing provinces to create new constituencies for local regime support while reaping the added benefit of donor support...but we could either equivocate and risk reform failure, or put our money behind [the military government] to gain a voice'.[81] Gain a voice they did. In fact, so enamoured have been external donors by Musharraf's 'readiness to confront issues that eluded the country since independence',[82] that some have openly violated even their own declared goal of 'local ownership' and 'stakeholder consultations'. While the overall objective of the UNDP Governance Program in Pakistan is 'to create an enabling environment within which the people of Pakistan can influence the direction and conduct of their governing institutions',[83] it virtually ignored civil society organizations, professional associations and political parties during the planning process for the local government plan.[84] Throughout the formulation, design, dissemination and even implementation of the devolution plan, the UNDP also bypassed public institutions, including the Ministry of Local Government, to support the NRB.[85] Meyer has analyzed donor-funded rural institutional development projects in the Dominican Republic which advanced short-term donor priorities rather than local needs and subverted existing institutions. Once donor support ended, the new institutions collapsed.[86]

Although criticized by most political parties and independent human rights groups, donor acceptance and ownership of the devolution plan has endowed Musharrraf's local government system with its own momentum and a semblance of legitimacy missing in the domestic context. In the process, the military's political engineering has put a fragile, multi- ethnic Pakistan under immense strain. Since provinces were also largely bypassed to centralize control over the lower levels of government, donor-funded devolution has fanned federal provincial tensions without bestowing internal legitimacy on military rule. Since the formal transfer of power to an elected civilian government in November 2002, frictions between elected politicians and local governments are growing. Criticisms of, and demands for restructuring of the local government from government ministers and opposition politicians alike have led to speculations about its survival. For now, international support and the coercive powers available to the military insulate devolution from dissolution by the political elite. But in the extreme case that the local government system was dismantled, external donors are likely to conveniently dissociate themselves from the project to look for new 'strategic governance interventions' in a possible repeat of donor policy practice in Pakistan.

Conclusion

External economic assistance is 'not a pretty thing when you look into it too much'. Aid is ultimately political in nature betraying a fundamental contradiction between short-term donor interests and the long-term development needs of Pakistan. Stringent conditionality attached to donor financing represents an additional set of external constraints on policymaking which detracts from the state's ability to deal with its central economic and political problems. Rather than fostering development, conditionality often evokes widespread public resistance and strains the popular legitimacy of democratically elected governments.

With low levels of internal and external accountability, aid agencies continue to put aid money after 'non-democratic' governance not only in stark contradiction of their own declared objectives and normative commitments, but even where the chances of failure and/or political contestation are high. By supporting the military regime's devolution plan, for instance, donors have further reinforced the anti-politics consensus espoused by Pakistan's dominant military-technocratic coalition, exacerbating inter-ethnic and provincial-federal tensions.

Despite the rhetoric of ownership, donors seem to have used bureaucratic corruption and inefficiency as a pretext to ignore existing institutions in project design, formulation and implementation. Instead of strengthening or reforming standing public sector institutions, aid agencies prefer to bypass them by investing in parallel institutions (like the NRB) and/or use their influence to shape the nature and direction of policymaking.

Given their influence over the policymaking process, the onus of bridging the gap between the good governance discourse (i.e. less corrupt, economically sound and more democratic governments) and its practice rests, at least in part, with the donors. Unless they assist governments in taking realistic steps to reduce poverty and strengthen democratic institutions, widespread and growing poverty and deprivation will continue to undermine societal cohesion and fuel religious extremism in Pakistan with far reaching negative repercussions for regional and international security. The complex nature of the country's developmental deficit means there can be no quick fixes. Sustainable development and poverty reduction will require sustained, long-term aid commitments delivered on favourable terms and tailored specifically to the peculiar development needs of Pakistan. But economic development is not just an economic problem which can be solved by getting 'aid' right. It rests ultimately on political stability and democratic legitimacy. Authoritarian regimes may initiate structural reforms but whether they can sustain them is an open question. Unless the authoritarian enclaves in the Pakistani state are subjected to civilian control and economic policy is brought under the purview of elected officials, Pakistan's lurch from one crisis to another is a more plausible outlook over the long haul than political and economic development.

Notes

1. United Nations Development Program, *Human Development Report 2004* (New York: UNDP, 2004). The index was constructed for a total of 171 countries ranked in high, medium and low human development country groups.
2. United Nations Development Program.
3. Economic Affairs Division, Government of Pakistan, Islamabad. *Economic Survey of Pakistan 2003-04.*
4. Economic Affairs Division, Government of Pakistan, Islamabad. *Economic Survey of Pakistan 2001-02.*
5. Deborah Brautigam, *Aid Dependence and Governance* (Stockholm: Almqvist and Wiksell International, 2000).
6. David Dollar and Lant Pritchett, *Assessing Aid: What Works, What Doesn't, and Why* (New York: Oxford University Press, 1998).
7. Shahrukh Rafi Khan, 'Do IMF and World Bank Policies Work', Monograph # 6 (Islamabad: Sustainable Development Policy Institute, 1997).
8. Robert Cassen et al., *The Effectiveness of Aid to Pakistan* (Islamabad: Economic Affairs Division, Pakistan and UNDP, 1990).
9. Cassen et al.
10. UK Department for International Development, Departmental Report 2002, <www.dfid.gov.uk>. OECD donor governments have committed to untying financial assistance to least developed countries from 1 January 2002, this commitment covers only certain types of aid and only 12 per cent of total OECD bilateral aid.

11. Shahid Kardar, *The Political Economy of Pakistan* (Lahore: Progressive Publishers, 1987), 259.
12. Economic Affairs Division, 2001-2.
13. Personal communication with a UN official, March 2003.
14. Cassen et.al.
15. Personal communication, March 2003.
16. Joseph E. Stiglitz, *Globalization and Its Discontents* (New York: WW Norton, 2002), 44.
17. For a discussion of these developments, see Olav Stokke, ed., *Aid and Political Conditionality* (London: Frank Cass, 1995).
18. European Union, Pakistan Country Strategy Paper, 2002-6) <http://europa. eu.int/comm/external_relations/pakistan/csp/02_06_en.pdf> (5 April 2003).
19. Alberto Alesina and David Dollar, 'Who Gives Foreign Aid to Whom and Why?' Working Paper 6612 (Cambridge, MA: National Bureau of Economic Research, June 1998).
20. Alberto Alesina and Beatrice Weder, 'Do Corrupt Governments Receive Less Foreign Aid', Working Paper 7108 (Cambridge, MA: National Bureau of Economic Research, May 1999).
21. A Report of the President's Committee to Study the United States Military Assistance Programme, Volume 11 cited in Omar Noman, *Pakistan: Political and Economic History since 1947* (New York: Kegan Paul, 1990), 35.
22. The PL 480 is a concessional sales program to promote exports of U.S. agricultural commodities. For a description of PL 480 titles see <http://www. fas.usda.gov/excredits/pl480/FOOD-AID.HTML>
23. Hamza Alavi and Amir Khusro, 'Pakistan: The Burden of US Aid' in R. I. Rhodes, ed., *Imperialism and Underdevelopment: A Reader* (New York: Monthly Review Press, 1970) cited in Kardar, 258.
24. In the 1970s, Pakistan largely relied on concessional financing from the oil producing Middle Eastern countries.
25. The Symington Amendment to the Foreign Assistance Act of 1961 prohibits most US economic and military assistance to any country delivering or receiving nuclear enrichment equipment, material, or technology not safeguarded by the International Atomic Energy Agency (IAEA).
26. Zia had earlier spurned the Carter administration's aid offer of US$ 400 million calling it 'peanuts'.
27. Kuldip Nayar, 'We have the A-Bomb, Says Pakistan's Dr Strangelove', *Observer* (London), 1 March 1987. A 1983 US State Department assessment claimed 'unambiguous evidence that Pakistan is actively pursuing a nuclear weapons development program'. US Department of State, 'The Pakistan Nuclear Program'. 23 June 1983, SECRET/NOFORN/ORCON released under the Freedom of Information Act to the National Security Archive (Washington, DC), 17 January 1991.
28. Glenn Amendment to the Foreign Assistance Act of 1961. This amendment proscribes US assistance to any non-nuclear weapon state (as defined by the

Non-Proliferation Treaty) that conducts a nuclear explosion. The Symington and Glenn amendments were not applied retroactively to India or Pakistan.

29. See Council for a Livable World 'India-Pakistan Sanction Legislation Fact Sheet http://www.clw.org/control/indopaksanctions.html

30. In November 2004, the US Congress authorized the first annual installment of approximately US$ 701 million for FY 2005.

31. Quoted in K. Alan Kronstadt, 'Pakistan-US Relations', Congressional Research Service Issue Brief, Updated 11 August 2004. <http://www.fas.org/man/crs/index.html> (29 August 2004).

32. The Poverty Reduction Strategy Paper (PRSP) articulates a country's 'strategic objectives for reducing poverty' and is a requirement for obtaining PRGF support from the IMF. The Bank and Fund insist that PRSPs are based on 'broad public participation and country ownership'. Interviews this author conducted with Pakistani officials in 2003 reveal that the reality of ownership lies somewhere in the narrow band between consultation with and dictation to them.

33. Stiglitz, 44.

34. Nadeem ul Haq and Peter Montiel, 'The Macroeconomics of Public Sector Deficits: The Case of Pakistan', Working Paper 673, World Bank, May 1991.

35. Haq and Montiel.

36. Fund and Pakistan.

37. See, for instance, Stiglitz, 'Globalization'. Stiglitz argues that IFIs (especially the IMF) remain unaccountable for their actions and insensitive to the social costs of their policies and their mistakes (especially in the sequencing of reforms) reflect a deep misunderstanding of the economic and political processes in developing countries which stems from their unwavering faith in the supremacy of the market.

38. Ayesha Jalal, 'Pakistan's Tangle: The Politics of Conflicting Security and Economic Interests', Government and Opposition, vol. 34, no.1, Winter 1999.

39. Dawn (Karachi), August 31, 1998.

40. Merilee Grindle and John Thomas, Public Choices and Policy Change. The Political Economy of Reform in Developing Countries (Baltimore: Johns Hopkins University Press, 1991), 62.

41. Ishrat Hussain, 'Pakistan and the IMF', paper presented at the International Expert Workshop organized by the German Foundation for Development (DSE) at Berlin, Germany, 1-2 July 2002, 2.

42. Author's interview with a former Finance Ministry official, Islamabad, April 2003.

43. Iqbal Akhund, Trial and Error: The Advent and Eclipse of Benazir Bhutto (Karachi: Oxford University Press, 2000), 52.

44. See Mushahid Hussain and Akmal Hussain, Pakistan: Problems of Governance (Lahore: Vanguard Books, 1993).

45. Zaidi, Pakistan's Economy, 316.

46. Ibid., 322-323.

47. Ibid.
48. International Monetary Fund and Government of Pakistan (GoP), 'Enhanced Structural Adjustment Facility Policy Framework Paper 1998-2001', 23 December 1998.
49. Fund and Pakistan.
50. The Bank, along with the Export-Import Bank of Japan (Jexim), had also contributed US$ 400 million each to the Long Term Credit Facility (LTCF) meant for longer term financing. For details of the IPP controversy, see Khaleeq Kiani, 'The Price of Power: High Energy Collisions', *Himal South Asian*, March 2002 <www.himalmag.com>.
51. Ibid.
52. World Bank, 'Press Statement on Pakistan Independent Power Producers', 11 July 1998 <www.worlbank.org>.
53. Mark Tran, 'IMF Threatens to Cut Funding to Pakistan', *The Guardian* online (London), 13 October 1999. (11 August 2004).
54. IMF Press Release, 'IMF Executive Board Completes Final Review Under Pakistan's PRGF Arrangement', 1 December 2004.
55. Ishrat Hussain, 'Why Pakistan Should Exit the IMF Programme', *Dawn* (Karachi), 29 February and 1 March 2004.
56. See Jay Solomon, Zahid Hussian and Saeed Azhar, 'As Growth Returns, Hopes Rise on Terror Front', *The Wall Street Journal* (Online), 9 November 2004.
57. In June 2004, Finance Minister Shaukat Aziz claimed on the basis of an official survey that the percentage of the population below the poverty line had fallen by four percentage points over the last three years. However, independent analysts (and even the IMF) have questioned the validity of the government's claim because the results from the survey are not fully comparable with earlier household surveys that the government used as its baseline. In this view, the reduction stems from differences in the sample design of the surveys rather than an actual change in the real magnitude of poverty. See Akmal Hussain, 'Poverty Reduction Figure is Fudged', *Daily Times* (Lahore), 14 June 2004.
58. State Bank of Pakistan, Monetary Policy Statement for July-December 2004. In its annual report 2003-4, the State Bank notes that the unemployment rate rose from 7.8 per cent in FY2000 to 8.3 per cent in FY2002.
59. Hussain, 'Why Pakistan Should Exit the IMF'.
60. This it did by securing PM Zafrullah Jamali's resignation and stage-managing Aziz's election to the national assembly (a requirement for the post of the Prime Minister) from two seats (one each in Punjab and Sindh) vacated by ruling party legislators.
61. IMF Staff Report, for the 2004 Article IV Consultation, Washington, D.C., 16 November 2004.
62. James Manor, *The Political Economy of Democratic Decentralization* (Washington, D.C. World Bank, 1999).
63. Ibid.

64. See Charles Kennedy, 'Constitutional and Political Change in Pakistan: The Military Governance Paradigm, 'Paper prepared for 'Prospects for Peace in South Asia' conference, Stanford University; 21 February 2003, p. 21. Also, see chapter six of this volume.

65. Government of Pakistan, Chief Executive Secretariat, National Reconstruction Bureau. *Local Government (Proposed Plan): Devolution of Power and Responsibility Establishing the Foundations for Genuine Democracy* (Islamabad: May 2000).

66. BBC, 'UK Halts Aid to Pakistan', 15 October 1999 <http://news.bbc.co.uk/1/hi/uk_politics/476091.stm> (20 April 2003).

67. 'Clinton Tours Indian Village, Pakistan Announces Local Elections', CNN online, 24 March 2000.

68. In fact, the NRB devolution plan virtually mirrored the latest development policy discourse in calling for 'devolution of political power, decentralization of administrative authority, de-concentration of functions, redistribution of resources and enhanced representation'.

69. World Bank, 54.

70. World Bank, 53.

71. Other short-term international consultants and inputs including information and communication technology support were also provided under the project. <http://undp.un.org.pk> (15 April 2003).

72. UNDP spearheads a US$50 million multi-donor Devolution Trust for Community Empowerment which aims to activate the community participation elements of devolution.

73. For instance, CIDA's Democratic Governance Program for Pakistan supports almost exclusively '... the devolution of power, the decentralization of administration, and the participation of citizens in local governance' which is expected to lead to 'improved local governance policies and policy implementation, effective local democratic institutions and practices, and effective citizens voice in setting local priorities and delivering social services'. < http://www.acdi-cida.gc.ca/CIDAWEB/webcountry.nsf/VLUDocEn/Pakistan-Projects#8>

74. Asian Development Bank, Press Release. 'Helping Pakistan's Devolution Program Improve Delivery of Social Services' Manila (Philippines) 21 November 2002, www.adb.org (12 April 2003).

75. This observation is based on the author's interviews with several *nazims* in the Punjab and Sindh provinces, April-May 2003.

76. See the report of the European Union Election Observation Mission (EUEOM) to Pakistan online at < http://www.eueom.org.pk/finalreport.asp> (7 April 2003).

77. For a project synopsis see <http://undp.un.org.pk>

78. UNDP Governance and Gender Unit Quarterly Progress Report: April - June 2002, <http://undp.un.org.pk> (2 April 2003).

79. Musharraf's LFO placed the four provincial Local Government Ordinances in the Sixth Schedule of the 1973 constitution which can only be amended or

repealed with consent of the president. Under Article 268 (2), 'the laws specified in the sixth schedule may not be altered, repealed or amended without the previous sanction of the president'.

80. World Bank, 'Devolution in Pakistan: Main Report: An Assessment and Recommendations for Action', 1 September 2004.

81. Author's confidential interview, Islamabad, June 2003.

82. Asian Development Bank, 'Pakistan: Country Strategy and Program 2002-2006'. <www.adb.org>

83. UNDP Governance Unit < http://undp.un.org.pk>

84. Kennedy, op. cit.

85. Funded by the Asia Foundation, the only visible attempt to solicit public views was a series of 'People's Assemblies' held under the auspices of Ministry of Local Government and Rural Development.

86. Carrie Meyer, 'The Irony of Donor Efforts to Build Institutions: A Case Study From the Dominican Republic'. *Journal of Institutional and Theoretical Economics*, 148 (1992): 628-44.

4

Hostage to History: The India-Pakistan Confrontation in the Nuclear Age

Rasul Bakhsh Rais

Introduction

India and Pakistan have never been friendly toward each other. There have been more than five decades of an uneasy peace, punctuated by wars, regular clashes on the borders and disruption of trade, communication and diplomatic ties. The India-Pakistan rivalry has proven to be the most stable crisis of the South Asian region which is further complicated by a costly conventional arms race, the acquisition of nuclear weapons and the insurgency in Kashmir. While the tensions between India and Pakistan, their nuclear capability and risk of nuclear war have received considerable attention in recent years, the question why India and Pakistan continue to remain confrontational has been generally ignored or addressed perfunctorily with reference to a single set of factors.

There are many complex dynamics of history, geopolitics, identity, national power, status and role perceptions that have constantly, but in varying degrees, influenced the patterns of confrontation between the two countries. Therefore, it would be instructive to examine the crisis in Pakistan-India relations against the backdrop of emotive issues of partition of British India, a complex geo-strategic legacy and a vast disparity in power and purposes of the two countries that have fomented hostility and deepened negative perceptions of each other.[1] In a world system based on national power, it would be natural for any power of the size of India with large economic resources and military power to entertain regional ambitions, which Indian elites unremittingly do, but that would certainly generates fears, apprehensions and intuitively defensive responses from Pakistan, as it does. Pakistan views Indian policies within the region and toward it as driven by hegemonic aspiration and power politics.[2] It finds India unwilling to address the legitimate aspirations of the people of Jammu and Kashmir or even enter into serious dialogue on a trilateral basis to resolve this dispute. India considers Pakistan's role as that of a revisionist state that is trying to redraw the territorial boundaries around the Jammu and Kashmir region by consistently staking claims on the disputed state.[3] In addressing the question why India and Pakistan continue to remain hostile to each other, we will argue that the incongruity between fundamental goals—security, identity, role, status—perpetuates tensions, mistrust, and conflict. Unless both sets of issues are settled through dialogue or, overtime, lose their relevance, mutual rivalry will continue to influence India-Pakistan relations.

Clash of Identities

The roots of the confrontation between India and Pakistan are found in the struggle for independence. Indian nationalist leaders opposed and resisted partition of the subcontinent on religious grounds, while the creators of Pakistan based their demand for partition on a conception of Muslim nationalism.[4] Hindu-Muslim relations during the last two decades of the British *Raj* were tense, often culminating in communal clashes and vengeance killings. The Hindu revivalist movement and Muslim separatism were the root-cause of communalism.[5] The intensity of the Hindu-Muslim rift grew stronger with the prospects of an independent Pakistan. At the heart of the tension were contradictory aspirations, as the dreams, ideals and identity of the two communities developed in opposite directions. Attempts to reconcile their differences and make one nation through constitutional means failed. When it became clear that the Muslims were going to have a country of their own in the eastern and north-western parts of India, communal frenzy engulfed the subcontinent.[6] The trauma of partition and transmigration of populations, during which an estimated two million men, women, and children lost their lives, have left deep scars on the psyche of these two nations.

Two states born out of bloodshed have not yet lost their collective memory of communal conflict.[7] Because states are human-made abstractions administered by individuals, prejudices cannot but impact the actions and policies of nations-states. India and Pakistan have been personified as essentially Hindu and Muslim. The communal experience of the first two generations of Indians and Pakistanis is responsible for transferring communal hatred between communities to ambivalence and hatred of the rival state.[8] The communal factor shaped attitudes, orientations and the policy responses of each state toward the other in their formative phase, and perceptions of the 'mid-night' children laid the foundation of India-Pakistan antagonism.[9] These memories have, unfortunately, survived through textbooks, the writing of history, and an enemy-consensus sustained by political actions and rhetoric.

The Kashmir Dispute

The question of Kashmir continues to be the major source of tension between India and Pakistan. The problem is enmeshed in conflicting theories of the origins of the two countries which began with confusion over the principles on which the partition of British India was to take place. Pakistan wanted to apply the concept of Muslim majority areas forming its part to the princely state of Kashmir. The princely states had the option to accede to either India or Pakistan on the basis of proximity and communal composition of the population.[10] India, supported by Lord Mountbatten, took full advantage of the anomaly in Kashmir. There, the ruler was a Hindu while over 78 per cent of the population was Muslim and the state was adjacent to Pakistan. In utter disregard of the wishes of the people of Kashmir, the Maharaja, in dubious circumstances, signed the Instrument of Accession with India.[11] India accepted the accession as provisional and committed itself to holding a plebiscite in Kashmir to determine the final status of the State.[12] Tragically, notwithstanding such unilateral promises and United Nations resolutions, India began integrating the State of Jammu and Kashmir into the Union after realising that the plebiscite would not go in its favour. Even Article 370 of the Indian Constitution, which was intended to protect the internal autonomy of Kashmir, has been 'reduced to a husk'.[13] Reneging on pledges to allow Kashmiris the right of self-determination, the rigging of successive elections to place pliant Kashmiri leaders in power, and the erosion of autonomy have served to alienate the Muslim population of Kashmir.

Pakistan has rejected Indian measures to assimilate the Kashmir State and has insisted that India must grant the right of self-determination to the people of Kashmir. It believes that if such a right is granted and the plebiscite is conducted under UN or third party auspices, the overwhelming majority of Muslims in Kashmir will vote to join Pakistan. At times, Pakistan has actively supported various groups in Kashmir seeking independence from India and has gone to war with India on two occasions over this issue. Pakistan's Kashmir policy has been consistent in demanding a plebiscite, but its level of support and level of involvement has varied depending upon the internal situation in Kashmir and the security climate in the region. After the separation of East Pakistan in 1971 and signing of the Simla Agreement with India in 1972, Pakistan preferred to put the issue on the backburner, keeping it symbolically alive for domestic political purposes. However, with the eruption of a mass movement in the 1990s leading to unrest and insurgency, the issue has been the cause of constant tension between India and Pakistan during the past decade, quite often boiling over into military clashes on the border.

In the present context, Pakistan sees the Kashmir uprising against India as a legitimate and popular movement that developed its own momentum largely in response to coercive and manipulative policies of the central government of India.[14] This view has been confirmed by Indian human rights activists, intellectuals and even some politicians. A celebrated Indian writer Khushwant Singh argues that India has totally lost the sympathies of Kashmiri

Muslims and that '...if there was a plebiscite, the vote would go heavily against India and in favour of Pakistan'.[15]

For the past eleven years, Indian forces have been faced with battling one of the toughest and most enduring insurgency movements occurring in various parts of the country. Though other insurgency movements in the North-East of India have disrupted the political process and kept different outfits of security forces engaged, the insurgency in Kashmir has involved by far the largest number of Indian army personnel, intelligence agencies and para-military forces. By some estimates, India has continuously deployed over half a million troops and depending on the severity of the crisis, it has added more troops. Indian held Kashmir contains the highest concentration of army as a percentage of the occupied population of anywhere in the world.

Unfortunately, India has chosen to deal with what is essentially a political issue with the use of brutal force. Through the use of the military and security agencies who have been given licence to kill, detain and torture, India hopes to eventually force the people of Kashmir to accept Indian rule. Such an assumption defies logic given the experiences of other similar insurgency movements around the world. India, itself, has had eleven years of experience, more than enough to question the wisdom of this strategy. Armed resistance and guerrilla warfare in modern history have symbolized the struggle of the weak against the strong. Many of these struggles have eventually forced powerful adversaries to negotiate a political settlement. Over time, states that fight popular insurgencies, like the one in Kashmir, tend to lose their moral authority and erode their own ability to maintain effective control over the population. The counter-insurgency campaigns that the Indian government has launched with fresh resolve each time to crush the Kashmiri resistance, have de-legitimized its rule and created enormous difficulties in restoring normal political order or re-engaging Kashmiri groups in the political process.[16] The destruction of villages, the arbitrary arrests through the application of Draconian laws on the pretext of 'special circumstances', torture and the disappearance of mostly young people without any trace,[17] is a sure sign of eventual political defeat.

The most important aspect of Indian policy is the effort to neutralize Pakistan's influence on the Kashmiri resistance, which if does by telling the world leaders that Pakistan is behind the militancy in Kashmir. India has exploited the post–9/11 environment to portray Kashmir as an issue of terrorism, accusing Pakistan of sending fighters across the border.[18] The Indian leaders also assert that Pakistan has no *locus standi* in the Kashmir conflict, which it argues is an internal matter. Both of these assertions are politically loaded. Ten years of conflict have attracted *jihadi* elements from Pakistan and other countries, however, these elements cannot operate inside Indian-held Kashmir without local co-operation. In addition, these fighters do not represent the numbers that would engage half a million Indian troops. If India continues to resist changes in its policy, the *jihadi* outfits from other countries, with highly motivated fighters, may increase their participation in the conflict. This may not auger well for India or for regional peace and stability. It is time for all three parties, India, Pakistan and the Kashmiri insurgents, to recognize that military means will not settle internal conflicts or interstate disputes. The lesson of its own failure in Kashmir should not be lost on India. Kashmir is the central problem between India and Pakistan and it has drained the economic resources of both countries and continues to push them to the edge of disastrous conflicts.[19]

The fact is that Kashmir is not simply a piece of territory, but a land inhabited by people with their own dreams and political aspirations, struggling to win their rights. It would be prudent to listen to their voices and discover what they want.

There are three parties that have a stake in the issue; the Kashmiris, India and Pakistan. Pakistan has a historical claim and geopolitical interests, clearly having a tremendous stake in the issue and it is unrealistic to contemplate leaving Pakistan out of any final settlement of the Kashmir dispute.

For many years Pakistan has insisted that once the Kashmir problem is resolved, relations between India and Pakistan will qualitatively improve. Trade, communications, and borders will open up and Pakistan is in the position to provide the transit routes for the supply of the gas and oil resources of Persian Gulf and

Central Asia to India. India requires these for its development and future industrial growth but the Indian leaders have continually ignored the positive geo-economic benefits of a reconciliation with Pakistan over the Kashmir problem, preferring to keep a shaky and doubtful hold over an unwilling population. The Indians have contemptuously rejected all suggestions of a resolution to the dispute to the satisfaction of all the parties. Rather than resolving the issue outright, India deflects the problem by approaching through trade and openness.

From Lahore to Kargil

The Lahore declaration that Mohammad Nawaz Sharif and Atal Behari Vajpayee signed in February 1999 was a landmark in the relations between the two countries for many reasons, but two deserve mention. First, the two countries committed themselves to holding a sustained dialogue and resolving all problems through negotiations.[20] There have been other, similar, agreements between the two countries stressing the importance of dialogue, but the difference is that the Lahore process came about in a time of peace and not at the end of a conflict. The change in attitude of the two leaders reflected a deep desire in liberal circles of the subcontinent that the two countries resolve outstanding issues now, rather than to pass them on to the next generations. The fact that Mr Vajpayee represented a conservative party that had previously taken an extremist position on bilateral problems, was seen in Pakistan as a sign of a new thinking among the Indian leadership.

A second important aspect of the Lahore declaration was the recognition by the Indian Prime Minister that Kashmir was a dispute between India and Pakistan that had yet to be resolved. It was agreed that the two countries would place the Kashmir problem on the top of agenda and would use all their energies to resolve it through negotiations. In a fundamental shift from holding talks through traditional channels of diplomacy, the two prime ministers decided to assign the Kashmir dispute to two respective nominees, hoping they would succeed in their efforts where others had failed.

The Lahore process focused on softening the borders, removing restrictions on visits, and facilitating trade and business transactions. There is a strong general perception within the region and in the western world that a peaceful resolution of the Kashmir problem would open up many opportunities for economic activity within the region, and that the dividends of peace would benefit all sections of society in both countries. It was with this objective in mind that Pakistan committed itself to the Lahore process.

The euphoria over a peaceful resolution of the Kashmir conflict and the possibility of a stable security environment in the region, did not last more than a few months. The Kargil conflict in the summer of 1999 buried such hopes as antagonistic images and rhetoric roared back into public debate in both countries. Kargil was a terrible episode in the history of India and Pakistan. Let us examine briefly its genesis. The episode cannot and should not be seen in isolation from the Kashmir issue in general and the Siachen conflict in particular. India and Pakistan had been locked in a costly struggle in Kashmir's Siachen area for the past twenty years. The line of actual control drawn up under the 1972 Simla Agreement left out the glacier region because delineation was considered impracticable.[21] Pakistan had been administering this area since independence; international mountaineering expeditions obtained authorization from Pakistan from 1957 to 1983. After a series of secret military expeditions, India moved its forces in the summer of 1984, occupying the Sia La, Belafond La, and Gyongla passes of the Saltoro range lying west and adjacent to the Siachen glacier.[22] The question is: why would India undertake a costly war with Pakistan to capture an area recognized by both as no-man's land, an area almost at the roof of the world (16,000–19,000 feet above sea level) that requires special equipment and logistics? A strategic offensive in line with regional ambitions is the answer to why India undertook such a military action. In no less significant terms, the Siachen conflict continues to literally bleed the two countries. It also serves as an important lesson to how vulnerable a militarily weak Pakistan would be under these present conditions. Several rounds of talks to disengage the forces and re-demarcate the ceasefire line over the glaciers have not produced any results so far.[23]

Pakistan had been planning to move its forces into the Kargil-Drass area for some time. By doing this, it hoped to monitor and, perhaps, restrict the Indian supply lines to the Siachen glacier. Another objective was to achieve a strategic advantage in an area that could be used as a point to retaliate against the Indian shelling in the Neelum Valley in Azad Kashmir. It made the move under three assumptions. First, that Pakistan will be able to hold on to the heights and establish a new line of control to which India would acquiesce. Second, the international community would intervene to arrange a ceasefire should the move provoke a military response from India. Third, the Kashmir issue would attract greater international attention than it did previously given the nuclearization of South Asia.

There are many questions about who actually started the conflict in Kargil. Were those who captured the heights the Kashmir Mujahideen, as Islamabad first claimed, or regular Pakistani forces? Was it an action plan executed without the knowledge of Prime Minister Nawaz Sharif? How much did Prime Minister Sharif know about the plan and at what stage? How was the move consistent with the policy to engage India in the peaceful resolution of the Kashmir conflict laid out by the Lahore process? Nawaz Sharif, after his removal and conviction by a court on charges of hijacking, revealed that he was kept in the dark by the military about the Kargil incursion.[24] By all subsequent evidence, Nawaz Sharif was in the picture throughout, but probably did not fully comprehend the complexity of the operation, or he was unwilling to confront the military brass on the issue. There is no doubt that Kargil was a reversal of what had been agreed upon in Lahore. It widened the distrust between the two countries.

The conflict was a reminder that without resolving the Kashmir dispute, progress in other areas may prove to be temporary, and that the risk of confrontation was ever present. When Nawaz Sharif began warming up to India, many in Pakistan had serious doubts about the rapprochement between the two countries because they feared that the Kashmir issue would cause a spillback. The events in Kargil proved them right.

Since the Kargil conflict, relations between India and Pakistan have sunk to their lowest level. The two countries are conducting 'diplomatic' relations through accusation and a propaganda war, shutting down all normal channels of diplomacy. India has generally taken the lead in launching offensives in the national and international media to malign Pakistan to which Pakistan has reacted in kind. Such a sorry state of affairs between the two nuclear powers sends a wrong signal to the world about their ability to maintain regional stability, strengthening global and domestic fears that they may remain locked in a costly arms race.

The opportunity to resume dialogue after it was broken off by the Kargil conflict came on 23 May 2001, when Prime Minister Vajpayee invited Pervez Musharraf to visit India and have talks in Agra.[25] This invitation marked a major shift in Indian policy from one of previously isolating Pakistan, to now engaging it without pre-conditions. Pakistan cannot meet or cannot prove it had met, for example, the restoration of democracy and/or cessation of support to the Kashmir militants. The Agra summit in June 2001 was one of the major events in the history of bilateral relations. The occasion raised the level of optimism about the hopes India and Pakistan have for settling their problems through dialogue. The Agra summit came very close to an agreement on a framework for future talks and according to a Pakistani version of the talks, a draft declaration was finalized with consensus of both sides. It was only at the last moment that an agreement failed due to differences among the Indian establishment.[26]

On the Brink of War

Having failed to crush insurgency in the disputed Kashmir region, India wanted to use the 13 December (2001) terrorist attacks on the Indian Parliament, while it was in session, to show the world that insurgency in Kashmir was nothing but the handiwork of terrorist groups in Pakistan. Nothing could be more misleading. Following the horrendous terrorist attack, India ordered the full-scale mobilization of troops on Pakistan's border to teach it a lesson for sponsoring 'terrorism'. India accused Pakistan of direct involvement in the incident.[27] Pakistan reciprocated by bringing its forces to the line to counter India's pressure. The armies of the two countries sat at striking distance from January to October 2002. Both sides quickly built up their war-fighting capability along the border by moving in everything needed to attack and counter-attack. In certain sectors along the Line of Control, India and Pakistan exchanged heavy machine gun and mortar fire causing a large number of casualties, the evacuation of civilians and the disruption of social and economic life. Every piece of military equipment and soldiers remained in place, minutes away from war, awaiting a signal from the top brass.

India's brinkmanship added to an already uncertain and volatile security situation, one even more unstable since the Kargil war. India moved two more mountain divisions into occupied Kashmir, pulled its strike aircraft to bases close to the Pakistani border, and ordered its navy to sail to the Arabian Sea. The Indian Prime Minister, Atal Behari Vajpayee, asked his troops to prepare for a 'decisive war' against Pakistan. Inside the country, Hindu nationalists whipped up war hysteria, accusing Pakistan of being the cause of everything that was wrong in India.

While Pakistan took the military steps that were required to meet the challenge on the borders, the Pakistan government assiduously avoided contributing to darkening the war clouds that could rain down disaster. Pakistan routinely conveyed to India that it wanted a resumption of dialogue to resolve tensions, asking India to pull back the troops at the border and return to the negotiating table. Islamabad also invited the attention and involvement of the international community, as Pakistan did not want to be pushed into the final step, for that would have spelled disaster. The consequences of war would be devastating for both nations. Unfortunately, some Indian leaders seem to live under the illusion that they would be able to absorb the economic and human costs of war due to their bigger economy and larger population.

Would they? Doubtful

The Indian leadership has come up with the dubious notion of 'limited war'. Former Army Chief General Malik has asserted that there is substantial 'strategic space' between a low intensity conflict and a nuclear war and that such a 'strategic space' could be used by India to respond to Pakistan's efforts to bleed India in Jammu and Kashmir.[28] We do not know if such a conflict could be limited in scale. Wars rarely remain limited because once armies are put in full operational gear, small accidents and provocations can easily trigger a full-scale conflagration. Adding to the uncertainty of India's assumption is the fact that the side that feels they are going down has all the incentives to up the ante.

A sobering lesson from other wars should instruct India and Pakistan that adversaries can inadvertently falter on their way up the rungs of the escalatory ladder. Operational strategies in the tense environment of warfare create their own dynamics: military commanders short of time and limited thinking space, blunder into ill-calculated gambles.

Nuclear Factor

The perception of threat from India compounded by the experiences of statehood confirms that India drives Pakistan's quest for nuclear status. Many Pakistanis, particularly in the political and policy-making circles, believe that nuclear capability is the best guarantee against a nuclear-capable and militarily superior India. Both countries, after years of ambiguity, emerged as *de facto* nuclear powers in May 1998.

There are, however, many questions about the stability of the deterrence, about both party's nuclear doctrines, and their systems of command and control. For example, under what conditions would either use nuclear weapons? Pakistan says it would use nuclear weapons only as a matter of last resort, which is a deliberately ambiguous statement. India asserts it will not be the first to use nuclear weapons, meaning that India would use nuclear weapons only should another country launch a nuclear attack against it. However, these declarations have no sanction of law nor do they create any binding obligation[29]—they are only statements of intentions. No leader of a nation would base security policy on the stated good intentions of a potential adversary.

Statements such as 'no sane person would discuss the prospect of nuclear war between the two countries', and that 'India and Pakistan are reasonable and responsible enough to prevent and avoid a nuclear conflict', should not be taken on face value.[30] Leaders are under many compulsions to make such statements and send words of assurance to the world community. Who is not looking at the mobilization of one million armed men in one of the poorest region of the world with trepidation. The global community fears that there is a real risk of war which could escalate to a nuclear one.

It is imperative for the men and women of our region and those outside to think the unthinkable. India's 'no first use' declaration is deceptive because its accumulation of conventional weapons in all areas of modern warfare is so colossal that it believes it can and would overwhelm Pakistan in a military confrontation. How could Pakistan sit back facing its destruction and not contemplate the use of nuclear weapons? Once Pakistan hits India with nuclear weapons, India would certainly retaliate, perhaps on a larger scale?

The apprehension is that both countries, probably starting with the tactical use of nuclear weapons, may end up destroying each other. This is a dreadful and frightening scenario but one should think about it now rather than the day after. The human, environmental, and economic cost of nuclear holocaust in the region would last for generations. It is time to think collectively and ponder the question of what the leaders of the two nations would accomplish by going that far. The answer is: Mutually Assured Destruction (MADness).

It is important to raise questions about fuzzy thinking occurring on two issues that dominate the strategic mindset of India and Pakistan. First, that nuclear deterrence always works. Pakistan thinks its nuclear deterrence would dissuade India from going to war. It may, it may not. The problem with deterrence is that its chances of success lie with the other side.[31] The question of rationality of decision-makers, the domestic compulsions of the leadership, and a false and real sense of superiority may tempt the other side to plunge in a deadly gamble.

Second, many Indians entertain the notion of nuclear superiority. They believe since they have a greater number of nuclear weapons, and can deploy them in multiple modes while having the capacity to survive Pakistan's first strike, they would win a nuclear war and ensure the total destruction of Pakistan. This type of thinking is insane. Should India and Pakistan ever blunder into using nuclear weapons against each other, both countries would stand defeated and destroyed.

Given the illogic of the premises that guide both nations' strategic thinking, a middle-ground must be found. Unfortunately, the leaders in both countries have disabled themselves from finding one by cultivating stubborn constituencies at home and playing a zero-sum game with one another. This has put top leaders into an extremely tight, narrow, and dark political box. From there, they are unable to see the light and strive for a compromise. In such a situation, global players have a role to play in bringing the leaders of the subcontinent onto the path of reconciliation.

Role of a Third Party

When neighbours armed with nuclear weapons will not talk, the intervention of a third party is necessary, even if their primary task is the carrying of messages from one side to the other hoping to restore normal ties. When neighbours refuse to talk after a fight, harmony is difficult to restore but the damage is contained. In the case of states, it is much more dangerous to disrupt all communications during times of conflict, because without communication hope for resolution becomes dim, the role of national diplomats becomes irrelevant and their presence in the capitals is reduced to redundancy.[32] Since the failure of the Agra summit, India and Pakistan have done much of their talking indirectly through the media and the emissaries from the United States, United Kingdom and the European Union. The question taken up here is how useful are third parties in defusing tensions and what role could they play in settling disputes between India and Pakistan?

India has a long tradition of resisting any third party intervention in conflicts with her neighbours. Its diplomacy within the region, which it considers a natural area of strategic interest, is based on bilateralism. What this means is that India would not allow any other power or world institution to mediate conflict with any of its neighbours. The diplomatic and security implications of this doctrine should be clear. India's position prevents the smaller South Asian states from having a neutral, honest broker to mediate disputes. Going by the well-known and well-practiced principle of power politics, India wishes to settle its problems with states in the region according to its own sense of justice and fairness. Others see in Indian bilateralism big power politics in which an extended notion of her interests determine the terms and conditions of any resolution, conflict or otherwise.

Pakistan, on the other hand, has been open to third party intervention, oftentimes insisting that the complex issue of Jammu and Kashmir receive a helping hand from the UN and other major world powers. Consistent with its policy, it has welcomed the role that the US and European countries have been playing since the massing of Indian troops on her border in early 2002.

How successful have these intermediaries been? What are the prospects of their efforts to normalize ties between India and Pakistan? It is very clear though, that the questions of war and peace are primarily determined by the states involved and not by third parties. It will be India and Pakistan that will ultimately choose whether to live in peace or in perpetual uncertainty.

There are three factors pushing the major powers to seek a third party role to intervene between India and Pakistan. First, conventional war on a limited scale can become a major war in which the use of nuclear weapons can not be ruled out. Second, the nuclear threat is real and will stay with us as long as we have the weapons and unresolved disputes such as Kashmir acting as a flash point. Third, Western interests in preventing war are genuine because of the escalatory factor, which no rational person would dismiss as a possibility in the hostile climate of the subcontinent.[33]

Why the US and others are interested in diffusing tensions can also be explained by the logic of events in Afghanistan where they are locked in a difficult task of flushing out the Taliban and Al-Qaeda fighters. A major war next door would divert international attention and seriously undermine the campaign, which is already faltering on the issue of internal security and nation building. A war in the subcontinent would waste much of the success that has been achieved so far. Also, equally important to consider from America's interests is what would be the nature of social and political movements that would emerge in the wake of war, feeding on the myths of victory and defeat. The score board tracking American efforts is mixed. The United States succeeded in bringing down the temperature between the two countries when they mobilized troops on the borders in 2002 and continued threatening each other. That is a positive point. But there is no guarantee that violent events in the murky world of armed resistance and state oppression in Kashmir will not push India and Pakistan to war. The problem of Kashmir needs to be settled and settling it requires greater attention by the third parties than it has been given. This is a point that weighs against the United States. What likely frustrates US efforts is that they have adopted a crisis management approach without a sustained interest in resolving the issue of Kashmir. Pakistan must end infiltration into Indian held Kashmir and in return India would take de-escalatory measures and re-engage in bilateral talks. Washington is engaged in a difficult balancing act; while insisting Pakistan must address the legitimate concerns of India over 'cross-border terrorism', the US counsels India to give primacy to diplomacy and 'begin dialogue over the issues that are at (the) root cause' of tensions in the region.[34]

The approach that the United States applies to India-Pakistan issues is vastly different from those employed in the case of the Arab-Israeli conflict or that in Northern Ireland. In the case of Kashmir, the United States does not wish to become a formal mediator unless requested to do so by both parties. The United States knows that India is not going to accept any direct or open third party intervention. It would, as it has during the past several years, prefer to work behind the scene to 'inspire' a settlement of the long-running Kashmir dispute and stay involved.[35] Contrary to this soft paddling, Pakistan would like the US and international community to play a central role in conflict resolution in South Asia, as the 'minimalist approach of crisis management' has failed to yield any durable results.[36]

One of the major concerns that the US has come to share with India is terrorist violence in Kashmir. Whenever a ghastly act is committed, India points its fingers at some *jihadi* group based in Pakistan. Some of the groups banned by the government of Pakistan have been found to be involved in terrorism against their opponents inside the country and have worked closely with the Afghan Mujahideen and some Kashmiri groups. In the wake of the war on terrorism, the United States seems to have evolved a long term view of the region and that of Pakistan in particular; a stable, preferably a democratic Pakistan with effective state institutions will contribute to regional security, and the stability of Afghanistan, and will also be able to protect itself better against home grown Islamic militancy and extremism that threatens its social cohesion, political order and prospects of economic growth. The ruling establishment of Pakistan has belatedly recognized the dangers of supporting militancy across the borders. By engaging Pakistan in new security arrangements, Washington has successfully persuaded Pakistan to address the issue of religious extremism at home and control the movement of militant groups into Indian-administered Jammu and Kashmir. This also raises some questions. Is this change an indication of failure of Pakistan's policy to force India to come to some reasonable terms on the settlement of the Kashmir issue; the premise that defined its Kashmir policy in the entire decade of the 1990s? Has Pakistan received some understanding that India would be serious and sincere about negotiating a settlement? Is this change tactical to weather the international storm on the question of Islamic terrorism? Is it a sign of success of India's coercive diplomacy toward Pakistan? These questions need to be kept in mind to understand the shift in Pakistan's internal and external policies under the military regime of Pervez Musharraf. If the change is real, Pakistan will like to see some payback. Its expectation will be that the United States remain engaged and play the role of honest broker. It is yet unclear if the US will act intrusively on the Kashmir issue, freeing India and Pakistan to focus on development, markets and economies. But whatever role a third party plays, it will be limited to delivering important signals through back channels and helping India and Pakistan narrow the gap in their negotiating positions. The real burden of resolving the Kashmir problem or any other issue is on the two countries.

A New Peace Process?

After a long decline in bilateral relations, and teetering on the brink of war for more than a year, following the attack on the Indian Parliament in December 2001, Pakistan and India have restored road, air and railways links. The high commissioners of the two countries have resumed their responsibilities and interaction between private groups and government functionaries has increased. This has generated a new optimism about reconciliation between the two traditional adversaries. How has this thaw come about and what promise does it hold for the future? The condition of virtual war that persisted for about a year and the severance of trade and diplomatic relations was hurting both countries. Both wanted to seek a way out. Under a vastly changed regional and international environment, Pakistan began to reassess its Kashmir policy in the year 2002. This timing is important for two reasons. First, international opinion turned against militancy, violence and killing by all groups, ethnic, sectarian or nationalist. Pakistan could no longer justify violence in the name of a freedom struggle. Also, it could not keep up the pretence that it was not supporting the insurgency. Second, Pakistan's Kashmir policy was not going anywhere. Its assumption that perhaps it could force India to settle the issue by raising its costs through support to the insurgency had not proved right. Islamabad wanted to pursue the same strategy that it had successfully applied to Afghanistan by aligning itself with the Afghan Mujahideen. In a way, it was a test of wills, or who would bleed more and back off. In the Kashmir insurgency, both the sides, the Kashmiris supported by Pakistan and the Indians, have bled profusely. This could be a factor in bringing them back to the negotiating table.

Pakistan, since the failed Agra summit, has been talking about the resolution of the Kashmir problem on the basis of what would be acceptable to both sides. This would require placing all the possible options on the table and eliminating all those which either side rejects. But the question is: what will be left to negotiate?[37] While Pakistan, under Musharraf, has been talking about exploring other options, India has been intransigent in its position. It does not want to negotiate a settlement outside the Indian union. Nor is there a fundamental change in the attitudes or strategic mind set of the two countries. What they have accomplished so far is limited to a general understanding on the reduction of tensions, taking measures to build confidence and re-engage themselves in the composite dialogue that includes a diverse range of issues including Kashmir. At the moment, this process is stalled and it is uncertain if they would be able to sustain it if India fails to show the flexibility that Pakistan has been asking for.

Conclusion

Pakistan considers Kashmir as the core issue with India and would like to settle it before it agrees to redefine the entire range of relationships. India has formally rejected the Pakistani position but tacitly does recognize that Kashmir is a problem. It does not accept the UN resolutions or Pakistani terms. India insists that another partition on communal lines is not acceptable, and that Kashmir is an integral part of India that no government would like to bargain away either through war or negotiations.[38] This is the formal position of India, but in fact, in several agreements and declarations, it has accepted Kashmir as a dispute and would like to resolve it without giving away any territory, preferring the Line of Control as an international boundary. While Pakistan believes that the time is ripe for resolving the Kashmir issue, India insists that the conditions necessary for the resolution of the problem simply do not exist.

Over time, India and Pakistan have moved toward a middle ground that all the problems between the two countries must be addressed simultaneously. After signing the Islamabad declaration on 5 January 2004, they have revived the composite dialogue. The changing regional and international environment presents opportunities to both the countries to normalize relations. Will India and Pakistan move away from confrontation to compromise on Kashmir? What is really driving India and Pakistan toward initiating a peace process? Will the process go ahead or collapse in the minefields of mistrust? An attempt to address these questions has been made in this chapter and a few more comments are necessary.

There is mounting pressure on Pakistan to end its support to the Kashmiri freedom fighters because the US and other powers are not willing to separate the insurgency there from global concerns on the rising tide of Islamic militancy and violence. It seems Pakistan has agreed as President Musharraf has declared on different occasions that no group will be allowed to use Pakistani territory to stage attacks against any other country. This clearly implies a change in Pakistan's Kashmir policy that it pursued for more than a decade giving whatever support the Kashmiri militants needed, but keeping its support below the threshold of provoking a full-scale war with India. There is also a change in Pakistan's conventional policy on Kashmir. General Musharraf has stated that Pakistan was prepared to 'put aside for now' its traditional insistence on holding a plebiscite, and would like to explore a new solution acceptable to all three sides—Pakistan, India, and the Kashmiris.[39] But he has conditioned this change to India showing flexibility on the issue.[40] This will mean that India gives up its stance that Jammu and Kashmir State is an integral part of the Indian Union, and Pakistan will give up its position that the dispute be resolved through a plebiscite. But that can only be the starting point.

India's decision to normalize relations is driven by economic and strategic considerations. Many Indians in top decision-making positions acknowledge that India's global economic and political ambitions cannot be realized quickly without settling problems with Pakistan. What makes many so hopeful about the present peace initiative is a growing understanding on both sides that: a) military means or use of force cannot, and will not resolve the Kashmir dispute; b) Peace is a necessity for economic and social development for both the countries.

One of the contentions, however, has been that if the core issues remain unsettled, the two sides will edge back to the line of confrontation. What is needed is a meaningful, sustained and focused dialogue that would lead to the resolution of the Kashmir dispute to the satisfaction of the three parties, the Kashmiris, India and Pakistan. The problem may be addressed independently or in conjunction with others issues, as agreed upon a few years ago. But it should be the object of unbroken, unconditional negotiations to reach a time-bound, final solution.

Notes

1. Also see, Ashok Kapur, 'The Indian Subcontinent: The Contemporary Structures of Power and the Development of Power Relations', *Asian Survey* Vol. 28, No. 7, July 1988, pp. 693-716.

2. Leo Rose argues that the 'basic principle underlying India's regional policy since 1947 has been its undeclared claim to hegemony in South Asia' in J.N. Rosenau *et al.*, (eds.) *World Politics* (New York: Free Press, 1976), p. 214.

3. One of the central arguments of Sumit Ganguly is that Pakistan's irredentism in Kashmir is the cause of escalating tensions. See his, *Conflict Unending* (New York: Columbia University Press, 2002).

4. There are many factors that are responsible for the development of two opposite identities, among them, religion was the most divisive. See, S.M. Burke, *Mainsprings of Indian and Pakistani Foreign Policies* (Minneapolis: University of Minnesota Press, 1974), pp. 7-21.

5. Much has been written on this subject. See Abdul Hamid, *Muslim Separatism in India* (London: 1967); Mushir ul Hasan, *Nationalism and Communal Politics in India 1416-1928* (New Delhi: 1979)

6. H.V. Hodson, *The Great Divide: Britain-India-Pakistan* (Karachi: Oxford University Press, 1985), pp. 403-418.

7. Gowher Rizvi, 'The Rivalry Between India and Pakistan', in Barry Buzan and Gowher Rizvi, *South Asian Insecurity and Great Powers* (London: Macmillan, 1986), p. 96.

8. On the generation dimension, see Stephen Philip Cohen in his ed., *The Security in South Asia* (Urbana and Chicago: University of Illinois Press, 1987), p. 231.

9. A public opinion survey conducted by the US Information Agency in New Delhi, Bombay, Madras and Calcutta in October 1995 of 1500 urban Indians,

including 766 college graduates finds that; a) Eight-in-ten (84 per cent) had have a very bad opinion of Pakistan as a country; b) Nine-in-ten blamed Pakistan for supporting terrorism in Kashmir. USIA, Office of Research and Media Reaction, *Opinion Analysis* (Washington, D.C.: USIA, 28 December 1995).

10. Viceroy Lord Mountbatten laid down the following criteria for the rulers of princely states for making their choice between India or Pakistan: 'Normally geographical situation and communal interests and so forth will be the factors to be considered'. *Time Only to Look Forward: Speeches of Rear Admiral the Earl Mountbatten of Burma* (London, 1949), p. 42.

11. See, Alastair Lamb, *Kashmir: A Disputed Legacy, 1846-1990* (Karachi: Oxford University Press, 1992).

12. P.L. Lakhanpal, *Essential Documents and Notes on Kashmir Dispute* (Delhi: International Books, 1965), p. 57.

13. Balraj Puri, *Jammu and Kashmir: Triumph and Tragedy of Indian Federation* (New Delhi, 1981).

14. Sumantra Bose argues that uprising in Kashmir, denial of democracy, tensions in India-Pakistan relations have all 'gradually fostered a firm belief among a large mass of Kashmiris, most visibly and dramatically in Indian-administered Kashmir but also in Pakistan-controlled Kashmir, that the route to popular, democratic government must first traverse the steep and treacherous pass of national self-determination'. See, his *The Challenge in Kashmir: Democracy, Self-Determination and a Just Peace* (New Delhi: Sage Publications, 1997), p. 109.

15. Khuswant Singh, 'The Valley of Tears', *The Telegraph*, 5 February 1990.

16. The All Parties Hurriyat Conference has boycotted all elections since the uprising, including the October 2002 general elections in Jammu and Kashmir.

17. *1947-1997, The Kashmir Dispute at Fifty Charting Paths to Peace* (The Kashmir Study Group, 1997), p. 20.

18. See a statement of former Pakistani ambassador to the US Dr Maleeha Lodhi. *Dawn* (Karachi), 24 June 2002.

19. Bose, op. cit., p. 109.

20. Lahore Declaration was singed on 21 February 1999. *Dawn*, 22 February 1999.

21. Robert G. Wirsing, 'The Siachen Glacier Dispute: Can Diplomacy Untangle It?' *Indian Defence Review*, July 1991, pp. 95-107.

22. Rita Manchanda, 'Frozen Waste', *Far Eastern Economic Review*, 26 November 1992, pp. 28-29.

23. Both sides have lost thousands of men. According to some earlier estimates, both sides spend $2 million per day on the troops there. See reports by Molly Moore, 'War on Top of the World', *Washington Post*, 2 May 1993, pp. A1, A 30; 'Siachen: The Forgotten War', *India Today*, 31 May 1992, pp. 87-101.

24. 'Nawaz vows to expose Kargil debacle', *Dawn*, 14 June 2000.

25. *The News* (Rawalpindi), 24 May 2001.

26. See, President General Pervez Musharraf's statement, *The News*, 22 June 2002.

27. *Dawn*, 14 December 2001.

28. G. Parthasarthy, 'Pakistan as a threat to India', *The Tribune* (Chandigarh), 13 March 2003.

29. Ashley J. Tellis, *India's Emerging Nuclear Posture: Between Recessed Deterrent and Ready Arsenal* (Santa Monica: RAND, 2001), pp. 250-365.

30. Such remarks are frequently expressed, both by leaders and intellectuals in South Asia. See for instance comments made by an Indian retired Admiral Ramdas. M.H. Askari, 'An admiral's viewpoint', *Dawn*, 15 November 2002.

31. On this point see two opposite views, Scott D. Sagan and Kenneth Waltz, *The Spread of Nuclear Weapons: A Debate* (New York: W.W. Norton, 1995).

32. Since the 13 December 2001 terrorist attacks on the Indian Parliament, the two countries have substantially reduced the number of diplomats in the capitals. The diplomatic relations have been downgraded to low levels. 'Crossing Bounds', (editorial) *The Telegraph* (Calcutta), 2 February 2003.

33. A study conducted by the Council on Foreign Relations sees inherent danger in the conflict in Kashmir spilling over to India-Pakistan borders 'conceivably one involving use of nuclear weapons', *New Priorities in South Asia: US Policy Toward India, Pakistan and Afghanistan* (New York: Council on Foreign Relations, 2003) p. 65.

34. US National Security Advisor, Condoleezza Rice, quoted in 'The balancing act' (editorial), *The Hindu*, 4 May 2002.

35. Statement of U.S. Deputy Secretary of State, Richard Armitage, *Dawn*, 25 June 2002.

36. Maleeha Lodhi, *Dawn*, 24 June 2002.

37. *South Asia Monitor*, Number 75, 1 October 2004.

38. K. Shankar Bajpai, 'Untangling India and Pakistan', *Foreign Affairs*, May-June 2003.

39. 'Musharraf calls for debate on Kashmir options', *Dawn*, 26 October 2004.

40. *Dawn*, 21 November 2004.

5

India-Pakistan Relations at a Crossroads

Robert G. Wirsing

Introduction

India and Pakistan, with 2004 population estimates, respectively, of
1, 065, 071, 000 and 153, 705, 000, are the world's second and sixth
most populous nations.* They have a history of bitter rivalry,
including four wars with one another (the most recent in 1999 over
Kargil) since achieving independence from Great Britain in 1947.
Their back-to-back detonations of nuclear explosives in May 1998
unequivocally demonstrated to the world the mounting muscularity
of their nuclear weapons programs. Their steady progress in the
development of ballistic missiles underscores the gravity of the
danger stemming from these programs. They are the two largest and
most powerful member-states of the South Asian Association of
Regional Cooperation (SAARC), the success of which in promoting
regional economic and social development has been held hostage
to their hostility since the group's founding in 1985. Unexpectedly,
during the past few years these two historic rivals are simultaneously
enjoying unusually close ties with the United States: India, having
largely abandoned its past commitment to non-alignment, has been
busily crafting a defense-oriented 'strategic partnership' with
Washington; and Pakistan, a vital member of Washington's post-
September 11 global counterterrorist coalition, found itself rewarded

---

* The views expressed in this article are those of the author and do not necessarily
reflect the official policy or position of the Asia-Pacific Center for Security Studies,
the US Pacific Command, the US Department of Defence or the US Government.

in spring 2004 with the prized status of 'non-NATO major ally'.[1] In short, Pakistan and India are significant players in global as well as regional politics; thus the question 'Is Peace Real This Time?', raised in a recent Carnegie Endowment for International Peace report on the warming trend currently in progress between them, points to a matter of enormous importance to the international community.[2]

Back from the Brink: India-Pakistan Relations 2001-2004

The pace of improvement in India-Pakistan relations since April 2003, when then Indian Prime Minister Atal Bihari Vajpayee offered a 'hand of friendship' to Pakistan in what he called a last effort to mend ties, has been breathtaking. In the space of a year, the two archrivals managed to:

- restore the rail, bus, and air links that had been cut in the wake of the terrorist attack on Parliament House in New Delhi in December 2001;
- agree to a cease-fire not only on the 740-kilometer Line of Control (LoC) dividing their forces in Jammu and Kashmir but also on the remote Siachen Glacier, where guns have not been silent since Indian forces took possession of the area in April 1984;
- commit themselves in early January 2004 at the close of the 12th SAARC summit in Islamabad, to revive bilateral talks broken off when the last peace initiative between India and Pakistan foundered at Agra in July 2001;
- lay the groundwork in spring 2004 for comprehensive and simultaneous negotiations with an eight-point agenda covering all major issues between them, including Kashmir; and
- successfully conclude on 13 April 2004 the Indian cricket team's first Test tour of Pakistan in fourteen years—the most public sign that a serious thaw was in progress.

The change in India-Pakistan relations is all the more remarkable considering the circumstances that immediately preceded it. Most dramatically, for a period of ten months in 2002, upwards of a million Indian and Pakistani troops had squared off menacingly against one another along the lengthy border separating their two countries. India and Pakistan seemed then on the brink of war. With that episode's peaceful conclusion, India and Pakistan have clearly stepped back from the brink. The question remains, of course, whether this undeniably momentous turn of events marks a permanent break with the past. One part of the answer can be sought in the unsettled issues that are likely to surface on the agenda of talks planned between them.

Agenda for Talks: The Issues

In a Joint Press Statement issued at the close of the 12th SAARC summit, Prime Minister Vajpayee and Pakistani President Pervez Musharraf committed themselves 'to commence the process of the composite dialogue in February 2004 ... confident that [its] resumption ... will lead to peaceful settlement of all bilateral issues, including Jammu and Kashmir, to the satisfaction of both sides'.[3] The foreign secretaries of the two countries worked out a preliminary timetable for the talks at a meeting in Islamabad on 18 February.[4] Due to India's intervening national elections, conducted in phases in late April to early May 2004, the meeting of the two countries' foreign ministers was postponed until August. Expert-level talks and further preparatory meetings of the foreign and defence secretaries were conducted in May and June. Judging from the last time composite talks were undertaken by the two sides in the so-called '6 + 2' integrated format of discussions begun in October 1998, longstanding disputes over the Wullar Barrage (Tulbul Project), Siachen Glacier, and Sir Creek were bound to receive attention, along with drug trafficking and cultural exchanges. Likely to top the list of issues on the agenda, however, were Kashmir, terrorism, nuclear confidence-building measures, and what Pakistanis were calling 'strategic stability'—the balance of nuclear and conventional weapons. Promotion of bilateral trade was also certain to be high on the agenda.

Kashmir

Between 1947 and the present, India and Pakistan have held direct bilateral talks in which Kashmir was an agenda item on nearly twenty-five separate occasions. A few of these talks (Karachi 1949; Tashkent 1966; Simla 1972) accomplished immediate objectives: they formally brought war to an end and provided for such things as repatriation of POWs, return of occupied territories, or establishment of ceasefire lines. They all failed on the larger issue of Kashmir's ultimate disposition. The only major discussions involving Kashmir that resulted in workable and sustainable agreements were those that led to the 1960 Indus Waters Treaty. That treaty still stands. However, it was internationally mediated and international funding was a pivotal element in its implementation.[5] If its historical record is any guide, talks on the subject of Kashmir in a strictly *bilateral* framework seem doomed from the start.

Is the time ripe for settling Kashmir? There are clearly some reasons to think so. One is that leaders from both sides have made explicit and repeated mention in recent months of their belief in the need to move away from irreconcilable stated positions. A second is that leaders on both sides appear genuinely dismayed by the baleful effects that more than a half-century of intransigence over Kashmir has had on their economies. With large sections of its population still mired in poverty, the South Asian region's attractiveness to foreign investors suffers from a global reputation as a nuclear flashpoint. A third is that there is strong evidence, including some polling results, indicating that Kashmiris themselves are insurgency-fatigued and willing to settle for much less than either accession to Pakistan or *azadi* (the state's complete freedom from either India or Pakistan). New Delhi's offer of direct talks with the militant Kashmiri Muslim leadership of the All-Parties Hurriyat Conference (APHC), another prong in its peace initiative, is almost certainly traceable to this perceived weakness in the separatist cause. A fourth and perhaps the most important reason for thinking that the time is ripe, if not for final resolution then at least for agreement to sustain the present ceasefire, is that Pakistan's foreign policy establishment seems to have come to the conclusion that coming to terms with India is the best of a number of largely unattractive strategic options available. Islamabad simply cannot contend all at once, in other words, with an irate India, a still chaotic Afghanistan, embarrassing disclosures about its past nuclear proliferation practices, and—a factor more than ever driving change in regional calculations of strategic alternatives—American expectations that Islamabad co-operate in the war on terrorism.

There are clearly also good reasons for pessimism over Kashmir. Still to be discovered, for instance, is whether the peace initiative can survive fundamental differences in the expectations and objectives each side brings to the discussions. The initiative has come as far as it has, Ashley Tellis cautions,

> because Pakistan surrendered on issues of process in order to begin formal negotiations through which it hopes to secure Indian concessions on matters of substance. India, in contrast, sought and accepted the Pakistani concessions on process principally in order to intimate the limits to future compromises that may be forthcoming on matters of substance. In other words, the fundamental problem between the two sides has still not been engaged: Pakistan seeks negotiations to alter the status quo, whereas India accepts negotiations primarily to ratify the same. Unless some way can be found to bridge this chasm, the long-run prospects for successful dispute resolution do not look promising.[6]

Tellis argues that the national strategies of the two sides will remain on a collision course until and unless Pakistan, by far the weaker side in the equation, decides to accept the current territorial *status quo* in Jammu and Kashmir—an extremely difficult step requiring a basic redefinition of Pakistan's national interest.

If Tellis is correct, the only realistic antidote to continued fighting over Kashmir is for the two sides to agree to the conversion of the LoC into a permanent international border. He is not alone, however, in believing that winning the agreement of both sides to that will be a most arduous exercise. Indeed, none of the many 'solutions' to Kashmir proposed over the decades inspires much optimism. Surveying them recently, Prem Shankar Jha, one of India's leading journalists, concluded that all of them were basically

non-starters. Included on his list of rejects were not only the
conversion idea along with the traditional favourites of Pakistan
(the holding of an internationally supervised plebiscite in the state
of Jammu and Kashmir to ascertain the people's wishes about
whether it should belong to India or Pakistan) and India (that the
whole of the state of Jammu and Kashmir, including Pakistani-
controlled Azad Kashmir and the Northern Areas, should belong
to India), but also the repartition of the state (transferring only the
Valley of Kashmir to Pakistan, leaving the rest with India), complete
independence for Kashmir, and some species of condominium or
quasi-sovereignty arrangement for the state. Unfazed by the paucity
of attractive options, Jha offered up a solution of his own—namely
the application to Kashmir of the Tyrol Model. That model
involved a grant of substantial autonomy to the German-speaking
trans-Alpine region of Tyrol, part of which falls in Italy, part in
Austria. The model's adoption managed to defuse a potentially
explosive territorial dispute between those two European neighbours.
Jha conceded that it had taken the better part of a half-century to
work out the model and also that the key element in the dispute's
successful resolution had been trust, a quality conspicuous in its
absence in India-Pakistan relations. Nevertheless, he insisted—
perhaps more out of frustration than conviction—that the time was
ripe to apply the Tyrol Model to Kashmir.[7]

Also on the darker side of the ripeness issue, perhaps, are the
results of India's Spring 2004 parliamentary elections. Defying
expectations, the ruling Bharatiya Janata Party (BJP) went down in
defeat, inevitably spreading a cloud of uncertainty over the nascent
dialogue process. After all, much of the credit for launching the
peace initiative belonged to the ousted Prime Minister Vajpayee,
whose towering popularity had enabled him to enlist the
acquiescence in the initiative of his Hindu nationalist political
allies. The newly appointed Prime Minister, Manmohan Singh,
promptly signalled his intent to carry forward the peace initiative
with Pakistan. 'We seek the most friendly relations with our
neighbours', he was reported to have said at his first news
conference, 'more so with Pakistan than any other. We must find
the ways and means to resolve all outstanding problems that have

been a source of friction and the unfortunate history of our relations with Pakistan'.[8] Nevertheless, the incoming Congress party-led coalition is likely to be preoccupied for some time with its own survival in power, and that preoccupation, while it may not actually derail the dialogue process, could well rule out the kinds of imaginative statesmanship and political risk-taking that many observers believe are essential to its success.

It is important to bear in mind, in any event, that neither side—regardless of who is in power—is likely to favour appeasing its old adversary on the issue of Kashmir without receiving major concessions in connection with other issues on the agenda, including some that almost certainly matter more in ruling circles than Kashmir. In other words, a resolution of the Kashmir issue—which in itself is complicated—depends upon progress on other contentious issues, which highlights the extraordinary difficulty of the path ahead.

Conventional and Nuclear Arms

Any attempts by India and Pakistan to negotiate bilateral arms agreements are likely to conflict with the considerable instability currently characterizing the existing arms balances, conventional and nuclear, between them. Current conventional and nuclear arms inventories and the actions of India and Pakistan indicate that they are not on an unrestrained peace binge. On the contrary, they are two of the largest spenders on defence in the world. The authoritative *SIPRI Yearbook 2003* ranked India 11th highest in 2002 when its defence outlay was measured in standard market exchange rates. Pakistan was not included among the top 15 ranked by SIPRI when market exchange rates were used. When the reckoning was done in terms of purchasing power parity (PPP), however, a different picture emerged. India ranked third in the world in defence expenditure, following only the United States and China, while Pakistan ranked 15th.[9]

Both countries are currently outfitting their military forces in ways that, while perhaps fully defensible on prudential grounds, inevitably appear threatening or even provocative to the other.

Given the considerable power disparity between them arising from the conspicuous asymmetries—geographic, demographic, economic, and military—in their relationship, it could scarcely be otherwise. The military balance between India and Pakistan, seen in this light, is at least as important as Kashmir.

Some of India's most recent planned arms acquisitions, including purchases from Russia of the $1.5 billion *Admiral Gorschkov* aircraft carrier and from Israel of three state-of-the-art Phalcon AWACSs could give India, according to some arms experts, a measurable military edge over Pakistan.[10] The edge would likely be further widened if India were to add both nuclear power and cruise missiles, potentially nuclear-tipped, to its growing submarine fleet. If recent reports prove accurate that Indian defence scientists have succeeded in developing mini-nukes or low-yield 'boutique' nuclear bombs for battlefield use, India's military equation with Pakistan might, in fact, be radically turned to Pakistan's disadvantage. India's diligent construction of new air and naval bases, along with its embryonic, but far from trivial, military connections with Iran and Northern Alliance-ruled Afghanistan, both in Pakistan's backyard, also carry serious warnings for Pakistan's defence strategists.[11]

Pakistani military planners are, of course, not without their own ambitions for increasing the reach, lethality, and efficiency of the country's conventional and nuclear weapons systems. In January 2003, the nuclear-capable medium-range (1,500 km) Ghauri missile came into service, bringing a huge expanse of India well within range. Pakistan's planned serial production beginning in 2006 of the JF-17 Thunder fighter aircraft, developed in close collaboration with the Chinese, naturally arouses concern in New Delhi, perhaps less because of its immediate combat potential than because of the long-range strategic implications of the Chinese connection.[12] Regarding China, Indians are bound to wonder about the implications of the opening in a year or two of the largely China-financed port and navy base at Gwadar on Pakistan's Balochistan coast, as also about China's plans to sell four warships to Pakistan.[13]

Pakistan's interest, then, in placing agreed bilateral restraints on weapons development and acquisition is readily understandable but it collides with India's great power aspirations and much larger strategic canvas. That canvas obviously includes China, whose superiority over India—arguably in conventional forces, unquestionably in nuclear forces—is a constant stimulus to yet greater exertion by India's defence planners. Confronting any imagined arms accord between Islamabad and New Delhi are thus two awkward asymmetrical arms relationships—that between India and Pakistan and between India and China.

Terrorism

At the SAARC summit in January 2004, India and Pakistan jointly signed a seemingly stringent *Additional Protocol to the 1987 SAARC Regional Convention on Suppression of Terrorism*. Most of the organizations banned by India in recent years under the Public Order and Terrorism Act (POTA) have been headquartered in Pakistan, however, and the Indian government officially claims that over 75 per cent of 'foreign terrorists' killed or arrested since the outbreak of the Kashmir insurgency in the early 1990s were from Pakistan. The Musharraf government has been under unusually strong pressure from Washington to halt activities of terrorist groups said to be operating from its soil; but scepticism is rampant, and not only in India, about the depth of Islamabad's determination to accomplish the job. As a scathing report issued by the International Crisis Group (ICG) within days of the signing of the new SAARC anti-terrorism protocol put it, the Musharraf government's pledge of sweeping reforms of Pakistan's *madrassas*—considered by some as key breeding grounds for radical Islamist ideologies and terrorist networks—had essentially come to naught. There was no presidential ordinance regulating the *madrassas*, no new national curriculum has been developed, and most *madrassas* remain unregistered. Moreover, tougher controls on the financing of extremist groups have not been implemented.[14]

Pakistani leaders appear well aware that their longstanding practice of labelling insurgents in Kashmir as 'freedom fighters' has been bled of virtually all its legitimacy since the events of 11 September. They have been reluctant, however, to crack down fully on the militant groups that target India while Pakistan's armed forces are still engaged in politically high-sensitive military operations against the Taliban and Al-Qaeda remnants along Afghanistan's border. It is also likely, moreover, that a complete shutdown of the anti-India militant groups based in Pakistan would come after, not before, Pakistan has secured equally important concessions from India.

Economic Cooperation

The incentives for India and Pakistan to pursue closer commercial and economic ties are considerable. They include major potential benefits to be gained not only from expanded trade but also from the sharing of energy and water resources. For instance, of the several natural gas pipeline routes that have been proposed in recent years to carry gas from Turkmenistan, Iran, or Qatar to gas-deficient India, by far the cheapest and technically most feasible route is the land route across Pakistan. That route has thus far won little support from India, whose leaders have appeared reluctant either to make its gas supply in any measure hostage to its political relations with Pakistan or to reward Pakistan with handsome conduit fees without first having wrung concessions from Islamabad on other unsettled issues between the two countries.[15]

Unfortunately, there is not much of a trading relationship between India and Pakistan to act as a foundation for added economic and commercial ties. The following tables present trade statistics for 2002. Arrestingly visible is the fact that major trading partners for both India and Pakistan are the world's more advanced industrial states—North American, European, and Asian—and not their South Asian regional neighbours with whom both their import and export trade are relatively miniscule. Other SAARC countries accounted for only 2.3 per cent of Pakistan's imports and only 3.0 per cent of its exports. The corresponding figures for India were 1.1 per cent of imports and 5.7 per cent of exports.

Economists have never tired of listing the huge structural impediments to heightened intra-regional trade in South Asia. Foremost on most every list are these reasons: The region's economies are low in per capita income and low in export potential, and for the most part, competitive rather than complementary in the range of goods produced. Allegedly, illicit trade between India and Pakistan runs upwards of $1 billion or so per annum, suggesting a potential for expansion not visible in the tables. Some economists claim that two-way trade could reach $6 billion once the South Asian Free Trade Area (SAFTA), which was agreed upon by the region's leaders at the 12th SAARC summit, comes into being in January 2006. For the moment, however, dramatic expansion in market opportunities between India and Pakistan is more likely to come as a reward for than as a cause of improved bilateral relations.

Table 1
Direction of Trade 2002
SAARC Countries, % of Imports

	Industrial States	Asia	SAARC
Bangladesh	25.4	55.1	15.6
Bhutan	n.a.	n.a.	n.a.
India	35.9	22.4	01.1
Maldives	18.5	63.3	33.7
Nepal	17.8	56.0	39.6
Pakistan	34.3	25.8	02.3
Sri Lanka	30.0	53.4	15.5

Source: Direction of Trade Statistics, Yearbook 2002 (Washington, DC: International Monetary Fund)

Table 2
Direction of Trade 2002
SAARC Countries, % of Exports

	Industrial States	Asia	SAARC
Bangladesh	74.1	04.9	01.4
Bhutan	n.a.	n.a.	n.a.
India	52.3	23.4	05.7
Maldives	70.2	26.8	13.5
Nepal	46.1	51.1	48.9
Pakistan	57.0	18.2	03.0
Sri Lanka	73.6	10.5	04.9

Source: Direction of Trade Statistics, Yearbook 2002 (Washington, DC: International Monetary Fund)

America in the India-Pakistan Relationship

The United States has been engaged for a half century in a delicate power-balancing act in the subcontinent. At times, as during the decade of war in Afghanistan following the Soviet invasion of 1979, it has tilted toward Pakistan; at other times, as during the second Clinton administration from 1996 to 2000, toward India. In a few instances, such as post-September 11, the United States has seemed to tilt simultaneously toward both of them. The closeness of current ties with Pakistan is obviously derivative of the war on terrorism: Pakistan shares a border and ethnic ties with Afghanistan and is intimately familiar with the Afghan political landscape. These factors along with its well-honed habits of collaboration with Washington have given Pakistan its natural geostrategic importance. In India's case, the habits of collaboration with Washington have been late in developing and have yet to reach the levels sometimes recorded in the history of US–Pakistan relations. Economic ties between India and the United States have expanded remarkably in recent years, however, and a spate of joint military exercises and arms agreements between them give promise of developing into a qualitatively new kind of strategic partnership. For some commentators in Washington and elsewhere, no small part of the motivation for building the partnership rests on India's potential role in the containment of China—a role that remains largely hypothetical.

By no means are Washington's present ties with Pakistan and India entirely trouble-free. For one thing, Pakistan's nuclear wheeling and dealing in the last several years has aroused substantial anxiety in the United States over the safety of Islamabad's nuclear weapons program.[16] Pakistan's wobbly commitment to democratic rule is also problematic for Washington, and both the Indian and Pakistani governments have reservations, so far largely muted in public, about Washington's Iraq policy. Over the long term, both governments remain deeply suspicious of Washington's intentions, especially of its willingness and ability to maintain current commitments.

Heavily preoccupied elsewhere, Washington has been extremely reluctant to assume a leading public role in conflict-resolving activities between India and Pakistan. Kashmir, in particular, has acquired a reputation in the United States as an unusually sticky tar baby; Washington has generally been content so far to rely on private appeals and the efforts of the two countries to resume bilateral talks. President Clinton's conspicuous involvement as informal mediator of the Kargil conflict in July 1999 stands as recent testimony of the potential for a more direct American role. Until India shows greater warmth for the idea, however, it is likely to remain essentially untested.

Maintaining friendly ties with the United States remains a matter of utmost importance to both India and Pakistan. Thus, pacifying the United States—avoiding actions that might upset the inherently delicate trilateral arrangement currently in place—naturally figures in calculations made in regard to their relationship with one another. This clearly gives Washington extraordinary advantage, including some capacity for stabilizing and even refashioning India-Pakistan relations. When compelling national interests are at stake, however, Washington's advantage is likely to prove somewhat illusory.

Conclusion: Prospects of Change

What about the question posed at the outset of this discussion—
namely, whether the undeniably momentous turn of events
witnessed in India-Pakistan relations during the past year marks a
permanent break with the past? Do these events mean that India
and Pakistan are on the verge of burying the hatchet once and for
all? Is there a new, peace and cooperation-oriented mindset
spreading through the region? Or is the world witnessing a
temporary suspension of the old rivalry—a laying aside of swords,
so to speak, rather than their conversion into ploughshares–brought
on by a rush of economic, political, diplomatic, and strategic
pressures that have elicited pragmatic adjustments from both
countries? Do these events represent, in Pakistan's case, little more
than a tactical retreat from a dangerously exposed position, and in
India's case, merely an expedient show of magnanimity toward its
outflanked rival? The answer, very likely, is that the break with the
past, to the extent that it is seriously underway at all, is in its
infancy—it faces huge and possibly insurmountable obstacles and
its ultimate fate, in any event, will be determined by far more than
the good intentions of the two countries' current leaderships.

Notes

1. 'U.S. Raises Pakistan's Standing to 'Major' Ally', *International Herald Tribune*
   (Internet edition), 18 March 2004. For background, see B. Raman, 'Pakistan as
   a Major Non-NATO Ally (MNNA) of US', *Paper no. 958* (Internet edition),
   South Asia Analysis Group, 22 March 2004.
2. *India and Pakistan: Is Peace Real This Time? A Conversation Between Husain Haqqani
   and Ashley J. Tellis* (Washington, DC: Carnegie Endowment for International
   Peace, 2004).
3. 'India-Pakistan Joint Press Statement', 6 January 2004, Press Release, Embassy
   of India (www.indiagov.org/press_release/2004/jan/07.htm).
4. 'Full Text of Indo-Pak. Joint Statement', *The Hindu* (Internet edition),
   19 February 2004.
5. For additional comment on the Indus Waters Treaty, see Robert G. Wirsing,
   Kashmir in the Shadow of War: Regional Rivalries in a Nuclear Age (Armonk: M. E.
   Sharpe, Inc., 2003), pp. 233-5; and Salman M. A. Salman and Kishor Uprety,
   Conflict and Cooperation on South Asia's International Rivers: A Legal Perspective
   (Washington, DC: The World Bank, 2002), pp. 37-61.

6. *India and Pakistan: Is Peace Real This Time?*, p. 14.

7. Prem Shankar Jha, 'Grasping the Nettle', *South Asian Journal*, no. 3, 14 April 2004 (Internet edition distributed by South Asian Media Net).

8. Amy Waldman, 'India's New Leader Vows Not to Tolerate Sectarian Riots', *The New York Times* (Internet edition), 21 May 2004.

9. *SIPRI Yearbook 2003: Armaments, Disarmament and International Security* (Oxford: Oxford University Press, 2003), Chapter 10: Military Expenditure.

10. 'Phalcon Sale to India of Utmost Seriousness: Pak', *The Times of India* (Internet edition), 23 May 2003.

11. On the Indo-Iranian connection, see Donald Berlin, 'India-Iran Relations: A Deepening Entente', *Asia-Pacific Security Studies* Special Assessment (Honolulu: Asia-Pacific Center for Security Studies, June 2004).

12. 'JF-17 Plane's Maiden Flight Next Week: Pakistan-China Joint Venture', *Dawn* (Internet edition), 31 August 2003.

13. 'China to Provide Four Warships to Pakistan', *The News*, 19 May 2004.

14. *Unfulfilled Promises: Pakistan's Failure to Tackle Extremism*, Asia Report No. 73 (Islamabad/Brussels, 16 January 2004).

15. For an optimistic (Pakistani) reading of pipeline prospects, see Nadeem Iqbal, 'For Iran, Pakistan, Gas Pipelines No Longer a Pipedream', *South Asia Tribune* (Internet edition), Issue no. 23, 30 December 2002-5 January 2003. For authoritative profiles of the energy situations of India and Pakistan, see the US Department of Energy (Energy Information Administration) country analysis briefings on these countries at Web site: www.eia.doe.gov.

16. There were innumerable accounts of Pakistan's alleged vulnerability to nuclear hijacking by fundamentalist terrorists. See, for example, Seymour M. Hersh, 'Watching the Warheads: The Risks to Pakistan's Nuclear Arsenal', *New Yorker*, 5 November 2001. The sensational expose in late 2003 of international nuclear-merchandising engaged in by Dr. Abdul Qadeer Khan, the father of Pakistan's nuclear weapons program, vastly increased the focus on Pakistan's proliferation habits. For an Indian narrative of these habits, see B. Raman, 'A. Q. Khan Shifted Iraq's WMD to Pakistan?', *Paper no. 916* (Internet edition), South Asia Analysis Group, 7 February 2004.

6

A User's Guide to Guided Democracy: Musharraf and the Pakistani Military Governance Paradigm

Charles H. Kennedy

Pervez Musharraf assumed power through a bloodless military coup on 12 October 1999. His assumption of power and the political course his regime has followed since is eerily familiar to the paths followed by his military predecessors. Perhaps this is owing to the limited options available to Pakistani military rulers; perhaps it is owing to a collective lack of imagination; perhaps it is owing to a 'Grand Strategy' formulated within the GHQ. In any case, Musharraf's government has followed very closely the familiar patterns of military regime development within Pakistan. In the pages that follow an explicit attempt will be made to analyze Musharraf's first five years in power in terms of the 'Pakistani military governance paradigm'. This paradigm has ten sequential or nearly sequential steps. We will look at each in turn.

Step One: Explain Yourself

The first step following a military coup is to establish a plausible, ideally compelling excuse for subverting the political process. After all, military coups should not be entered into lightly. Pakistan's first coup, staged by President Iskandar Mirza and General Ayub Khan set a precedent by justifying their actions in terms of countering what they typified as a wholesale breakdown of the process of governance in the state. Evidence for such a 'breakdown' was provided in that each of the four previous post-1954 governments (headed by Chaudhary Muhammad Ali, Huseyn S. Suhrawardy, I.I. Chundrigar, and Feroz Khan Noon) were pathetically weak. Such weakness it was alleged had led to the growing civil unrest in East Pakistan, which threatened to deteriorate into chaos. Mirza's and Ayub's case was strong; and Ayub's case for subsequently ousting Mirza (the latter had presided over the 1954-58 mess and he had subverted his own government) was compelling.[1]

Perhaps not as compelling in retrospect were the motives of Ziaul Haq's 'Operation Fair Play'. Zia claimed that the political system of Pakistan had come unglued following Bhutto's rigging of the 1977 general election. The Pakistan National Alliance (PNA) was leading a nationwide campaign calling for Bhutto to step down and for a new election to be held, and Bhutto had, for all intents and purposes, admitted electoral misdeeds by promulgating the Seventh Amendment to the constitution. The latter amendment allowed for the holding of a national referendum—ostensibly to seek popular support for continued confidence in the Prime Minister. Before such a referendum could be held, and before Bhutto could reach an accord with the PNA, the military struck. To Zia and his apologists they had no choice but to intervene.

Pervez Musharraf's motives for staging the 12 October 1999 coup were several.[2] The immediate motive was to counter Nawaz Sharif's dismissal of Musharraf as Chief of Army Staff and the appointment of General Khawaja Ziaduddin in his stead. On its face this is a less than compelling rationale as the Prime Minister possessed the competent authority to dismiss a COAS—indeed in 1998, Nawaz Sharif had done just that by dismissing General Jehangir Karamat and replacing him with General Musharraf. A more compelling motive was the growing concern that Nawaz Sharif was systematically overstepping his bounds and challenging the corporate interests of the military; interests which included sharing in Pakistan's governing structure. Nawaz Sharif's successful abrogation of Article 58(2)(b)—the passage of the Thirteenth Amendment—had left his government immune from civilian dissolution. Such civilian presidential dissolutions had been greatly influenced by the military. Also, a compelling motive was the military's rift with Nawaz Sharif over what many in the military viewed as the latter's capitulation in Kargil. For good measure Musharraf's government also contended that Nawaz Sharif's government was significantly corrupt and as a consequence was subject to removal. This argument was made most forcefully before the Supreme Court in the *Zafar Ali Shah* case.[3]

In any case, the test of a successful excuse is if it is accepted by its recipient—if it can be sold to the public. When measured by this yardstick it seems apparent that Ayub's and Musharraf's coups were more 'successful' than Zia's. There was virtually no public outcry against the dismissals of Iskandar Mirza and Nawaz Sharif. Zia's dismissal of Bhutto was a far more difficult sale. It is also important to note that the 1999 coup followed in the tradition of being bloodless. Coups, in Pakistan, are fairly polite occasions; they are the result of consensual decision-making by the officer corps. Violence would mar the proceedings; upset the paradigm.

Step Two: Avoid Legal Chaos

Following the presentation of plausible excuses, the next step is to provide continuity of government—to avoid legal chaos. Each of Pakistan's coup makers has followed a similar path.

On 10 October 1958, Ayub Khan promulgated the Laws (Continuance in Force) Order. The general effect of this was to validate laws, other than the 1956 constitution, that were in force prior to the 7 October coup. It also restored the jurisdiction of all courts including the Supreme Court and High Courts, and directed that the government of Pakistan should act as nearly as possible in accordance with the abrogated constitution. But the Order made clear that 'no court or person could call or permit to be called into question (i) the proclamation of 7 October, (ii) any order in pursuance of the proclamation or any martial law order or martial law regulation, (iii) any finding, judgment or order of a Special Military Court or a Summary Military Court'.[4]

A nearly-identical pattern was followed in Zia's Laws (Continuance in Force) Order, 1977. It repeated Ayub's formulary.

'Pakistan shall, subject to this order and any order made by the president and any order made by the Chief Martial Law Administrator (CMLA) be governed as nearly as may be, in accordance with the constitution'. The courts were also allowed to function normally except they would have no jurisdiction to challenge the actions of the CMLA or Martial Law Administrators or any person exercising authority on behalf of either.[5]

General Musharraf (by then the self-styled 'Chief Executive') followed suit in his promulgation of the Provisional Constitution Order of 1999 (PCO):

> 'Notwithstanding the abeyance of the provisions of the constitution of the Islamic Republic of Pakistan, ... Pakistan shall, subject to this Order and any other Orders made by the Chief Executive, be governed as nearly as may be, in accordance with the constitution. Subject as aforesaid, all courts in existence immediately before the commencement of this Order, shall continue to function and to exercise their respective powers and jurisdiction provided that the Supreme Court or High Courts and any other court shall not have the powers to make any order against the Chief Executive or any other person exercising powers or jurisdiction under his authority'.[6]

Step Three: Make Things Legal in the Short Term

Military coups and the abrogation or suspension of relevant constitutions are likely to draw the attention of and engender opposition from amongst the members of the judiciary. Pakistan's coupmakers have proven adept at encouraging the superior judiciary to be compliant and to mandate their 'extra-constitutional' practices.

Ayub Khan inherited a cooperative superior judiciary. In the *Moulvi Tamizuddin* case, the Federal Court had upheld the dissolution of the Constituent Assembly by the Governor-General. More importantly in a subsequent case (1955) the court relied upon the 'doctrine of state necessity' to validate laws made invalid by the court's earlier decision.[7] With such recent legal precedents Ayub did not risk serious legal challenge against his declaration of martial law. Indeed, when his declaration of martial law was challenged the Supreme Court (the 'Federal Court' became known as the 'Supreme Court' under the terms of the 1956 constitution) in the *Dosso* case ruled that a successful *coups d'etat* is an internationally recognized legal method of changing a constitution.[8] Justice Muhammad Munir wrote the leading decision in all three cases.

Ziaul Haq faced a more complex situation. Zia's coup had displaced a populist prime minister at the peak of his power, having led the PPP to an overwhelming, albeit tainted, victory in the 1977 general elections. Moreover, Bhutto had loyalists within the superior judiciary including the Chief Justice of the Supreme Court, Yakub Ali. Zia, nothing if not clever, seized upon the expedient of placing into abeyance the operation of the Bhutto-inspired Fifth and Sixth amendments to the constitution. The introduction of the latter amendments had been bitterly resented by Pakistan's superior judiciary as an infringement upon their authority.[9] The timely abrogation of these amendments also served to remove Yakub Ali from the post of Chief Justice and to elevate Justice Anwar-ul-Haq to the position.[10]

Subsequently, in a unanimous decision written by the new Chief Justice, the Supreme Court ruled that Zia's assumption of power must be maintained as a matter of 'state necessity' as Zia's actions had been necessitated in turn by a prior usurpation of power by Bhutto. Moreover, the Court ruled that Zia's actions were designed, in part, to prevent the further deterioration of the civil order. The Court drew a distinction between the current case and Ayub's coup in that Zia's coup did not abrogate the relevant (1973) constitution.[11]

Musharraf faced the trickiest situation of all. The 'doctrine of state necessity' had fallen out of favour within Pakistan's legal circles, and the superior courts, although harmed by Nawaz Sharif's recent meddling were still activist and at least episodically independent. Moreover, international public opinion by 1999 had largely dismissed the *coups d'etat* as an acceptable means of changing government.

Accordingly Musharraf and his advisors devised a plan to make the judiciary *ex post facto* 'co-conspirators' in the coup. On

31 December 1999 he introduced an ordinance that required superior court judges to take a fresh oath of office under the terms of the PCO, *not* the 1973 constitution.[12] Six justices of the Supreme Court and nine judges of the High Courts refused to take the new oath and stood retired.[13] The reconstituted and now ostensibly more cooperative Supreme Court quickly consolidated the numerous writ petitions that had been filed challenging the constitutionality of the military coup, and on 12 May 2000 issued their landmark finding— the *Zafar Ali Shah* decision.[14] The decision among other things provided legal cover for Musharraf's actions. It also granted the regime a three-year grace period (until 12 October 2002) to hold general elections and to restore the national and provincial assemblies. When the dust settled following the decision the military (and the Chief Executive) had held the field. First, Musharraf's seizure of power had not been defined as constituting an act of 'martial law'. An adverse finding would have occasioned a variety of domestic and international problems. Second, the military coup was defined as regrettable but justifiable. Finally, Musharraf's regime had been granted legitimacy, and given an extra-constitutional 'grace period' of three years. Appeals against the *Zafar Ali Shah* decision were rejected by the Court in the *Wasim Sajjad* case.[15]

Step Four: Eliminate Political Opponents

By their very nature military coups displace former political leaders, who have typically been elected and who as a consequence have some degree of popular legitimacy. Clearly it is imperative for the successful coupmaker to discredit and ideally to 'get rid' of such former leaders.

Ayub's task proved quite simple in this regard. Iskandar Mirza had not been elected by the people to the presidency; and his legitimacy was tarnished as he had been one of the principals in the 1958 coup. Ayub deftly had him arrested and negotiated and enforced his safe passage and exile to England.

Zia's task was far more complicated. The process that led to the legal acceptance of Zia's coup was the *Nusrat Bhutto* case. But, even after the court's decision, Z.A. Bhutto remained a powerful force with which to be reckoned: Zia had promised to hold elections within ninety days of the coup; if such elections were held, Bhutto would almost certainly be re-elected as Prime Minister; and Bhutto had made it clear that he intended to invoke Article 6 of the constitution ('High Treason') against Zia once he regained his post.[16]

Zia's approach was two-fold: (1) He amassed extensive information detailing the misdeeds of Z.A. Bhutto and his regime and published the data in the several volume *White Papers*.[17] (2) He pursued an unlikely abetment to a murder charge against Bhutto, in which Bhutto was implicated in the inadvertent murder of Nawab Muhammad Ahmad, the father of Ahmed Raza Kasuri (a political opponent of Bhutto), the actual target of the alleged 'hit'. Both approaches bore fruit. Bhutto's legacy was tarnished by the publication of the *White Papers*. But, the legal procedures proved even more 'effective'. Bhutto and four co-conspirators were convicted of murder by the Lahore High Court on 18 March 1978.[18] After a lengthy appeal before the Supreme Court, the Court eventually upheld the conviction in a 4-3 decision on 6 February 1979[19] and Bhutto was sentenced to death. He was hanged on 4 April 1979 in the Rawalpindi Central jail.

Chief Executive Musharraf faced a similar dilemma to that of Zia. Nawaz Sharif was a popular and elected leader. He could not be allowed to remain a viable politician. Fortunately for Musharraf, Nawaz Sharif had paradoxically provided a vehicle for his own undoing, his controversial anti-terrorism laws.[20] On 2 December 1999, Musharraf introduced two amendments to the Anti-Terrorism Ordinance. The first extended the schedule of offences cognizable by the Anti-Terrorism courts to include several other provisions of Pakistan's criminal code. The courts' expanded jurisdiction would now include:

1) Section 109—abetment of offence;
2) Section 120—concealing a design to commit an offence;
3) Section 120B—criminal conspiracy to commit a crime punishable by death or with imprisonment greater than two years;

4) Section 121—waging or attempting to wage war against Pakistan;

5) Section 121A—conspiracy to commit certain offences against the state;

6) Section 122—collecting arms with the intent to wage war;

7) Section 123—concealment with intent to facilitate waging of war;

8) Section 365—kidnapping;

9) Section 402—being one of five or more persons assembled for the purposes of committing dacoity; and

10) Section 402B—conspiracy to commit hijacking.[21]

The second 2 December amendment established two new special courts, one to be located at the Lahore High Court, the other at the Karachi High Court. Each of these new courts would be headed by a High Court judge and each would have the power to 'transfer, claim, or re-admit any case within that province'. These courts would also serve as Appellate Tribunals for the Anti-Terrorism courts.[22]

With these two amendments in place, the government turned its attention to the disposal of the case brought against Nawaz Sharif and his co-conspirators. The government's case against the former Prime Minister was designed to bring both criminal charges against Nawaz Sharif, which if successful would effectively end his political career, and to absolve Chief Executive Musharraf from any liability associated with staging the military coup of 12 October. The actual charges brought by the government, seem on their face, to have been problematic at best. Essentially the facts presented were that Prime Minister Sharif had made the decision to remove General Musharraf from his position as Chief of Army Staff; but delayed the execution of that decision until Musharraf was out of Pakistan. Therefore, when Musharraf went to Sri Lanka in order to attend a conference, Nawaz Sharif struck. Allegedly, Sharif was hopeful that by the time Musharraf had returned the unpleasantness associated with the dismissal of the COAS would have subsided. However, Nawaz Sharif's plans were foiled when key personnel within the military remained loyal to Musharraf, and refused to accept the orders of the Prime Minister. When Nawaz learned that his orders were not being followed, and in light of Musharraf's imminent return to Karachi (the latter had boarded a commercial PIA flight destined for Karachi), Sharif struck. He ordered that the flight not be allowed to land in Pakistan. Various officials of PIA and the airport authority cooperated with the Prime Minister's directive, while others refused, but in any case, the airplane, carrying not only General Musharraf, but also more than one hundred other passengers was diverted from its original flight path. The diversion, in turn, 'threatened the lives' of the passengers as the aircraft was running low on fuel and as a result could not comply with the directive to land outside Pakistan. Eventually, the relevant airport authorities relented, perhaps owing to the involvement of military personnel who had in the meantime occupied Karachi Airport. The plane landed, its passengers, inconvenienced, but safe. No one was hurt, let alone killed, owing to the events.

Therefore, given the charges outlined above to be brought against the ex-Prime Minister, the 2 December amendments to the Anti-Terrorism Ordinance were crucial to the government's case. The crimes for which Nawaz Sharif would be charged (Sections 109, 120B, 121A, 122, 123, 365, and 402B) were not cognizable before Anti-Terrorism courts prior to the amendments. Ostensibly, then, without the amendments such charges would have had to be filed with the regular courts. Moreover, the ostensible venue of such a prospective trial would have been Lahore *not* Karachi—Lahore is Nawaz Sharif's hometown. That is, the aforementioned amendments were designed to increase the probability of the timely conviction of Nawaz Sharif. Accordingly, one of the main defence strategies of Nawaz Sharif's attorneys was to challenge the standing of the Karachi Anti-Terrorism court, to which his case was assigned. This petition was rejected on 12 January 2000, and the trial was held. On 6 April, the Karachi Anti-Terrorism court announced its verdict—Nawaz Sharif was convicted of conspiracy to hijack the PIA flight and was sentenced to life imprisonment. Charges against his seven co-defendants were dropped.[23]

One could speculate that if this case had been brought before the regular court system the outcome may have been different. The thread of evidence linking Nawaz Sharif to the 'hijacking' was weak, at best. Certainly, a trial conducted through the regular courts would have taken far longer to complete. In any event, Nawaz Sharif appealed the decision to the Appellate Tribunal of the Sindh High Court. But, the appeal was never heard for while it was pending, the government struck a deal with Nawaz Sharif and his family. In December 2000, the Sharif family were allowed to leave the country for Saudi Arabia. It was reported that the Sharif family was fined more than Rs 20 million ($400,000) and agreed to the forfeiture of property worth in excess of Rs 500 million ($10 million) as part of the deal.[24] This conviction and exile has likely ended Nawaz Sharif's political career. Indeed, neither he nor any of his family members were allowed to contest seats in the October 2002 general elections.

It is also important to note that the other main political threat to Musharraf—Benazir Bhutto—has been largely neutralized owing to the earlier actions of the Nawaz Sharif government. Following the latter's landslide victory in the 1997 elections, numerous indictments were issued against both Benazir Bhutto and her husband Asif Ali Zardari, charging them with, *inter alia*, corruption and financial impropriety. Zardari was also indicted for complicity in the 1996 murder of Murtaza Bhutto (Benazir's brother).[25] After having been convicted *in absentia* in 1998 and facing a five-year jail sentence, Benazir lives in self-imposed exile, dividing her time between Europe and the Gulf.[26]

Step Five: Arrange to Become President

Each of Pakistan's coup makers faced a similar dilemma: how to transform and legitimize their unelected status as a CMLA or a Chief Executive into an elected President. Their respective remedies have been eerily similar. Each has decided to hold a referendum.[27]

On 14 February 1960, the CMLA Field Marshal Ayub Khan presented the approximately 80,000 Basic Democrats with the choice: 'Have you confidence in President Field Marshal Mohammad Ayub Khan?' If he was 'elected' (if a majority said 'yes') he would then be empowered to make a constitution; and to hold office for the first term under the constitution so drafted. Basic Democrats at 75, 283, representing 95.6 per cent of those voting, voted 'yes'.[28] *Voila!* Pakistan had a President!

On 20 December 1984, Ziaul Haq followed suit, although his referendum question was a bit more complex and convoluted. Pakistani voters were asked, in keeping with Zia's then much-publicized Islamic agenda, the following question: 'Whether the people of Pakistan endorse the process initiated by General Muhammad Ziaul Haq, the President of Pakistan, for bringing the laws of Pakistan in conformity with the Injunctions of Islam as laid down in the Holy Quran and *sunnah* of the Holy Prophet (PBUH) and for the preservation of the ideology of Pakistan, for the continuation and consolidation of that process, and for the smooth and orderly transfer of power to the elected representatives of the people'.[29] When the votes were tallied the Chief Election Commissioner announced that 62 per cent of the electorate had cast their ballots and 97.7 per cent of those had voted 'yes'.[30] Pakistan had another President!

On 1 May 2002, Musharraf, not to be outdone, held a third referendum.[31] This time the Chief Executive asked the voters to elect Musharraf for a five-year term to enable him to consolidate his 'reforms and the reconstruction of institutions of state for the establishment of genuine and sustainable democracy, including the entrenchment of the local government systems, to ensure continued good governance for the welfare of the people, and to combat extremism and sectarianism'.[32] Musharraf won handily, though he fell slightly short of the 'margin of victory' of Zia, *only* 97.5 per cent voted 'yes'. However, it was reported by the Chief Election Commissioner, former Chief Justice Irshad Hasan Khan (who wrote the lead decision in the *Zafar Ali Shah* case), that 71 per cent of the electorate exercised their right of franchise by participating in the exercise.[33]

Of course, few, if any, have been fooled by the practice of staging presidential referendums—however, they have served their purpose. As if by magic, Field Marshals, Generals, and Chief Executives have been transformed into Presidents with none of the fuss of untidy electoral competition and the unpleasantness associated with opposition candidates.

Step 6: Re-invent Local Government

Pakistan's system of local government has never been particularly robust. The British were far more concerned with governing its colony from the top-down rather than developing grassroots democracy. Since independence successive decision-makers have typically spent a good deal of time and political capital on constructing local governmental institutions, but their efforts have been reversed by successor regimes, who have typically seen merit in scrapping the structures of their predecessors and starting over again. There is a compelling rationale for this process. Namely, Pakistani decision-makers have seen the construction of local governmental institutions as a mechanism to enhance their respective regime's political authority and legitimacy. The main goal is not to develop representative or democratic institutions, nor to effectively govern, nor to deliver services more efficiently at the local level. Rather the main goal of deconstruction and reconstruction of local government is linked to regime survival. To Pakistan's military leaders the construction of local governmental institutions serves three functions: (1) to provide a source of patronage; (2) to open up an avenue for demonstrating the process of 'democratization' and/or for holding 'elections'; and (3) to serve as a mechanism to develop new and loyal political leaders who will challenge, if not replace, the existing political leadership. The task is to create friends and displace enemies.

Ayub Khan's scheme of Basic Democracies, introduced in 1959, is a case in point.[34] Ayub did not believe that Pakistan was ready for democracy. Therefore, the Basic Democracies programme was designed to 'teach democracy' from the grassroots. Under the BD programme, local councils were constituted at the union, *tehsil* (district), and *thana* (sub-district) levels. Such councils were partially constituted by direct election, but above the union level a majority of each council's membership was appointed. The Basic Democrats also served as an electoral college for members of the provincial and national assemblies and the president. Ayub's government also introduced land reforms touted to reduce the power of landlords. The reforms placed ceilings on the individual holdings of agricultural land, but most analysts agree[35] that the reforms were ineffective and were developed in part to target political opponents. Basic Democracies was disestablished during the successor regime of Yahya Khan.

Ziaul Haq re-introduced Local Government by promulgating four provincial ordinances in 1979.[36] Like Basic Democracies, Zia established three tiers of local government in rural areas: (1) union councils—consisting of village(s); (2) *tehsil* committees; and (3) *zila* (district) councils. In urban areas 'town committees' were established for small towns; 'municipal committees' for bigger towns; and 'municipal corporations' for major cities. Elections based on universal adult suffrage were instituted to select Muslim members of the union councils (80 per cent of total); while the remaining 20 per cent were reserved for peasants (5 per cent), workers (5 per cent), tenants (5 per cent), and women (5 percent). The chairman and vice-chairmen were selected by the members of the respective union councils to serve as members of the *zila* (chairmen) and *tehsil* (vice-chairman) councils. All elections were conducted on a political party-less basis. The duties of the councils were extensive but their funding base was limited with the bulk of their funds to be derived from federal and to a lesser extent provincial 'awards'. Also, similar to BD, Zia's 'Local Bodies' system maintained overall control of the elected councils through relevant civil bureaucrats (federal and provincial) who served in various capacities within the councils. Unlike BD, Zia's system did not utilize the Local Bodies officials as an electoral college rather elections were based on universal adult suffrage. Elections to union councils/town committees were held in 1979, 1983, and 1987.

Zia's Local Bodies system well-served the three functions listed above—they created a vast source of patronage; provided ample scope for the staging of elections, albeit non-partisan; and most importantly served to nurture new political elites. Indeed, a majority of the Majlis-i-Shura appointed by Zia in 1985 had prior experience serving in Local Bodies. Also, the basis of the *Islami Jamhoori Ittehad*

(IJI-Islamic Democratic Alliance), the political party that became associated with Zia and Nawaz Sharif, drew most of its membership from those who had served in Local Bodies. Unfortunately, as is the tradition, however, Zia's creation was allowed to die, a victim of malign neglect, during Benazir Bhutto's first term as prime minister.

Like his predecessors, General Musharraf saw merit in reviving a system of local government. But, his intentions, at least originally, were far more ambitious. As early as 17 October 1999, Musharraf announced that one of his regime's top priorities was the 'devolution of power to local government', and on 16 November he charged the high-powered National Reconstruction Bureau (NRB) with the task of developing an appropriate plan. The NRB took its mission quite seriously releasing a draft proposal in May 2000.[37] The draft proposal was a remarkable document. Like Zia's LB and Ayub's BD, it called for the reestablishment of a three-tiered system of elected councils established at the union, *tehsil*, and *zila* levels. But, unlike the earlier programs it suggested that such councils be given extensive authority, and comparable budgetary resources to address such additional responsibilities. Even more revolutionary the plan called for the directly elected district '*nazims*' (mayors; chairs of *zila* councils) to be accorded authority to transfer or dismiss deputy commissioners (top civil bureaucrat in the district). It also called for the abandonment of the division-level of the administrative system. Therefore, the Local Government Plan envisaged the reversal of the relationship between civil bureaucrats and elected politicians, a relationship that has been a dominant feature of local government in South Asia since the mid-Nineteenth Century. The LGP also called for a wholesale revision of the local governmental departments—creating new department and eliminating or merging others. It also proposed significant revisions in legal administration of the districts and sub-districts. It also called for the reservation of one-half of all seats in the union councils for women. Nonetheless, it mandated that elections to the councils be held on a non-party basis.

During the next several months some of the more radical features of the original LGP were worn away: (1) *nazims* were stripped of their prospective power to unilaterally transfer or dismiss recalcitrant DCs; (2) the election of *nazims* and *naib-nazims* (vice-mayors) was made indirect (such officials were to be elected by the members of the union councils); and (3) the reservation of posts for women in the union councils was reduced from 50 to 30 per cent.[38] But the thrust of the reform remained intact. *Nazims* still maintained formal authority over civilian bureaucrats; district councils were provided additional funds to enable them to meet, at least partially their expanded functions; district-level departments were significantly restructured; the division-level of administration was abandoned; and women were elected, albeit indirectly, in unprecedented numbers to the union, *tehsil* and *zila* councils. And, the NRB has promised additional policies which will lead to further devolution in the future.[39] The first elections to union councils were held on 31 December 2000; two subsequent phases of elections were completed by May 2001. Elections for *nazims* and *naib-nazims* were completed in July 2001.[40]

The fate of the LGP and the more recently proposed 'Devolution Plan' is uncertain. The implementation of the latter directly challenges the vested interests of members of Pakistan's provincial and national assemblies; and the LGP is deeply resented by Pakistan's senior bureaucracy (particularly by members of the All-Pakistan Unified Grades). Nevertheless, the NRB won a significant battle when the Seventeenth Amendment was passed by the National Assembly on 31 December 2003. The latter amendment validated actions taken by Musharraf's government including the LGP and the LFP.

Step 7: Intimidate the Civil Bureaucracy and the Superior Judiciary

With politicians effectively weakened by the actions of the coup makers: leaders exiled or worse; political parties banned; assemblies dissolved; etc, the only remaining challenge to the authority of the military dictators was the civilian bureaucracy and the courts. But unlike the services of politicians which can be dispensed with, military governments need the services of bureaucrats and judges. The task therefore, was more subtle—to intimidate *not* eliminate.

Ayub worked very closely with the civil bureaucracy continuing a tradition that pre-dated independence. Most favoured and important were the members of the Civil Service of Pakistan (CSP), the premier cadre of the bureaucracy. Officers of the CSP came to dominate virtually all aspects of Pakistan's government during Ayub's tenure. Indeed CSP officers constituted the overwhelming majority of Ayub's political and administrative advisors. Accordingly, attempts to reform the bureaucracy, most notably the Pay and Services Commission chaired by Justice A.R. Cornelius (1959–62)[41] were successfully thwarted by the machinations of the CSP. For instance, the 'Cornelius Report' was kept confidential and not released (and then it was classified) in 1969. During the course of the Disturbances in 1968–9, which led to the departure of Ayub, the Pakistani bureaucracy and particularly its elite cadres were targeted as corrupt and responsible for the breakdown of civil order. After Yayha Khan displaced Ayub in 1969, one of his first acts was to dismiss ('purge') Pakistan's bureaucracy of 303 Class I officers— thirty-eight were members of the CSP and a total of seventy-eight members of the Central Superior Services. Such a widespread purge was unprecedented and violated the well-established principle of the insulation of the bureaucracy from political control.[42]

Ayub was also favourably disposed to the judiciary. Ayub's constitutional re-engineering was never seriously challenged by the courts. And, the 1962 constitution largely a product of former Chief Justice Muhammad Shahabuddin, provided for a powerful and independent judiciary.[43]

Like Ayub, Zia did not target the civil bureaucracy directly—as had his predecessors Yahya Khan and ZA Bhutto.[44] But, Zia extended and institutionalized the practice of military recruitment to the civil bureaucracy. In 1980 he established a 10 per cent reservation of posts for retired or released military personnel in entry-level (BPS grades 17 and 18) officer level ranks of the bureaucracy. Such military recruits became regular members of the bureaucracy. Similarly he introduced a reservation of 10 per cent for military lateral recruitment to senior bureaucratic ranks (BPS grades 19 and above) on a three-five year contractual basis.[45] The effects of such institutionalized military recruitment have been profound. Since Zia's initiative retired or released military officers have become a regular *part* of the civilian bureaucracy; thereby directly challenging the autonomy and the career prospects of its officers. Members of the civil bureaucracy have greatly resented this intrusion into their domain.

Ziaul Haq's policies of intimidation were even more extensive and creative with respect to the judiciary. Zia deftly abrogated the Fifth and Sixth amendments of the 1973 constitution, reversing the unpopular policies of ZA Bhutto, and allowing Anwar-ul-Haq to become Chief Justice. Zia was rewarded with a favourable decision in the *Nusrat Bhutto* case. Zia stayed formally aloof from the Bhutto trial, but the opportunity presented to the judiciary—to stand in judgment over a prime minister who had done all in his power to weaken the judiciary—apparently proved too difficult for the superior judiciary to resist. The bizarre conviction and execution of Bhutto did incalculable damage to Pakistan's superior judiciary and made them subsequently an easy target for Zia. Following ZA Bhutto's trial, Zia's government went out of its way to harass and humiliate the judiciary. In 1979 Zia established military courts, which were placed beyond the jurisdiction of the regular courts. Subsequent Martial Law Orders prohibited the Supreme Court from entertaining appeals against the decisions of such courts. Also in 1979, the establishment of the Federal Shariat Court, served to reduce the jurisdiction of the High Courts. In 1980 Zia started the practice of 'punishment promotions'. The Federal Shariat Court, hierarchically situated above the High Courts, became a dumping ground for High Court judges who ran afoul of Zia.[46] Zia also introduced the practice of the rapid transfer of judges from posting to posting—the latter made particularly threatening when Zia established 'permanent benches' of the High Courts in inconvenient locations.[47] In effect, judges were placed under the chronic threat of being transferred from Lahore or Karachi to remote locations like Dera Ismail Khan or Sukkur. Finally after introducing the Provisional Constitution Order in 1981, Zia forced superior court judges to take a fresh oath of office under the terms of the PCO, occasioning the early retirement of several judges.[48]

Zia's policies worked. The superior judiciary did not pose a significant deterrent to Zia's bold constitutional changes. He was able to wholly change Pakistan's constitutional structure as we will see with hardly a cautionary whimper from the superior judiciary.

One of Musharraf's first acts after assuming office was to assign standing military officers to 'shadow' the activities of civilian bureaucrats. Musharraf's actions were justified as part of this accountability process—designed to reduce corruption. But, their immediate effect was to demonstrate who was boss; to intimidate the officers of the civil bureaucracy. Far more significant than this to civil bureaucratic—military relations has been the Local Government Plan. The LGP gives the elected district *nazims*, effective authority over district commissioners. The LGP also dissolved the administrative tier of the division. Both actions directly challenged the domain of Pakistan's federal bureaucracy; and particularly of the District Management Group, the lineal descendent of the CSP. Also, Musharraf significantly increased the number of former military officers recruited to the civilian bureaucracy, filling the military recruitment quotas which had been established by Zia, but which had remained unfilled during the civilian interregnum.[49]

Also quite early on, Musharraf showed the judiciary who was in charge by forcing superior court judges to take a fresh oath of office under the PCO. In this he was most likely inspired by Zia's 1981 oath taking exercise. Musharraf's actions served to factionalize the courts, and considerably weakened their prospective opposition to Musharraf's constitutional engineering. The *Zafar Ali Shah* case was decided by a court which consisted of judges who had taken the PCO oath. On 1 January 2003, Musharraf provided further ground for discord within the superior courts by implementing a heretofore unimplemented amendment to the Legal Framework Order (LFO),[50] to raise the retirement age of superior court judges from 65 to 68 years of age. The immediate effects of such changes extended the terms of all fourteen members of the Supreme Court including the term of the current Chief Justice, Sheikh Riaz Ahmad, who had been due to retire in March 2003; the enforcement of the provision also extended the terms of the standing judges of the four high courts and the FSC. Musharraf's actions could be interpreted as a transparent attempt to influence the outcome of the cases pending against the constitutionality of the LFO. Put most simply, if the Supreme Court ruled that the LFO is unconstitutional, many standing judges of the superior judiciary, including the then Chief Justice of the Supreme Court, Sheikh Riaz Ahmed, would stand retired and all superior court judges would lose three years of their prospective tenure.[51] Further it could be argued that similar considerations may have played a role in the Supreme Court's (Shariat Appellate Bench) ruling in the *United Bank Ltd.* (2002) case remanding the issue of prohibition of *riba* back to the Federal Shariat Court.[52] Significantly the latter case has effectively derailed the government's obligation to implement interest-free banking in the state.

Paradoxically however, one of the provisions of the LFO abandoned by the Musharraf/Jamali government (ostensibly as part of the 'deal' with opposition to gain passage of the Seventeenth Amendment) was to effectively 'rescind' the 'revision' of Article 179 which had raised the retirement age of superior court judges by three years.[53] Consequently, three judges of the Supreme Court (Chief Justice Sheikh Riaz Ahmed, Justice Munir A. Sheikh, and Justice Qazi Muhammad Farooq) stood retired. Obviously, this process has served to both humiliate and discredit Pakistan's superior judiciary.

Step Eight: Re-write the Constitution

If one has successfully accomplished the foregoing steps, it is time to address the actual purpose of the elaborate exercise—to construct a new constitutional system. All three of our coup makers gave birth to a new system.

Ayub Khan went about the process of constitution-making deliberately and systematically. His task was simpler than that which faced his successors in that he had abrogated the 1956 constitution, and he could start over again with impunity.

Accordingly in February 1960, he appointed a Constitution Commission chaired by former Chief Justice Muhammad Shahauddin. The Commission deliberated until April 1961 submitting their report to President Ayub.[54] Subsequently, Ayub appointed a drafting committee headed by Manzoor Qadir to put together the actual draft of the constitution, which was finally approved on 1 March 1962.

It is important to note that Ayub Khan had the ultimate authority to accept or reject the terms of the constitution throughout. Indeed, the most significant change which Ayub made to the Constitution Commission's recommendations was with respect to the method of elections. The Constitution Commission had called for the direct election of the president and National Assembly through restricted adult franchise. The 1962 constitution replaced direct elections with an electoral college consisting of the Basic Democrats.

Zia's re-writing of Pakistan's constitution was far more complex and confused. This was partially owing to the fact that Zia, unlike Ayub, could not abrogate the constitution and start from scratch. Therefore, he re-wrote the constitution in bits and pieces. New Islamic provisions which brought about *inter alia* the creation of the Federal Shariat Court and the Shariat Appellate Bench of the Supreme Court were introduced by series of Presidential Ordinances promulgated between 1979 and 1984.[55] On 12 August 1983, Zia made his constitutional plans known in an address before the Majlis-i-Shura. His plans called for the 'restoration' of the 1973 constitution but such a restoration would introduce a presidential-dominant form of government in which the president would be empowered to appoint the prime minister, the chiefs of the armed services, the chief election commissioner, and the provincial governors. The president would also be empowered to dissolve the National Assembly. Zia also imagined the creation of a National Security Council.[56] These ideas were later incorporated into the Revival of Constitution Order (RCO) in 1985.[57]

Musharraf has drawn inspiration from both Ayub and Zia in his process of constitutional re-engineering. Like Zia, Musharraf has been confined within the parameters of maintaining the 1973 constitution; like Ayub Musharraf has undertaken his self-assigned task of constitutional revision systematically. Musharraf has relied on his curious creation, the National Reconstruction Bureau (NRB) throughout to formulate constitutional change. The NRB, as we have seen, also formulated the Local Government Plan, and the Devolution Plans. It also produced the two-part 'Conceptual Framework of Proposals of the Government of Pakistan on the Establishment of Sustainable Federal Democracy'[58] in June-July 2002, which formed the basis of the Legal Framework Order, 2002. The LFO suggested the following changes:[59]

1) Establishes Musharraf as president for five years;
2) Increases the number of seats in the national and provincial assemblies;
3) Increases the number of seats reserved for women and minorities in the national and provincial assemblies;
4) Places additional restrictions which could serve to disqualify would-be candidates to the national and provincial assemblies;
5) Establishes a National Security Council;
6) Re-establishes the power of the president to dissolve the National Assembly; and of the governors to dissolve the provincial assemblies;
7) Validates all laws and actions taken by the government under Chief Executive Musharraf. This would include the Local Government Ordinances, the Accountability Ordinance, and the Political Parties Act.

Most of these provisions were incorporated into the Seventeenth Amendment.

Step Nine: Orchestrate Elections

With plans for constitutional reform formulated, the next step is to validate these plans—to have them endorsed officially by a competent authority. But, given the fact that the relevant competent authority (the National Assembly) has been dissolved, it is imperative to create competent authorities, to hold elections.

As we have seen, Ayub owing to his abrogation of the 1956 constitution and the 1960 referendum, was *the* competent authority to accept the 1960 constitution. There was no necessity to hold elections.

Zia, however, needed to stage elections. The Majlis-i-Shura, Zia's creation, had been appointed by Zia in late 1982, but it had no real legislative function and no political legitimacy. Accordingly, following the 1984 referendum which had 'elected' Zia President, Zia announced that elections would be held for the national and provincial assemblies in February 1985. The elections were to be held on a non-partisan (party-less) basis. Candidates with partisan affiliations were prohibited from contesting. The PPP and other political parties boycotted the elections. Nevertheless, the turnout was relatively high. Those elected to the 1985 National Assembly by the very nature of their candidacy were deemed to be generally supportive of Zia's regime—by definition they did not belong to any political party, they did not constitute an opposition.

With a friendly National Assembly in place, Zia placed the Restored Constitution Order (RCO), 1985 before them for incorporation into the constitution. The National Assembly complied with the passage of the Eighth Amendment. Virtually the entire text of the RCO was incorporated into the constitution accordingly. However, two important departures from the RCO, perhaps a result of compromise were embedded in the Eighth Amendment: (1) The president's power to dissolve the National Assembly was made conditional. Before the president could dissolve the National Assembly, he was obliged to be convinced that the government could not carry out actions in accordance with the constitution; and that following dissolution he would be obliged to hold fresh elections within ninety days. (2) The provision of the creation of the National Security Council was dropped.

Musharraf's position was even more problematic than Zia's. The *Zafar Ali Shah* case had validated the 1999 PCO but it had conditioned its acceptance upon the understanding that Musharraf would hold elections within three years of the coup (12 October 2002). Also, Musharraf for reasons yet partly unclear announced as early as August 2001[60] that prospective elections to the national and provincial assemblies would be held on a partisan basis. Therefore, unlike his predecessors, the outcome of the prospective election was not a foregone conclusion.

Of course, Musharraf and his ever-creative NRB were not without resources. The former on the advice of the latter introduced the Political Parties Ordinance, 2002[61] which re-defined the electoral rules of the game to favour an appropriate outcome. First, it extended the scope of provisions that disqualified those who were under investigation or who had been implicated by the National Accountability Bureau.[62] Second, it required political parties to develop a party manifesto (a time consuming and divisive exercise) before being deemed eligible to contest the election. But, more creatively the NRB suggested the establishment of educational requirements for those seeking political office. Would-be candidates for the national or provincial assemblies would now have to possess a Bachelor's degree or its equivalent.[63] Ostensibly, the target of the latter was the numerous standing politicians, particularly from the PML-N who did not possess the requisite qualifications. It is also important to note that the issuance of the Political Parties Ordinance in late June 2002 and the requirement to hold elections by 12 October placed a severe time constraint on political parties to comply with regulations in order to contest elections. Musharraf's government also successfully resisted the return of the Bhuttos and the Sharifs to Pakistan's political scene.

Musharraf's goal throughout was to ensure an outcome in which no one party would dominate and in which political parties that supported Musharraf would be able to form the government. The results of the election challenged Musharraf's goals, but the outcomes seem to have ultimately served his policy interests. Most surprising was the unexpected success of the MMA (*Muttahida Majlis-i-Amal*—a six party alliance of religious parties), which secured the third largest batch of seats in the National Assembly; and which was able to gain a plurality in the NWFP and later to form a government in that province. Also surprising was the strong showing of the PPP, despite the absence of Benazir Bhutto. Shortly after the election, but before the National Assembly was convened,

Musharraf took an oath of office as President under the terms of the LFO.

Finally, on 21 November 2002 a government was formed by Mir Zafarullah Khan Jamali, Pakistan's first Baloch prime minister. Jamali is a member of the Pakistan Muslim League (Quaid-i-Azam)—a party deemed loyal to Musharraf. His coalition consists of the PML(Q), numerous small parties, and defectors from the PPP, the so-called 'Forward Bloc'.

The reconstituted Parliament, however, found itself deeply divided over the appropriate approach to take regarding the validity of Musharraf's system and the constitutionality of the LFO. Indeed for thirteen months (November 2002-January 2004) the activities of the National Assembly and Senate were beset by chronic and frequent protests, walkouts, planned disturbances, and other unpleasantness occasioned by the opposition's demands that the LFO had no constitutional standing until and if, the Parliament passed relevant legislation. However, the government's 'hole card' was that the general election of 2002 had been conducted under the terms of various provisions of the LFO. Therefore, MPs were ultimately caught in the web of a carefully crafted Catch-22—if the parliamentarians decided that the LFO was unconstitutional then the election which had brought them to power would as a consequence be null and void. Some compromise was inevitable in such a situation, although the 'negotiations' with the opposition proved far more difficult for Musharraf and Jamali to accomplish than had Zia's and Junejo's experience with introducing the Eighth Amendment. But, when the dust finally settled, Musharraf and Jamali had convinced the MMA to 'support' (in reality to abstain from countering) a creative package solution of constitutional revisions which among other things kept the Jamali government in power and avoided a constitutional meltdown. The main features of the compromise were that: (1) Musharraf would be obliged to relinquish his position as Chief of Army Staff (COAS) by the end of 2004; (2) plans for the creation of a National Security Council would be scrapped; and (3) the extension of the tenure of superior court judges (see above) would be abandoned. In exchange for these 'concessions' by the government the MMA would begrudgingly

endorse (abstain from opposing) the provisions of the LFO
including:

- The re-introduction of the power of the President and
  governors to respectively dismiss respectively the National
  Assembly and provincial assemblies (Articles 58(2)(b) and
  119(2)(b)
- The confirmation of Musharraf's election as President for five
  years
- The confirmation of the general election of 2002 and the
  creation of the Jamali government

The crowning achievement of the 'deal' was the blanket
endorsement of Musharraf's actions since assuming power in
October 1999. The revised Article 270AA of the revised constitution
reads:

> '(2) All orders made, proceedings taken, appointments made,
> including secondments and deputations, and acts done by any
> authority, or by any person, which were made, taken or done,
> or purported to have been made, taken or done, between the
> twelfth day of October 1999, and the date on which this
> Article comes into force (both days inclusive), in the exercise
> of the powers derived from any Proclamation, President's
> Orders, Ordinances, Chief Executive's Orders, enactments,
> including amendments in the Constitution, notifications,
> rules, orders, by-laws or in execution of or in compliance with
> any orders made or sentences passed by any authority in the
> exercise or purported exercise of powers as aforesaid, shall
> notwithstanding any judgment of any court, be deemed to be
> and always to have been validly made, taken or done and shall
> not be called in question in any court or forum on any ground
> whatsoever'.[64]

Step 10: Implement the System

However effective Pakistan's coup makers have been at seizing
power, subverting respective constitutions, and establishing new
constitutional structures, they have been signal failures at

institutionalizing the systems they have introduced with such effort and cost.

Ayub's attempts at institutionalization of his constitutional system were particularly awkward. The 1962 constitution mandated that national and provincial assemblies be elected indirectly by the basic democrats. Accordingly, such institutions were established in June 1962, formally terminating martial law. Ayub's intent was not to significantly transfer power or authority to the newly-constituted legislature bur rather to maintain control through his well-developed system of civil-military authoritarianism. But, Ayub's plans were foiled by the interests of politicians, even if selected indirectly, serving in the assemblies.

Accordingly, Ayub was forced to reluctantly accept the legalization of political parties, banned since the 1958 coup, through the passage of the Political Parties Act, 1962 in July. With the lid lifted on political party activity, political parties were reconvened, and Ayub was 'forced' to become involved and later to become president of his own political party—the 'Conventionist' Muslim League. Despite such developments, however, political activity within Pakistan remained highly controlled, the press muzzled, and political opposition subject to significant restrictions. But, Ayub's carefully crafted authoritarian system would eventually unravel.

Under the terms of Ayub's constitution, presidential elections were mandated to be held within five years of the incumbent's assumption of office. Therefore, Ayub, who had been elected president in 1960 was required to seek re-election in 1965. The 80,000 Basic Democrats would serve as an electoral college for the selection of the president. Ayub's political opponents decided to join forces to contest the election forming an umbrella group, the Combined Opposition Party (COP). The COP nominated Fatima Jinnah, Mohammad Ali Jinnah's sister, to head their party and to contest the election. The ultimate outcome of the election was a foregone conclusion—Ayub could not lose given the nature of the indirect electoral process, the nature and self-interests of the Basic Democrats, and Ayub's profound 'incumbent advantages'. But, Fatima Jinnah and the COP did extraordinarily well. Ayub prevailed, receiving 49, 951 votes to Jinnah's 28, 691.[65] More important than this electoral outcome, however, were the long-term consequences for the Ayubian system. The COP claimed that the election had been rigged both structurally, owing to the nature of the indirect electoral process, and physically by vote buying and tampering. The public largely accepted the COP's verdict; Ayub had no defence against such charges. Although Ayub had won the election, the legitimacy of his system had been significantly undermined.

Subsequent to this election until Ayub's resignation from office on 25 March 1969, Ayub's regime came under increasing pressure both international and domestic. The misadventure of the Pakistan Army's 'Operation Gibraltar', the resultant disaster of the 1965 war with India, and the humiliating Tashkent Agreement did irreparable harm to Ayub's stature as a statesman, and emboldened domestic opposition. The growing secessionist sentiment within East Pakistan as evidenced by Sheikh Mujib's Six Points, and Ayub's ill-conceived ruse of introducing the Agartala Conspiracy case, further weakened the government. But, the disturbances of 1968–9, proved to be the final straw that broke the government's back.

For our purposes what is important to note is that after Ayub resigned his carefully crafted system was easily and perhaps carelessly abandoned by his military successor. General Yahya Khan, the Chief of Army Staff who assumed power following Ayub's resignation, promulgated his own Legal Framework Order on 28 March 1970, which savaged the Ayubian system. (1) It disestablished the Basic Democrats. (2) It replaced One Unit in West Pakistan by establishing four provinces. (3) It mandated direct popular elections under universal adult suffrage for the national and provincial elections.[66] In retrospect Yahya's actions were perhaps the most ill-considered of all of Pakistan's LFOs: direct elections to the National Assembly were a certain recipe for the horrors of the civil war and the eventual dismemberment of the state.

Zia's constitutional system proved even more short-lived. To Zia his selection of Muhammad Khan Junejo as prime minister in 1985, to preside over the National Assembly, did not signal a transfer of power from the military to a civilian government. The RCO had 'restored' the constitution but it left Zia, as president, in charge (see above). But, as was the case with Ayub's indirectly elected National Assembly, the best-laid plans of Pakistan's coup makers can come unglued.

In short, Prime Minister Junejo took his role seriously and his growing independence from presidential (read military) dominance spelled his downfall. The example of Junejo's 'negotiation' with Zia which resulted in the revision of the RCO (the Eighth Amendment) curtailing the establishment of the National Security Council has already been cited. More importantly, Junejo encouraged the emergence of parliamentary groupings reflecting different political affiliations in open defiance of Zia's ban on political parties. Also, Junejo proved none too eager to advance Zia's Islamic agenda, nor to press for the passage of a Shariah bill in the National Assembly.[67] But the immediate cause of Zia's decision to invoke Article 58(2)(b) and to dissolve the National Assembly seems to have been provided by Junejo's unwillingness to halt the National Assembly's investigation into the Ojheri army munitions depot explosions. Such investigations would prove embarrassing to the military. In any case, on 29 May 1988, Zia issued an order dissolving the National Assembly and called upon the four respective provincial governors to follow suit in the provinces.

Zia did not fear that his order would be challenged. The framers of the 1985 RCO had consciously and thoroughly introduced a text that established a presidential-dominant system. Zia had been elected as president of that system before the RCO was formulated. Clearly, Zia's 1988 dissolution order was made by a chief executive confident of his powers, firm in his belief that his office and person were unassailable. One can speculate as to what Zia's next act would have been. He was contemplating adopting another set of constitutional reforms which if implemented, would have significantly altered Pakistan's federal structure,[68] if this had transpired it would have likely required new elections and a new electoral system. But fate proved unkind. On 17 August Zia was assassinated. His death precipitated a constitutional crisis of epic proportions. Pakistan was left without a president, prime minister, National Assembly, chief ministers, and provincial assemblies. The

Chairman of the Senate (the Senate was not subject to dissolution by the President), Ghulam Ishaq Khan, was mandated by the constitution to assume the post of president. His first official act was to schedule elections for the national and provincial assemblies.

The death of Zia effectively ended his constitutional system. Political parties were allowed to openly contest the ensuing general elections; Prime Ministers gained increasing authority; the military returned to the barracks.

Musharraf's current efforts can be viewed as an attempt to restore a version of Zia's constitutional system. But, Musharraf's intentions have proven hard to realize. As chronicled above the passage of Musharraf's Seventeenth Amendment proved far more difficult than the passage of Zia's Eighth Amendment. Unlike Zia, Musharraf faced an active partisan opposition which insisted on concessions from the government as a *quid pro quo* for support of the Amendment. The thirteen month standoff between the National Assembly and Musharraf following the election of the National Assembly was finally broken when the MMA accepted the face-saving compromise with the government which resulted in the three 'concessions' (see above). It has proven easy for Musharraf's government to meet the conditions of two of the concessions regarding judges' tenure and the disestablishment of the National Security Council but Musharraf intends to renege on his prospective promise to resign his position as COAS by 31 December 2004 (see chapter one in this volume).

One victim of the tussle between the National Assembly and Musharraf has been the government of Prime Minister Jamali. The latter was asked to resign by Musharraf on 26 June, and he was replaced by the self-styled 'interim Prime Minister' Chaudhry Shujaat Hussain until the heir-apparent, then Finance Minister Shaukat Aziz, could win a seat in a by-election and consequently be eligible to become Prime Minister. This complicated plan actually worked and on 18 August Shaukat Aziz became Prime Minister.

The deft, albeit complicated, replacement of Jamali with Shaukat Aziz demonstrates among other things that Musharraf has been able to successfully maintain his power—he is clearly calling the shots. That is, the President successively dismissed two standing Prime Ministers (Jamali and Chaudhry Shujaat Hussain) and replaced them with his hand-picked successor, Shaukat Aziz. Musharraf's actions went beyond the system imagined by the Seventeenth Amendment in that Musharraf had no need to invoke Article 58(2)(b) in order to change the government. Unlike presidential dismissals during the civilian interregnum (Ishaq Khan; Farooq Leghari) which required the involvement of the superior judiciary and ultimately fresh general elections—Musharraf was able to orchestrate the change the change of government autonomously with no need for such procedures.

Caveats and a Reluctant Conclusion

Before offering a conclusion, I have three caveats with the foregoing analysis. First, is the obvious omission of foreign policy from considerations of the military governance paradigm. Pakistan's military leaders have been more enthusiastically wedded to seeking the support of the international community (read US) than their civilian counterparts. This is an important, perhaps crucial, policy consideration of Pakistan's coup makers. I have ignored it here, as I deemed it beyond the scope of this exercise. Second, by focusing on the ten steps of the Pakistan *military* governance paradigm I did not mean to imply that Pakistan's civilian leaders had not engaged in similar strategies of regime survival. Perhaps this exercise should/could be revised to include the Bhuttos and Sharifs? Finally, I want to disabuse the reader of the notion that the actions of Pakistan's three military leaders have been solely motivated by cynical considerations of regime survival. Each of the three martial law regimes—Ayub, Zia, and Musharraf—have significantly and sincerely engaged in the attempt to address issues of 'governance' of the state. One can certainly have differences with the nature of their visions—but it is hard to find fault with the depth of their efforts. For instance, as Braibanti so meticulously demonstrated, Ayub empowered thirty-four separate commissions of inquiry between 1958 and 1964; each produced at least one report; some of the reports still stand as definitive on their respective topic.[69]

Similarly, Zia's attempts to bring Pakistan's laws into conformance with the Injunctions of Islam, produced an extraordinary scholarship, centred on the decisions of the superior judiciary. Finally, one has to be an admirer of the National Reconstruction Bureau. Its voluminous writings, represent a very significant and serious attempt to come to grips with Pakistan's seemingly insoluble problems of governance. No comparable attempts at addressing Pakistan's political dilemmas have been undertaken by any of Pakistan's civilian regimes.

Reluctantly, I offer the following conclusion. Pakistan's failure to develop a stable constitutional system is the fault of both Pakistan's military and civilian leadership. There is plenty of blame to go around. Clearly, constitutional stability can only be achieved if there is an accommodation between the interests of the two sets of actors. Neither the corporate interests of the military nor the ideological interests and representational proclivities of political parties can be ignored in such an accommodation—neither side can be allowed to win. Given this, tidy and well-defined constitutional systems that provide no constitutional role for the military (such as Nawaz Sharif's post-Thirteenth amendment system); or no scope for political party activity (such as Zia's RCO) can hope to provide long-lasting solutions to Pakistan's constitutional dilemma. Rather what is needed are untidy constitutional accommodations; accommodations in which neither the military nor the political parties 'wins' or 'loses', but one in which the interests of both are partially accommodated.

Pakistan stumbled upon, perhaps invented, such a system during the civilian interregnum of 1988–1997—a system, that can best be typified as the '58(2)(b) system'. The system was based upon the 1973 constitution as modified by the RCO and the Eighth amendment. In this system the civilian President (Ghulam Ishaq Khan; Farooq Leghari) was empowered, as had been the late Ziaul Haq, to dissolve the National Assembly under Article 58(2)(b). But, unlike Zia's system which envisaged untrammelled authority for the president, the 58(2)(b) system, as it developed, placed the burden of proof for the dismissal of a government on the shoulders of a civilian president. Such civilian presidents typically had the backing of the military but such presidents had to show clear and convincing evidence of why they had to take the extreme action of dismissing an elected government. The referee between the President and the Prime Minister was the Supreme Court. Four dismissals of the National Assembly and their respective prime ministers occurred during this period—Zia of Junejo, G.I. Khan of Benazir Bhutto, G.I. Khan of Nawaz Sharif; and Farooq Leghari of Benazir Bhutto. The Supreme Court upheld the two dismissals of Benazir Bhutto; took issue with Zia's dismissal of Junejo but let it stand for want of a political remedy; and overturned G.I. Khan's dismissal of Nawaz Sharif.[70] Coupled with the attendant and numerous dismissals of provincial assemblies, the system was anything but tidy. *But*, the constitutional system had the merit of keeping the military in the barracks *and* provided some degree of accountability to civilian governments. The system was dealt a fatal blow when Nawaz Sharif's PML was able to win a two-thirds majority in the 1997 election, and was consequently able to amend the constitution by passing the Thirteenth amendment. Following the passage of the Thirteenth amendment the only recourse for the military, if its corporate interests were violated, was a military coup—hence the unfortunate events of October 1999.

Perhaps the re-introduction of an idealized version of 58(2)(b) is a viable alternative to Pakistan's tortured constitutional history. Ideally, in such a system the President would be a duly-elected civilian; the superior courts would be free from political interference in undertaking their responsibility as referees of the process; and the President would be loathe to exercise his authority except in extreme cases. However flawed such a system may be it seems preferable to the continuance of Pakistan's military governance paradigm. It is for this reason that it is crucial, in this author's opinion, for Musharraf to fulfil his promise and to resign his position as COAS—the alternative would be the indefinite continuation of military governance.

Notes

1. This is a revised version of Charles H. Kennedy, 'Constitutional and Political Change in Pakistan: The Military Governance Paradigm', in Rafiq Dossani, ed., *Prospects for Peace in South Asia* (Stanford: Stanford University Press, 2005).
2. See Ayesha Jalal, *The State of Martial Rule* (New York: Cambridge University Press, 1990), pp. 273-6.
3. His official explanations for his assumption of office were expressed in his speech of 17 October 1999 the text of which is found in *Dawn* Internet edition (18 October 1999).
4. *Zafar Ali Shah v. Parvez Musharraf, Chief Executive of Pakistan* PLD 2000 SC 869. Especially see Articles 223, 228, and 232-236, pp. 1129, 1140, and 1145-7.
5. Hamid Khan, *Constitutional and Political History of Pakistan* (Karachi: Oxford University Press, 2001), p. 212.
6. Laws (Continuance in Force) Order, 1977 PLD 1977 Central Statutes 325.
7. Provisional Constitution Order, 1999 PLD 1999 Central Statutes 446.
8. *Federation of Pakistan vs. Moulvi Tamizuddin Khan* PLD 1955 Federal Court 240; *Reference by HE the Governor-General* PLD 1955 Federal Court 435. See discussion in Paula Newberg, *Judging the State* (Cambridge: Cambridge University Press, 1995), pp. 42-68 and Hamid Khan, pp. 136-54.
9. *State vs. Dosso* PLD 1958 SC 533. See discussion in Newberg, pp. 73-78.
10. The Sixth Amendment had permitted sitting Chief Justices of the Supreme Court and the High Courts to serve beyond their normal age of retirement—65 year and 62 years respectively. The Fifth Amendment among other things had set the term limits for the Chief Justice of the Supreme Court at five years and that of Chief Justices of High Courts at four years. Hamid Khan, pp. 530-5; 538.
11. Justice Yakub Khan, a Bhutto appointee, had reached the age of retirement but had not completed his five-year term as Chief Justice of the Supreme Court. [See note supra] The suspension of the Sixth Amendment forced him to retire and allowed the appointment of Justice Anwar-ul-Haq to the post of Chief Justice. The latter justice was to prove to be very sympathetic to Zia-ul-Haq's assumption of power and to his subsequent regime.
12. *Begum Nusrat Bhutto vs. Chief of Army Staff* PLD 1977 SC 657. Also see Newberg, pp. 167-70.
13. Oath of Office (Judges Order), 1999 PLD 2000 Central Statutes 38. Musharraf seems to have borrowed the idea of forcing the superior judiciary to take a fresh oath of office from the ever-resourceful Ziaul Haq. In 1981, after Zia promulgated his own Provisional Constitution Order, he required the superior judiciary to take a fresh oath. Four Supreme Court justices (Chief Justice Anwar-ul-Haq, Maulvi Mushtaq, Dorab Patel, and Fakhruddin Ibrahim) did not take the oath and stood retired. See Hamid Khan, pp. 649-51.

14. Those refusing to take the oath in Supreme Court were: Chief Justice Saeeduzzaman Siddiqui, and Justices Mamoon Kazi, Khalilur Rehman Khan, Nasir Aslam Zahid, Wajihuddin Ahmad, and Kamal Mansur Alam. Justice Irshad Hasan Khan, who took the new oath, became the new Chief Justice.

15. *Zafar Ali Shah vs. Pervez Musharraf,* Chief Executive of Pakistan PLD 2000 SC 869.

16. *Wasim Sajjad v. Federation of Pakistan* PLD 2001 SC 233.

17. Article 6 of the constitution reads: '(1) Any person who abrogates or attempts or conspires to abrogate, subverts or attempts to subvert the Constitution by use of force or show of force or by other unconstitutional means shall be guilty of high treason. (2) Any person aiding or abetting the acts mentioned in clause (1) shall likewise be guilty of high treason'.

18. Three 'White Papers' were issued in six volumes each published by the Government of Pakistan. *White Paper on the Performance of the Bhutto Regime* (3 volumes)—Vol I 'Mr. ZA Bhutto, Family and Associates' (January 1979), Vol II 'Treatment of Fundamental State Institutions' (January 1979), and Vol III 'Misuse of the Instruments of State Power' (January 1979); *White Paper on the Misuse of the Media* (August 1978) and *White Paper on the Conduct of the General Elections in March 1977* (July 1978). The latter volume was 1449 pages. A 118 page *Summary of White Paper on the Conduct of the General Elections, March 1977* was also published.

19. *State vs. Zulfiqar Ali Bhutto* PLD 1978 Lah 523.

20. *ZA Bhutto vs. State* PLD 1979 SC 53.

21. For details see Charles H. Kennedy, 'The Creation and Development of Pakistan's Anti-Terrorism Regime, 1997-2004' (unpublished manuscript, March 2004).

22. Anti-Terrorism (Second Amendment) Ordinance, 1999 PLD 2000 Central Statutes 8.

23. Anti-Terrorism (Third Amendment) Ordinance, 1999 PLD 2000 Central Statutes 78.

24. The trial was covered extensively by the major Pakistani dailies. See internet editions of *Dawn* and *The News*.

25. *Dawn* (internet edition) (10 December 2000).

26. Murtaza Bhutto, politically estranged from his sister, had formed a rival faction of the PPP—the PPP (Shaheed Bhutto), in alliance with their mother, Nusrat Bhutto. The PPP (SB) fielded candidates in the 1997 election.

27. The 1998 conviction of Asif Zardari and Benazir Bhutto for involvement in kickback payments involving the Swiss company SGS Industries was overturned in 2001, and was remanded to the Lahore High Court for a fresh hearing. *Asif Ali Zardari v. State* PLD SC 568.

28. It is instructive to note that civilian leaders have also attempted to utilize the vehicle of the referendum as a device to legitimize their authority. Following the 1977 general election, the Pakistan National Alliance (opposition to ZA Bhutto) alleged widespread rigging of the results. In the midst of

disturbances which followed Prime Minister Bhutto promulgated the Seventh Amendment to the constitution which established provisions for a referendum to be held which would ask the voters to voice confidence in his government. The Seventh Amendment proved short-lived, however, as Zia's military coup took place before the National Assembly could ratify the amendment. See discussion in *Qazi Hussain Ahmed v. Pervez Musharraf* PLD 2002 SC 853, pp. 876-7. Also see Hamid Khan, p. 566.

29.	Hamid Khan, p. 221.

30.	Hamid Khan, p. 660.

31.	Ibid. Of course, the reported turnout was inflated. The author visited three polling stations near my residence in Islamabad on election day in 1984. At mid-afternoon, the time of my visit to the respective stations, a total of only six people had cast their ballot. At one polling station no one had cast their ballot.

32.	On 20 June 2001 Musharraf had dismissed President Rafiq Tarar through the vehicle of the Proclamation of Emergency (Amendment) Order, 2001 PLD 2001 Central Statutes, 391; and had assumed the duties of the Office himself through President's Succession Order, 2001 PLD 2001 Central Statutes, 392.

33.	Referendum Order, 2002 PLD 2002 Central Statutes 218, quoted p. 220. The dismissal of Rafiq Tarar; the assumption of the Office of the President by Musharraf; and the referendum that led to the election of Musharraf for a five-year term were validated by the Supreme Court in *Qazi Muhammad Hussain v. Pervez Musharraf* PLD 2002 SC 853.

34.	International Crisis Group, 'Pakistan: Transition to Democracy?' ICG Asia Report # 40 (Islamabad/Brussels, 3 October 2002), p. 20.

35.	Basic Democracies Order, 1959 PLD 1959 Central Statutes 364.

36.	See for example Ronald Herring, *Land to the Tiller: The Political Economy of Land Reforms in South Asia* (New Haven: Yale University Press, 1983).

37.	Punjab Local Government Ordinance, 1979 PLD 1979 Punjab Statutes 101; Balochistan Local Government Ordinance, 1979 PLD 1980 Balochistan Statutes 26; Sindh Local Government Ordinance, 1979 PLD 1980 Sindh Statutes 1; and NWFP Local Government Ordinance, 1979 PLD 1980 NWFP Statutes 1.

38.	Government of Pakistan, Chief Executive Secretariat, National Reconstruction Bureau. *Local Government (Proposed Plan): Devolution of Power and Responsibility Establishing the Foundations for Genuine Democracy* (Islamabad: May 2000).

39.	Government of Pakistan, The *Local Government Ordinance 2001—Promulgated by Provinces (13 August 2001)* <NRB website>. For a discussion of the process see Charles H. Kennedy, 'Analysis of Pakistan's Devolution Plan'. Paper prepared for Department for International Development (UK) (September 2001). The original provincial ordinances each of which has been subject to numerous amendments subsequently are in found in PLD as under: Balochistan— Balochistan Local Government Elections Ordinance, 2000 PLD 2001 Balochistan Statutes, 4; NWFP—NWFP Local Government Elections Ordinance, 2000 PLD 2001 NWFP Statutes, 20; Punjab—Punjab Local

Government Elections Ordinance, 2000 PLD 2001 Punjab Statutes, 1; and Sindh—Sindh Local Government Elections Ordinance, 2000 PLD 2001 Sindh Statutes, 38.

40. Government of Pakistan, Chief Executive Secretariat, National Reconstruction Bureau. *Devolution: Local Government and Citizen Empowerment (14 August 2001)* <NRB website>.

41. For an analysis of the first phase of elections see Farzana Bari, '*Local Government Elections December 2000 (Phase One)* (Islamabad: Pattan Development Corporation, 2001).

42. Government of Pakistan, Cabinet Secretariat, *Report of the Pay and Services Commission, 1959-1962* (Karachi: MPCPP, 1969).

43. Charles H. Kennedy, *Bureaucracy in Pakistan* (Karachi: Oxford University Press, 1986), pp. 75-8.

44. Hamid Khan, pp. 274-6; 245-7.

45. In 1972, Bhutto purged 1828 officers of the bureaucracy and later introduced significant administrative reforms which targeted the bureaucratic elite. See Kennedy, *Bureaucracy*, esp. p. 80.

46. Ibid., pp. 122-25.

47. During the author's affiliation with the Federal Shariat Court (1984-1986) none of the FSC regular judges (non-*ulema* judges) had sought appointment to the Court.

48. The Lahore High Court had benches established in Bahawalpur, Multan, and Rawalpindi; the Sindh High Court in Sukkur; the Peshawar High Court in Abbottabad and Dera Ismail Khan; and the High Court of Balochistan in Sibi. Hamid Khan, p. 643.

49. See note 12.

50. This is becoming an increasingly contentious issue subsequent to the election of a civilian regime in late 2002. Prime Minister Jamali does not have the same scope for the provision of political patronage as did his predecessor civilian regimes. See for instance, Ansar Abbasi, 'Performance of 600 Khakis being reviewed', *The News* internet edition (18 January 2003) and Irfan Husain [Mazdak], 'Jobs for Boys', *Dawn* internet edition (5 October 2002).

51. The Legal Framework Order, 2002 was introduced on 21 August 2002, PLD 2002 Supplement Central Statutes, 1604. It was amended to include the provision for the extension of terms for the superior judiciary on 10 October 2002 as Legal Framework (Amendment) Order, 2002 PLD 2002 Central Statutes, 1698. The constitutionality of the LFO was challenged in *Watan Party v. Chief Executive of Pakistan* PLD 2003 SC 74. Chief Justice Sheikh Riaz Ahmed writing for the Court rejected the plaint on the grounds that the Watan Party had no legal standing to bring the suit.

52. See Zeeshan Siddique, 'Judges Get Extension', *Dawn* internet edition (5 January 2003).

53. *United Bank Ltd. v. Farooq Brothers* PLD 2002 SC 800. For a full discussion see Charles H. Kennedy, 'Pakistan's Superior Courts and the Prohibition of *Riba*' paper presented to Woodrow Wilson International Center (27 January 2004).

54. The Seventeenth Amendment purportedly amended Article 179 (the terms of superior court judges). However, since this provision of the LFO was not validated, the Article was technically never actually revised.

55. Government of Pakistan. *Report of the Constitution Commission, 1961* (Karachi: MPCPP, 1961).

56. Between 1980 and 1985 provisions relating to the operation of the Federal Shariat Court were modified twenty-eight times, through the mechanism of twelve separate presidential ordinances and were incorporated into the constitution in fourteen subsections. For details of Zia's Islamization policies see Charles H. Kennedy, *Islamization of Laws and Economy: Case Studies on Pakistan* (Islamabad: Institute of Policy Studies, 1996).

57. *Dawn* 13 August 1983. Also, see Hamid Khan, pp 656-7.

58. Revival of Constitution of 1973 Order, 1985 PLD 1985 Central Statutes 456.

59. Government of Pakistan, Chief Executive Secretariat, National Reconstruction Bureau, *Conceptual Framework of Proposals of the Government of Pakistan on the Establishment of Sustainable Democracy Package I (26 June 2002); Package II (14 July 2002)* <NRB website>.

60. Legal Framework Order, 2002 PLD 2002 Supplement Central Statutes, 1604.

61. The promise was made in the August 14 address to the nation. Most likely Musharraf felt that this announcement would demonstrate his sincerity to democratize the political process to domestic and international critics.

62. Political Parties Order, 2002 PLD 2002 Central Statutes, 250.

63. For a detailed discussion of National Accountability Bureau see *Khan Asfandyar Wali v. Federation of Pakistan* PLD 2001 SC 607.

64. This was made law through the promulgation of the Conduct of General Elections (Second Amendment) Order, 2002 on 25 June 2002. PLD 2002 Central Statutes, 249. The relevant section reads: 'a person shall not be qualified to be elected or chosen as a member of the Majlis-i-Shura or a provincial assembly unless he [sic] is at least a graduate possessing a bachelor degree in any discipline or a degree recognized as equivalent by the University Grants Commission'. Quoted on p. 250. The Supreme Court rejected a constitutional challenge to this clause in *Pakistan Muslim League (Q) v. Chief Executive of Islamic Republic of Pakistan* PLD 2002 SC 994.

65. 'Text of the 17th Amendment Bill' in *Dawn* (internet edition—30 December 2003). Also see the useful analysis of the 17th Amendment I.A. Rehman, 'Grand Deal 2003' in *Dawn* (internet edition—5 January 2004). The text of Article 270AA closely follows Zia's Article 270A introduced in 1977.

66. Hamid Khan, p. 312. Hamid Khan's discussion of the 1965 election is particularly useful, pp. 301-19.

67. Ibid., pp. 377-8.

68. See Charles H. Kennedy, 'Repugnancy to Islam—Who Decides? Islam and Legal Reform in Pakistan' *International and Comparative Law Quarterly* Vol. 41, no. 4 (October 1992), pp. 769-787.

69. His plan derived from the Ansari Commission Report would have replaced Pakistan's four provinces with its 20-odd divisions. See Government of Pakistan, Cabinet Division, *Ansari Commission's Report on Form of Government 24th Shawal 1403* (Islamabad: MPCPP, 1984).

70. Respectively (Benazir Bhutto dismissals): *Abdul Tariq Rahim vs. Federation of Pakistan* PLD 1992 SC 646, *Benazir Bhutto vs. Farooq Ahmed Leghari* PLD 1998 SC 388; (Junejo dismissal): *Federation of Pakistan vs. Muhammad Saifullah Khan* PLD 1989 SC 166; (Nawaz Sharif dismissal): *Mian Nawaz Sharif vs. President of Pakistan* PLD 1993 SC 473.

7

Validating Educational Qualifications as a Prerequisite to Hold Elective Office: The Supreme Court and the Pakistan Muslim League (Q) Decision

Cynthia A. Botteron

The Holy Prophet (PBUH) always selected educated
and learned men for important assignments,
therefore, learning and knowledge are the basic requirements.
The value of knowledge and education cannot be undermined.[1]
– Maqbool Ellahi Malik, Advocate-General, Punjab

Introduction

In 2001 President Pervez Musharraf, staying true to his commitment to devolve power to local government, adopted the Local Government Ordinance 2001. In this package of sweeping reforms he introduced the criterion whereby individuals seeking to contest elections for a position in local government were to have completed their certificate of Matriculation, the equivalent of a high school diploma. There were few voices of protest. However, when President Musharraf raised the bar on qualifications for those seeking to contest election to the Majlis-e-Shura (Parliament) and Provincial Assemblies to a bachelor's degree from an accredited university through the Conduct of General Elections Order (2002), the protest was vociferous. As expected, the Chief Executive's Order was brought before the Supreme Court in June 2002. After three days of hearings, the Supreme Court dismissed the petitions in July of 2002, concluding that the requirement for educational qualifications did not violate the principles of Pakistan's Constitution or democracy.

This chapter undertakes several tasks. The first is to place, briefly, into historical context the decision undertaken by Musharraf. The second will be to present and summarize the case for and against the alteration to Pakistan's constitution. Lastly, the chapter concludes with a discussion about the practical implications of the change and prospects for the future of democracy in Pakistan.

Whose History?

How history comes to judge regimes that take power through extra-constitutional means is not of immediate concern here. What is of concern is how present power-holders perceive the affair. Needless to say, a history of the events leading up to an extra-constitutional play for power will likely always remain contested. It is not the aim of this chapter to provide or derive the definitive story of General Musharraf's rise to power. For the purposes here, only a bare bones history of the ascension of Musharraf from General to President is needed. However, recognizing the possibility that readers may misinterpret any rendition of Musharraf's extra-constitutional move as either sympathetic or hostile to the regime, the decision was taken to draw heavily upon the very detailed history of regime change provided in the Supreme Court case against Musharraf.

Over its history, Pakistan's Supreme Court has overseen and ruled on extraordinary cases; the determination of whether to sanction the extra-constitutional moves of the military are among the most important such nation-shaping issues undertaken by the court. A tradition of the court, when ruling on these difficult cases, is to provide a detailed history that elucidates trends leading to whatever inescapable conclusion the court believes it needs to make. I do not claim that the historical reconstruction of Pakistan's failed democracy provided by the Justices is 'objective' or that it does not serve a very real political purpose, because clearly it is not and it does. The only claim made here is that the history provided in the

Supreme Court's ruling is critical to highlight because it is the foundation on which the Supreme Court of Pakistan rested its case.

The Failure of Electoral Politics: The Story that Continues to Conclude with Military Rule

Placed before the Supreme Court, was the request to consider whether President Musharraf's Conduct of General Elections Order 2002 violated both the spirit of Pakistan's constitution and the heart of Pakistan's democracy. The Justices, in their comments, went so far as to say that their decision on this issue 'would go a long way to carve out the path on which the politics of Pakistan is to run'.[2]

The Justices began their rendition of the failure of Pakistan's electoral politics from the beginning. They selected the very beginning because Pakistan struggled with how to conceive of its statehood right from the start. The first Constituent Assembly was dissolved in 1954 because it failed to give the new nation a Constitution. The 1956 Constitution was abrogated by General Muhammad Ayub Khan who dissolved the National and Provincial Assemblies upon the declaration of Martial law, ostensibly due to the lack of law and order in the nation. Under the 1962 Constitution, marshaled in under Ayub Khan, elections were held but in place of political parties were the Basic Democrats, individuals appointed by Khan to serve as electoral representatives for their districts. The job of the Basic Democrat was to cast votes for the leadership that had selected them. Needless to say, 'the general feeling of the public was that they had nothing to do with the same (elected bodies) and neither were they allowed to participate in the affairs of the government nor their problems had been solved'.[3]

After the elections, Ayub Khan, in violation of his own Constitution, asked General Yahya Khan to assume power rather than appoint the Speaker of the National Assembly. Yahya Khan then dissolved the government, imposed Martial law, and promulgated the Legal Framework Order, 1970 (1970 LFO), which served to legitimize his rule. Under the 1970 LFO, elections were held. However, intractable conflicts between West and East Pakistan soured the newly elected Assemblies. As might be expected, the Awami party that led in the elections and the citizens of East Pakistan were furious after the decision was taken to postpone calling the Assembly to order. The rancour between the two wings of Pakistan signalled the beginning of the end, the finale being the permanent secession of East Pakistan and the emergence of Bangladesh.

Zulfikar Ali Bhutto, who led the Pakistan People's Party (PPP), held the majority in the provinces of the Punjab and Sindh. He assumed the presidency of Pakistan in 1972. The 1973 Constitution was framed and came into force on 14 August 1973. However, the problems of the country continued to defy government efforts and the 1977 elections were charged with fraud on a broad scale. This led to such agitation against the PPP that the army was forced to intervene, imposing Martial law. The Constitution was put in abeyance and the government dissolved.

It was not until 1985 that another general election was held. General Ziaul Haq, who had steered Pakistan from 1977 to 1985, nominated Muhammad Khan Junejo as the Prime Minister. However, between 1985 and 1988:

> the law and order in the country (had) broken down to an alarming extent resulting in tragic loss of innumerable valuable lives as well as loss of property; And whereas the life, property, honour and security of the citizens of Pakistan (had) been render(ed) totally unsafe and the integrity and ideology of Pakistan (had) been seriously endangered.[4]

General Ziaul Haq dissolved government again, calling for a new round of elections. However, he died in an airplane crash before the elections could be called.

In November 1988, elections were called by Ghulam Ishaq Khan, Chairman of the Senate who had assumed the Presidency after Zia's death. These elections were held on a party basis. Benazir Bhutto headed the PPP victory, forming a government at the centre and in the provinces of Sindh and the NWFP. The rival party, the Muslim League, formed the government in the Punjab.

It is at this point in the history of Pakistan's failed electoral process that the Supreme Court Justices appear to focus their greatest attention:

> ...an unfortunate period of confrontation between the two rival parties and their leaders started. The two leaders were at daggers drawn with each other. Hardly any tolerance was shown and instead of solving the problems of the country and the people, they were trying to malign and humiliate each other.... The stories of corruption, maladministration, nepotism, favouritism, etc. were rampant.[5]

In 1990, Ghulam Ishaq Khan dissolved the National and Provincial Assemblies. The grounds on which Mr Khan dismissed the government take up two full single-spaced pages in the Court document. To summarize the Court's discussion of the most notable misdeeds of the Bhutto government: internal dissension, corruption, and 'scandalous horse-trading for political gain', corruption to such a degree that the utility of the National Assembly was undermined. Additionally, because of the widespread corruption and nepotism in the Federal Government, credibility was lost. The superior judiciary had been publicly ridiculed and its integrity attacked. Finally, mentioned again by the Justices, the authority, resources, and agencies of government were used for political ends and personal gain.[6]

Elections were held, again, and the Pakistan Muslim League, headed by Mian Muhammad Nawaz Sharif formed the government while the PPP sat in opposition. 'There was utter personal hostility between the leaders of the two factions, which escalated the confrontation'.[7] On account of this acute confrontation, according to the court, the leadership failed to arrive at a consensus or to improve 'the lot of the man on the street' or the deteriorating economy. Because of these general failures, Ghulam Ishaq Kahn was led to dissolve government, yet again, in 1993.[8]

The dissolution order reproduced in this court document took up two-plus single-spaced pages. Among the notable grievances listed were: in the 17 April 1993 speech, the Prime Minister diverted citizen attention away from the numerous problems faced by the nation to focus on demeaning the President of Pakistan, the Prime Minister's speech being 'tantamount to a call for agitation... and conduct amount(ing) to subversion of the Constitution'.[9] Further, maladministration, corruption and nepotism had reach such proportions it was determined that the oaths taken by Public representatives, the Prime Minister and Ministers of State had been fundamentally violated. The Prime Minister had 'unleashed a reign of terror against the opponents of the Government'.[10] And again, the resources of government were used for political ends and personal gain, accompanied by the massive waste of public funds.

The Supreme Court at the time restored the Assembly rather than holding another election, but new elections were called for when it appeared the Assembly would not 'work'. Elections were held in 1993 and Benazir Bhutto, leading the PPP, once again formed the government. However, in 1996 President Farooq Ahmed Khan Leghari was led to the decision that the Bhutto government had to be dismissed.

This dissolution order was three pages long, chronicling primarily the failure of government to rein in the police, who had killed thousands either during street protests or while in custody. The Bhutto government was warned by the President that the extra-judicial killing must stop and those in the police force who were guilty had to be brought up on charges. However, 'The killings continued unabated. ...Instead of ensuring proper investigation... the Government has taken pride that, in this manner, the law and order situation ha(d) been controlled'.[11]

The Bhutto government, according to present-day Supreme Court justices, continued their campaign of malfeasance by accusing the brother-in-law of Nawaz Sharif of killing Benazir's brother as part of a conspiracy that reached all the way to the Presidency. The Mir Murtaza Bhutto murder became more scandalous when his widow and friends accused Benazir's husband Asif Ali Zardari, the Chief Minister of Sindh, the Director of the Intelligence Bureau and other highly placed individuals of his murder:

A situation has thus arisen in which justice, which is a fundamental requirement of our Islamic Society, cannot be ensured because powerful members of the Federal and Provincial Government who are themselves accused of the crime, influence and control the law-enforcing agencies.[12]

Other violations necessitating dissolution were: Benazir ridiculing the Supreme Court's decision on the 'Appointment of Judges' case in a speech before the National Assembly, violating Article 14 of the Constitution guaranteeing the right of privacy by phone-tapping and eavesdropping on Supreme Court Justices, leaders of political parties, and high ranking military and civil officers.[13]

And whereas corruption, nepotism and violation of rules in the administration of the affairs of the Government... has become so extensive and widespread that the orderly functioning of Government ... has become impossible and in some cases, national security has been endangered. Public faith in the integrity and honesty of the Government has disappeared.[14]

Elections were held again in 1997 and the Pakistan Muslim League won by a strong majority. Soon after assuming power, Nawaz Sharif undertook several critical Constitution reform measures. First, he introduced and the National Assembly passed the 13th Amendment whereby Article 58(2)(b) was dropped from the Constitution. Article 58(2)(b) gave the President the power to dissolve the National Assembly while empowering the Prime Minister to appoint Services' Chiefs. Also, Nawaz Sharif introduced the 14th Amendment, which forbade individuals in a party elected to the Assembly from speaking out against the policies of the party. This was challenged as an abridgement of freedom of speech, to which the Supreme Court agreed. The Amendment was later suspended. The Prime Minister, taking cues from Bhutto, ridiculed the Court's decision and instigated a mob attack on the Court forcing the Justices to leave the courtroom. During this same time, Chief of Army Staff General Jehangir Karamat delivered a speech suggesting that a National Security Council ought to be formed for the purpose of advising the Prime Minister in his reform efforts. Apparently, this suggestion was met with intense disfavour and

Jehangir Karamat was forced to resign. Sharif then appointed General Pervez Musharraf to the post of Chief of Army Staff.[15]

Resolving the debate as to what the true source of conflict was between Sharif and Musharraf is not relevant here, but it is clear that their very public dispute over Kargil was the most publicized link in a chain of events directly leading to Sharif's descent and Musharraf's ascension to power.

Initially, it appeared that the rift caused by their conflict over Kargil seemed to have been mended, the Prime Minister going so far as to appoint Musharraf to the Joint Chiefs of Staff Committee. However, only a few days later the Prime Minister issued an order to remove Musharraf from the position of Chief of Army Staff. According to the history rendered in the Supreme Court's judgment,[16] the army took exception to what it saw as an attempt by Sharif to politicize and destabilize the military. The final straw was the order by the Prime Minister to forbid Musharraf's entry back into Pakistan upon his return from a trip to Sri Lanka. The army acted quickly to subvert the orders and removed Sharif from office. General Pervez Musharraf then assumed control of the nation:

> When General Pervez Musharraf took over the reins of power, there was a sigh of relief because the people were fed up with the confrontation and lack of understanding between the two leaders (Benazir Bhutto and Nawaz Sharif) and their followers. The takeover by General Pervez Musharraf was challenged before this court and... was validated on the basis of doctrine of State necessity.[17]

After assuming power, on 17 October 1999, Chief Executive Musharraf announced his seven-point agenda for the nation. It was his chief aim to:
- Rebuild national confidence and morals;
- Strengthen the federation, remove inter-provincial disharmony and restore national cohesion;
- Revive the economy and restore investor confidence;
- Ensure law and order and dispense speedy justice;
- De-politicize State institutions
- Devolve power to the grass roots level; and
- Ensure swift and across the board accountability.[18]

Staying true to his stated objectives, Musharraf began undertaking quite a number of reforms. One might be optimistic about the eventual prospect for a sustainable democracy in Pakistan were it not for the fact that the path taken by Musharraf was a well-trodden one.

Local Government Reform: The First Step in Constitutional Revision

There is a similarity in the steps taken by nearly all Pakistan's military rulers when conducting the essential task of stabilizing and legitimizing their power grab. Many have commented that Pervez Musharraf appeared to be reading the script written by the last General who took power—Zia-ul-Haq.

As a first task, undertaken by all Pakistan's constitutional revisionists, is the knotting together of the primary threads of power, consolidating them under the office of Chief Executive, Prime Minister, or President. Consolidating power under a single office ensures critical veto power at any time.[19] The next move is to create extra-constitutional consultation bodies over which the primary power-holder presides. Then comes the task of adjusting the number of seats and the distribution of power among the national and provincial assemblies. The final task is the reconstruction or re-invention of local government.[20]

Affectionately called the 'Devolution Plan', the Local Government Ordinance is a textbook scheme for divesting authority and responsibility from the centre to the periphery. The Ordinance creates multiple layers of relatively autonomous, though connected, governing councils. The purpose of the scheme, according to the National Reconstruction Bureau (NRB), is: 'To achieve an efficient, transparent and responsive administrative system capable of delivering high quality public services to common people'.[21] Clearly, this is consistent with two of Musharraf's stated objectives: first, to devolve power to the grass roots level; and second, to ensure swift and across the board accountability.[22]

It is under the Local Government Ordinance that Musharraf or one of the NRB planners embedded twenty-one suggested qualifications for individuals seeking public office. These qualifications can only be suggestions because local government has no official standing in the Constitution; therefore, the provinces must adopt their own provisions. At present, the provinces have largely followed the recommendations of the Central Government and the National Reconstruction Bureau (NRB) with few modifications to the original list.

So as not to test the patience of the readers, the twenty-one suggested qualifications have been organized into three basic categories (The full set of qualifications is presented in APPENDIX A). These categories are: Citizen as Office-Seeker, Office Seeker as Upstanding Citizen; and Office Seeker as Appropriately Skilled.

I)   **Citizen as Office-Seeker:** Musharraf followed Ayub Khan's lead by forbidding those seeking local office from running on a party platform. Office seekers had to appeal to voters on the basis of name recognition, promises as to what they would accomplish in office, personal charisma, vision for the future, expertise, or any number of traits not associated with a political party.

II) **Office Seeker as Upstanding Citizen:** Pakistan's Constitution is unique in that there are dozens of qualifications that an individual must meet in order to run for national or provincial office. Many of the qualifications appear to address a desire to minimize government corruption. The qualifications identify such issues as potential political and/or economic conflict of interest, soundness of character and mind, criminality and trustworthiness, knowledge of the Quran and commitment to refrain from violating Islam's most important edicts (See APPENDIX B for the Constitution's Article on Qualifications). Many of the qualifications for running for national office were incorporated into the Local Government scheme (See APPENDIX B for the qualifications required for public office in Pakistan's 1984 Constitution and compare to those for local office in APPENDIX A).

III) Office Seeker as Appropriately Skilled: It is under this category that the educational requirement of Matriculation is introduced. The fact of the matter was that when the NRB began contemplating the actual structure and function of local government, it was brought to their attention that the duties being turned over to local boards were extraordinarily complex ones. The probability that that these tasks would be handed over to individuals who were, as a worst-case scenario, illiterate or, as a best-case scenario, simply lacking the necessary skill sets to govern, was quite high.

The complex tasks of governance, such as budgeting, institution building, management, policy creation, and conflict resolution, were devolved to the local level on the pretence that it would increase service delivery, transparency, and accountability. Not only were the tasks complex, but there was the additional pressure that the job of government had to be done better than it had been done before. And, if allowed to speculate about politics a bit, unskilled elected officials would be no match for a professional and entrenched civil service who would not give up power or resources easily. Musharraf had stated his intention to reform the civil service and this may have been one step in that direction.

It was concluded that a necessary, but not sufficient, condition for effective governance had to be literacy and minimal analytic skills. Rather than administering exams to all hopefuls, the most efficient criterion was thought to be Matriculation.[23] However, literacy and basic analytic skills do not guarantee that one knows how to negotiate the process of policymaking, budgeting, planning, or conflict resolution. In that, the next requirement for holding public office was to attend basic training courses in governance.

In the list of qualifications it is stated that an elected official could 'not fail to attend a training course'.[24] The training program administered by the NRB is not only intensive, but impressive. The book of procedures and rules given to *Nazims* (head of the council) is over 400 pages, that of *Naib Nazims* (deputy or next in line) and Council members is between 300 and 400 pages.[25]

The reason or reasons Musharraf introduced educational qualifications for those seeking election to the National or Provincial Assemblies can only be speculated upon. Perhaps it was because there was no significant protest against the policy at the local level or it might have been that institutional reformers he trusted, supported the move. His decision may have been driven by sheer logic; that is, individuals holding office at the provincial or national level would be faced with issues exponentially more complex, therefore, they should be more educated than those holding office at the local level. Regardless, the educational requirements for holding public office were introduced in the Conduct of General Elections Order, 2002.

Conduct of General Elections Order, 2002

The Conduct of General Elections Order, 2002[26] was the legal forum where the majority of the qualifications for public office reforms were instituted (See **APPENDIX C** for text). At present there have been eight amendments to this Order. In Article 8A the educational requirement is stated:

Educational Qualification for a member of Majlis-e-Shoora (Parliament) and a Provincial Assembly. Notwithstanding anything contained in the Constitution of the Islamic Republic of Pakistan, 1973, the Senate (Election) Act, 1975 (LI of 1975), The Representation of People Act, 1976 (LXXXV of 1976), or any other law for the time being in force, a person shall not be qualified to be elected or chosen as a member of Majlis-e-Shoora (Parliament) or a Provincial Assembly unless he is at least a graduate possessing a bachelor degree in any discipline or any degree recognized as equivalent by the University Grants Commission under the University Grants Commission Act, 1974 (XXIII of 1974)'.[27]

In addition to the qualifications for members of the National Assembly (MNA), out of the 100 allocated seats in the Senate, four from every province are reserved for technocrats and *ulema*. Chief Executive Order No. 21 of 2002 sets out the educational requirements for technocrats:

> A technocrat means a person who is the holder of a degree requiring conclusion of at least 16 years of education, recognized by the University Grants Commission or a recognized statutory body, as well as at least twenty years of experience, including a record of achievement at the national or international level.[28]

This is the sum total of the educational requirement that now graces the Constitution of Pakistan. It is to the court case we now turn.

The Challenge: Constitution Petitions Number 29–33

Under Constitutional Petitions Number 29 through 33, filed by the Pakistan Muslim League (PML-Q), the Awami National Party, Pakistan Awami Party, Jamhoori Watan Party, and Muhammad Ilyas respectively, the Supreme Court of Pakistan was challenged to rule on the constitutionality of Article 8A of the Conduct of General Elections Order, 2002.[29]

Numerous technical challenges were made in this petition that relate to issues such as whether the order violated specific articles of the Constitution, whether it was permissible based on the precedent established in the Syed Zafar Ali Shah case, whether the conditions for declaring state necessity were met, and so forth. Although compelling, the discussion before us will focus on the challenge that this requirement not only violates the intent of Pakistan's Constitution but strikes at the very heart of Pakistan's fragile democracy.

Petitioner's Case:

Syed Hussain Gilliani, who represented the PML-Q, argued that the educational qualification violates the principle of democracy as a 'government of the people, by the people, and for the people'. How, precisely, it violates this principle was not well defined. However, pulling together the disparate threads of his and other petitioner's arguments, the meaning becomes clearer.

One challenge as to the constitutionality and consistency with the principles of democracy was based on the claim that the requirements violated the principle of equal protection under the law. The charge was stated that restricting someone from running for public office hindered their guarantee of equal political rights, thus, violating equal protection. Equal protection was understood to mean that the order made it impossible for individuals to stand for election due to no fault of their own; that is, all citizens were not equally protected due to a factor over which they had no control. What was meant, specifically, by this claim?

Making a comparison to another qualification will help to make this argument more distinct. In articles 62 and 63 of the 1984 Constitution (See **APPENDIX B**), for a person to run for public office they must:

- be of good character and not commonly known as one who violates Islamic injunctions;
- have adequate knowledge of Islamic teachings and practices, and obligatory duties prescribed by Islam as well as abstain from major sins;
- be sagacious, righteous, non-profligate, honest and *ameen*.[30]

The charge is that, unlike the educational qualification, it is wholly within one's power to meet these qualifications. One chooses whether and when to indulge in a major sin or to refrain from that sin, to become profligate or not, to lie or not, to reject the obligatory duties prescribed by Islam or not. Should one make the decision to indulge, the loss of their right to run for public office was a known potential consequence of that decision.

However, the Petitioners argue that the educational qualification is a restriction of a different type. Gilliani charges that the state has failed in its obligation to properly educate its citizens. It has violated its promise to 'promote the educational and economic interests of backward classes or areas, remove illiteracy and provide free and compulsory secondary education... and higher education equally accessible to all on the basis of merit'.[31] To drive home the issue, in Pakistan, barely 2 per cent of the population graduates from University, which means 98 per cent of Pakistan's citizens, are denied the opportunity of running for public office *due to no fault of their own*. Gilliani argues they have been denied their full participatory political rights, their right for equal protection because of a failure of government not a failure of the individual.[32]

Qazi Anwar, representing the Awami National Party, supports Gilliani's argument by bringing forth the situation in the NWFP, FATA and Balochistan. In these areas, there are no degree-granting colleges for women. The educational facilities in the areas of Swat, Dir, Jharkhand, and Chitral are sparse.[33] The upshot is that these citizens are additionally alienated from their full participatory rights because the bar is set too high given the particular institutional constraints of the area. Few are able to meet the requirements; thus, the potential pool of citizens who can run for office is extraordinarily small.

Women are additionally impacted because of the extreme paucity of educational opportunities for them. If one believes in the importance of identity representation, the chances of having women represented by women approaches zero. The conclusion is that if so few have full participatory rights due to no fault of their own, a government 'of the people' is one in name only because the chances are great that the few who are able to participate may not be of the type that citizens would choose if they had a greater pool of candidates available.

The question then arises, would a greater pool of candidates necessarily be a more diverse one? Moreover, if the education qualifications were not enacted, would the pool of candidates be of a type quite different from those who can run under the qualifications? If they are of a different type, would it be a difference that made a difference? In other words, the question to ponder is whether the educational qualification denies elected office to a group of individuals who are uniquely situated in terms of dedication, public spiritedness, wisdom, skill, identity similarity, or insight garnered from shared experience?

I believe this is the question that Gilliani and Aftab Gul, attorneys for Muhammad Ilyas, answer in the affirmative. Their argument against the education requirement is that educated legislators cannot 'represent' an uneducated constituency. Because approximately 65 per cent of Pakistan's citizens are illiterate and 98 per cent have not graduated from university[34], Gilliani argues that the fundamental premise of representative government, that 'qualifications for members of Parliament have to be prescribed with reference to the conditions of the people whom they represent'[35] is violated.

Aftab Gul elaborates further by arguing that democracy means rule by majority, but 'Article 8A takes away the right of the majority to choose their representatives who reflect the aspirations of the people',[36] The article so widens the gap between the elected and electors that '... the spirit of democracy envisaged by the Constitution will be eroded'.[37]

At the foundation of Gul and Gilliani's argument is a philosophical quandary posed by democratic theorists: can one individual truly represent the interests and needs of another? In this context is the issue of identity politics: that is, how can someone who experiences life through one set of circumstances ever truly comprehend the needs, interests, and urgencies of someone who is not from that background? Are these differences in life experiences— gender, class, faith, region, language, race, education—significant enough to demand representation by individuals 'similarly situated'? Gul and Gilliani would have to argue yes, it does have profound policy implications.

Perhaps the importance can be illuminated by the following. For instance, 'Security' to someone coming from a privileged background may bring to mind issues such as: personal property, trust, and sanctuary. Whereas, 'security' to someone not living in a home surrounded by walls and guards, may mean the provision of food, and freedom from injury and illness. Gul and Gilliani's argument is grounded on the belief that a representative from a background very different from their constituency will have a radically different understanding of problems facing those they represent. That is, how can a representative who understands security as having trust in a personal bodyguard legislate for those who see security as primarily self-help and freedom from injury? Their conclusion is inescapable; would not a policymaker have greater insight and serve as a truer representative if their background were similar to those of the community they represented?

It is this difference in perception and experience of the world that makes 'identity' politics such a powerful force in democracy. Incommensurability of understanding leads some scholars to the conclusion that in representative politics, only the poor understand and can represent the poor; only illiterates understand and can represent the illiterate; only women understand and can represent women. Unless one wishes to go the distance with this logic to conclude that only I understand and can represent myself, the challenge for us is to discover which aspects of 'shared background' are relevant so as to increase the chance that critical interests are more accurately understood and pursued in the political process.

Certainly, there is great concern here and democracies have struggled mightily to increase 'identity' representation. The problem, I believe, with Gul and Gilliani is that they fail to provide an explanation as to why education, specifically, is the cause of the great divide. I suspect the reason for this failure is because they conflate the categories of education and class, arguing that Article 8A seeks to 'usher an elitist and oligarchic dispensation; and create political segregation and establish elector apartheid'.[38] It is not entirely clear that in Pakistan, privilege and education go hand in hand. As a matter of debate, it is argued that the wealthy tend not to pursue higher education because they do not need to; with wealth comes privilege, with privilege comes power, and with power comes additional wealth. In addition, the view that 'representation' is improved when electors and elected share 'identity' is still contested by democratic theorists. Several of these issues are picked up by the Respondent, to which we now turn.

The Respondent's Case:

The attorneys representing the Government of Pakistan began their defence by addressing the charge that individuals who could not meet the qualifications were denied their full participatory rights. To recall the Petitioner's case, when an individual is faced with overcoming intractable obstacles in order to run for public office, the promise of democracy as a government of, by, and for the people is violated because 'the people' cannot fully participate.

In the opinion of the court, there is no 'right' for each and every citizen to run for public office. The standing precedent in Pakistan is to view the 'right' to stand for public office as a statutory right; thus, regulated by law, not a fundamental one. In order to build their case on this point, the Petitioner's had relied on previous cases that challenged the government's ability to deny political parties from contesting an election. However, the Supreme Court justices concluded that political parties had not been hindered in this case, and thus, the cases referred to by the Petitioners were not relevant to the question about the standing of individuals.[39]

Further, Article 62 of the Constitution (replicated in APPENDIX B) gives lawmakers the power to change qualifications for those running for office, of which this change is wholly consistent. Therefore, it was not outside of the powers accorded in the constitution.

However, the curiosity of this case is the question of why now. Why is this specific qualification receiving the attention that it is; after all, the list of qualifications is quite extensive and burgeoning with character stipulations that are extremely difficult to verify (For example, adequate knowledge of the Quran, of good character, righteous, and non-profligate). A Bachelor's degree is easy to verify, so why is it more contentious than a qualification that relies on the subjective judgment of one person as to the authenticity and incorruptibility of the moral character of another? Perhaps the reason why no one has challenged these subjective qualifications is that, in all but the worst cases, they are wholly subjective and cannot truly be enforced with any rigour or consistency. The question, then, is why tag on to the Constitution a purely symbolic statute of this type?

As the history of Pakistan amply demonstrates, corruption of the policy process has been a notable problem. Whether the corruption was real or the perception of it manipulated for obvious political purposes, corruption has been a consistent thread running through Pakistan's political discourse; it was the claim of rampant corruption that served several times as justification for the military to step in and save the state. Including character-based qualifications for those running for public office is easily seen as a logical response to this endemic challenge to the state's legitimacy and credibility.

However, this does not get at the heart of the Petitioner's challenge. The most serious claim is that the social and educational conditions in Pakistan make it very difficult for most citizens to qualify; thus, an elitist brand of rule will follow on the heels of this qualification. In other words, the gap between citizen and representative will be so wide as to negate any appearance of a democracy of, by, or for the people.

Justice Makhdoom Ali Khan argues that the Constitution of Pakistan is consistent with other state's constitutions in that there is always a qualitative gap between voters and office holders. For example, the voting age in Pakistan was lowered to 18 years of age, but a Member of Parliament must be at least 25 because, 'a higher level of maturity is required'.[40] The question is whether the gap is truly necessary and whether the type of qualifications that set the office holder apart from the citizen is non-arbitrary; that is, relevant and related to the task and relationship at hand.

Makhdoom Khan and the defence, in general, argue that not only is the difference between the voters and members of the Assembly important, but the type of difference they are seeking to establish through this extraordinary measure is essential for democracy and good governance. Their argument is based on two premises: first, that office holders are faced with an increasingly complex set of tasks that demand critical thinking and an openness to new information. Second, education is a means to reducing corruption because education is one step on a long road to change, and the change sought is one whereby the political culture becomes increasingly intolerant of the types of abuses witnessed in Pakistan's history. Each premise of the argument is discussed below.

When drawing an analogy between the educational requirements and age requirement, Makhdoom Ali Khan pointed out that a 'higher level of maturity' is required from those seeking public office than from those casting a vote because 'the business of the State requires a certain level of competence as is required in other professions'[41] and '... it is high time that the Legislature should have persons who can understand the intricate problems with which the country is faced'.[42]

There is an important issue here. One of the common justifications for representative government is that citizens simply do not have the time, energy, and/or skill/knowledge to conduct the business of the state alongside their other life demands. Representatives are expected to serve as full-time watchers and promoters of their constituency's interests. It is their job to become experts in policy areas and intimately familiar with the nuances and subtleties of legislation. It is not that citizens, with proper time and effort, could not carry out the same mission but given that citizens have other work, they cannot. The expectation that legislators should have superior knowledge skills does not fly in the face of the common understanding about representative democracy. However, the radical and controversial aspect of Pakistan's legislation is whether such 'superior knowledge' can only be defined with regard to the attainment of specific educational degrees.

The court rides a slippery slope when making the case for the educational requirement; they move almost seamlessly from arguing for it because it would raise the level of deliberation and intellectual autonomy of representatives to the argument that it is an effective means of staving off corruption. The Advocate-General of Punjab, Maqbool Ellahi Malik, states, 'Being uneducated the members of the legislative chambers did not assert themselves and easily succumbed to allurements and indulged in floor crossing for reasons altogether ulterior'.[43] Assemblies were dissolved, rather than dissolving government, in four instances because the Assembly was not performing its duty or responsibility.[44] Malik directly attributes failure to lead, deliberate, and perform in the national interest on the lack of education. Other justices do not make the argument that the lack of education is a necessary and sufficient condition for corruption, but it appears that all the justices are willing to accept some correlation:

> No doubt it is the privilege of the public representatives to side with their party in power but it does not absolve them of their responsibility and look at the degree of irresponsibility that the 13th and 14th amendments were bulldozed (sic) and nobody raised his little finger against the proposed legislation.... A constitutional amendment requires sane thinking, deliberation and composition, which were totally absent and none took it seriously.... Of course, it cannot be totally attributed to lack of education but nevertheless it was one of the most important factors owing to which the representatives had allowed themselves to be driven by their leaders.[45]

The history of Pakistan's elected bodies, as constructed by the Supreme Court, highlighted their belief that the will of party leaders had become a proxy for the will of the citizen. Because the will of party leaders demonstrated interest in private rather than public affairs, corruption was rampant. It was so pervasive, the justices argue, that the State itself was threatened by the loss of legitimacy.[46] The manoeuvrings by one administration after another, the performances of party members:

> demonstrated utter disregard for the parliamentary values and (sic) deliberate attempt to injure the soul of democracy. The establishment of a democratic order and the institutions therein requires utmost responsibility on the part of the elected representatives of the people but the record of most of the elected representatives of the four dissolved National and Provincial Assemblies speaks volumes about their psyche, lack of education and sense of responsibility. It also shows that the political field was dominated by a coterie of individuals representing a special class of vested interests, which ensured that if not they, their kith and kin were elected as members of the Assemblies. Regardless of the ideal standards, their main effort was directed to have their hegemony in the political field.[47]
>
> ... it is crystal clear that the political scenario in Pakistan is a sad tale of failures on the part of the public representatives.[48]

The Court does not find fault solely in the character of the elected officials. Rather, it is found in a 'political culture, which leaves much to be desired'.[49] Educational requirements are thought to be only a first step in a very long journey of reform that begins with bringing about a general change in how Pakistan's political system operates.

How political culture is understood by the administration is critical to the argument. The Court, quoting from David Sills' article in the *International Encyclopedia of the Social Sciences*, see political culture as:

> the set of attitudes, beliefs, and sentiments which give order and meaning to a political process and which provide the underlying assumptions and rules that govern behaviour in the political system. It encompasses both the political ideals and the operating norms of a policy. Political culture is thus the manifestation in aggregate form of the psychological and subjective dimensions of politics.[50]

Clearly, the Justices believe that Pakistan's political culture is characterized by narrow-mindedness, a lack of public spiritedness, short-term thinking, and failure to follow constitutional or democratic principles; choosing instead political expediency and a willingness to sacrifice others in pursuit of one's own interests.

> The making of new laws in the light of the changing circumstances and social and political values is an uphill task. In this view of the matter, it is all the more necessary that the public representatives are well versed with the modern trends, changing social order and the events on the international scene. No doubt wisdom is not related with degrees but this is an exception to the rule. Education certainly broadens the visions, adds to knowledge, brings about maturity and enlightenment, promotes tolerance and peaceful coexistence and eliminates parochialism. We are convinced that the educational qualification prescribed for membership of Assemblies will not only raise their level of competence and change the political culture but will also be an incentive to education.[51]

With education, then, comes inter-provincial harmony and national cohesion, depoliticized state institutions, a government not afraid of accounting for its actions; thus, restoration of state legitimacy, national confidence and morale. In other words, the additional qualification is not whimsical, meaningless, nor arbitrary.

On the issue of 'equality before the law', to find in favour of the Order the Justices must conclude that the principle of equality before the law has not been violated. Article 25 of Pakistan's Constitution enshrines the 'equality before the law' clause, much like the 'equal protection under the law' clause found in the US Constitution. The challenge is to find that citizens who do not have a bachelor's degree are being unfairly classified by the state in such a manner that their full participation rights are being violated.

The justices find that all citizens are equal before the law and are entitled to equal protection, but that the State can treat citizens differently on the basis of a reasonable classification.

In order to make a classification reasonable, it should be based—

a) on an intelligible differentia which distinguishes person or things that are grouped together from those who have been left out;

b) that the differentia must have rational nexus to the object sought to be achieved by such classification.[52]

The object sought, in this instance, was good governance, 'the hallmark and soul of democracy'.[53] Therefore, the Election Order establishing the educational qualifications becomes the first step in a transformation of political culture that throughout its history has tolerated the violation of the spirit of democracy and consequently meets the second requirement. Meeting the first requirement, the Court concludes that the order equally applies to all graduates and is therefore deemed once again, 'reasonable and not arbitrary or whimsical'.

The petitions against the Conduct of General Elections Order (2002) were summarily dismissed.

Conclusion

A number of interesting issues arise when considering the long-term implications of Musharraf's Conduct of General Elections Order (2002) apart from its constitutionality: first, the immediate electoral implications of the Order; second, the related but unforeseen rise of the MMA; and, lastly, prospects for the future. Each will be taken up briefly.

Upon seizing power in 1999, the Supreme Court lent support to Musharraf on the condition that he would hold general elections by October 2002. It was clear that Nawaz Sharif's and Benazir Bhutto's parties were plotting a strong campaign, Sharif's party (PLM-N) was thought to pose the greatest threat. The question for Musharraf was how to weaken the opponent and usher in the party most friendly to his rule. Given the degree of international attention to this elections, outright fraud was unthinkable, tinkering with the election rules to weaken an opponent may have been.[54]

The impact of the Conduct of General Elections Order is interesting and telling. To assess the effect, the logical place to start would to look at those who were likely to run for office in the October elections, primarily those who held seats in the 1999 Parliament; seventy-nine members of the National Assembly and twenty-two senators did not possess a Bachelor's degree. Twenty-five per cent of former members of the National Assembly (MNAs) would now be ineligible, while 22 per cent of those in the Senate were.[55] Although these figures are not staggering in their magnitude, a different picture emerges when one assesses the impact of the Order on specific parties.

Bhutto's PPP lost only five former MNAs and none of their nineteen former Senators lost eligibility. The Awami National Party was relatively more weakened than the PPP. In the 1999 National Assembly they had eight senators and ten MNAs, of those four MNAs and three senators lost eligibility, nearly half of their contingent. The PML(N) took the biggest hit: fifty-three former MNAs did not qualify for filing nominations and eight of its past twenty-six Senators were prohibited from contesting the election. Not only did the PLM(N) lose the greatest number of seats, but as a result of the Order they lost their party's senior leadership including the former Speaker, the deputy chairman of the Senate, and Secretary General.[56] It is the clear the educational requirement had significant impact, at least temporarily, on Musharraf's most daunting opponent.

As to the correlation of the rise of the MMA and the educational qualification, the explanation must begin in 1980 with Ziaul Haq's Islamization program. To gain support for the reforms, Zia courted the *madrassas*, and in one series of concessions, he directed the University Grants Commission to draw up criteria of equivalence for degrees and certificates for *madrassa* education. The highest certificates of *wafaq* boards were recognized as an MA in Arabic or Islamiyat; the upshot is that *madrassas* were provided equivalent status to the formal, secular educational system.

After the Conduct of General Elections Order was passed, if the Awami Party is any indication, it is likely that secular regional party organizations were weakened. It is also very likely that regional religious party organizations remained intact given the educational equivalence concessions. I am not arguing that the Elections Order was the only reason why the MMA ascended to power; however, I would argue it was a contributing factor. If contending secular party organizations lost their leadership, they would be unable to effectively channel public sentiment away from an Islamist sentiment about the war in Afghanistan, fury at America, and Pushtun solidarity. How long the MMA is able to take advantage of this current situation remains to be seen.

To conclude, I would like to speculate briefly on what might be the impact of this reform beyond its immediate impact on the recent elections. First, I believe it is likely that the reform will stand because those presently in power have benefited from it and will protect it as it protects them. Good politicians across the world know that you do not tinker with the rules that put you in power and shield you once there. However, the brilliance of the human animal is our ability to adapt. If educational qualifications are now one more obstacle to overcome in the quest for political power, it is very likely that those who are able will seek degrees and those who are not will press for education reform based on the strongest argument possible—the deepening of democracy.

I anticipate that competing political parties will slowly rebuild and eventually contest elections on an equal footing. The long-term impact of this reform may be that the lure of power through education will indeed forever alter Pakistan's political culture. Whether it alters it in the way envisioned by Musharraf and the Supreme Court is unknown.

Second, the *madrassas* may rue the day that the MMA achieved notoriety because, I predict, public scrutiny will become focused on them again. There is a long history of efforts to reform the *madrassas* and certainly the content of *madrassas* education takes on added import given their new role in the political process. The *madrassas* have managed to evade reform efforts up to this point; however, citizens within Pakistan may begin to question whether the curriculum of the *madrassas* equips their graduates with the necessary skills and outlook to be effective and even-handed political leaders. In addition, it may become a national security imperative for Pakistan to further dilute the appearance of influence by religious parties in government given the international society's increasing intolerance for shades of grey in the war against extremism. The relative autonomy of the *madrassas* may eventually become one victim of this reform effort.

Lastly, is the reform a difference that makes a difference in a nation struggling against an established history of rather non-democratic practice? Musharraf flouts democratic processes and principles at will. In 2004, he replaced the Prime Ministers in the state without benefit of an election, he has gone back on his promise to step down as head of the military, and he continues to dominate the means of public discourse. At present, it would appear that the educational qualification reform has no immediate impact; but then, it was not expected to. Recall, the Justices argued that it was one step in a very long journey. What was expected at the conclusion of that journey? That education would bring about an intolerance of corruption by citizens. Education would inculcate in elected officials a desire to further the public interest rather than their private interest. Because public officials would be working for the common good, trust would eventually emerge as a public virtue binding together citizen and representative. Indeed, if this is the outcome, then not only will military rulers lose the justification for seizing power, but Pakistan will be able to teach established democracies a thing or two about good governance.

Appendix A

LOCAL GOVERNMENT ORDINANCE 2001
QUALIFICATIONS OF CANDIDATES AND ELECTED MEMBERS

A person will qualify to be elected or to hold an elective office or membership of a local government, if he:
- Is a citizen of Pakistan
- Is at least twenty five years of age
- Is enrolled as a voter in the electoral rolls of the relevant ward;
- Is of good character and is not commonly known as one who violates Islamic injunctions; has adequate knowledge of Islamic teachings and practices, obligatory duties prescribed by Islam as well as abstains from major sins; provided that these qualifications will not apply to a person who is a non-Muslim, but such a person will have a good reputation;
- Has academic qualifications of not less that matriculation of secondary school certificate or equivalent from a recognized institution, for contesting the election of a Nazim or a Naib Nazim;
- Has not been declared by a competent court to be of unsound mind;
- Is not in the service of the Federal, a provincial or a local government or, any statutory body of a body which is controlled by any such government or, in which any of such government has a controlling share or interest, except the holders of elected public office and part-time officials remunerated either by salary or fee; provided that in case of a person who has resigned or retired from such service, a period of not less that six months has elapsed since his retirement;
- Has not been dismissed, removed or compulsorily retired from public service on the grounds of moral turpitude;
- Does not possess assets which are inconsistent with his declaration of assets or justifiable means, whether held in his own name or of the dependents or any other person or

corporate body in whose name arrangement whereby the de-facto control of such assets including their sale, transfer or pecuniary interest, is retained by him;

- Has not been adjudged a wilful defaulter of any tax or other financial dues owed to the federal, a provincial, or local government or any financial institution, including utility bills outstanding for six months or more;
- Has not been convicted by a court of competent jurisdiction on a charge of corrupt practice involving moral turpitude or misuse of power or authority under any law for the time being in force;
- Has not been sentenced to imprisonment for more than three months for an offence under any law and, a period of not less than five years public office, has not been sentenced to imprisonment;
- Has not failed to file the required return of election expenses or is not convicted for exceeding the limits of election expenses prescribed under the electoral laws;
- Has not been declared an un-discharged insolvent by any court;
- Does not engage in any transaction involving pecuniary interest with the local government of which he is a member;
- Does not absent himself without reasonable cause from three consecutive meetings of the council of which he is a member; provided that a member will not be disqualified if the absence was necessitated by a national emergency or *force majeure*;
- Does not fail to attend a training course as required under section 189 of the Local Government Ordinance 2001;
- Has not been and is not involved, in activities prejudicial to the ideology, interest, security, unity, solidarity, peace and integrity of Pakistan and its people, and the good order and harmony of society; and
- Has not used, directly or indirectly, for his election the platform, flag, symbol, affiliation and financial or material resources or support of a political, religious, ethnic or sectarian party, formation or organization.

Whoever –

- is found by the Chief Election Commissioner to have contravened above provisions will stand disqualified from being a candidate for election to any office of the local governments for a period of four years;

or

- Having been elected as a member of local government or is a holder of an elective office of the local government is found by the Chief Election Commissioner to have contravened the above provisions will cease forthwith to be an elected member or to hold the office of such member and stand disqualified from being a candidate for election to a local government for a period of four years.

Local government elections will be held on a non-party basis.

Appendix B

PRESIDENT'S ORDER 14 of 1985
REVIVAL OF THE CONSTITUTION OF 1973 ORDER, 1985
[Gazette of Pakistan, Extraordinary, Part-1, 2nd March 1985]
No. F 17(3)/85-Pub.

For these Articles 62 and 63 the following shall be substituted, namely:-

62. Qualifications for membership of Majlis-e-Shoora (Parliament).

A person shall not be qualified to be elected or chosen as a member of Majlis-e-Shoora (Parliament) unless—

a) he is a citizen of Pakistan;

b) he is, in the case of National Assembly, not less than twenty-five years of age and is enrolled as a voter in any electoral roll for election to a Muslim seat or a non-Muslim seat, as the case may be, in that Assembly;

c) he is, in the case of Senate, not less than thirty years of age and is enrolled as a voter in any area in a Province or, as the case may be, the Federal Capital or the Federally Administered Tribal Areas, from where he seeks membership;

d) he is of good character and is not commonly known as one who violates Islamic Injunctions;

e) he has adequate knowledge of Islamic teachings and practices obligatory duties prescribed by Islam as well as abstains from major sins;

f) he is sagacious, righteous and non-profligate and honest and *ameen*;

g) he has not been convicted for crime involving moral turpitude or for giving false evidence;

h) he has not, after the establishment of Pakistan, worked against the integrity of the country or opposed the ideology of Pakistan; Provided that the disqualifications specified in paragraphs (d) and (e) shall not apply to a person who is a non-Muslim, but such a person shall have good moral reputation; and

i) he possesses such other qualifications as may be prescribed by Act of Majlis-e-Shoora (Parliament).

63. Disqualifications for membership of Majlis-e-Shoora (Parliament).

(1) A person shall be disqualified from being elected or chosen as, and from being a member of the Majlis-e-Shoora (Parliament), if —

a) he is of unsound mind and has been so declared by a competent Court; or

b) he is an un-discharged insolvent; or

c) he ceases to be a citizen of Pakistan, or acquires the citizenship of a foreign State; or

d) he holds an office of profit in the service of Pakistan other than an office declared by law not to disqualify its holder; or

e) he is in the service of any statutory body or any body which is owned or controlled by the Government or in which the Government has a controlling share or interest; or

f) being a citizen of Pakistan by virtue of section 14B of the Pakistan Citizenship Act, 1951 (II of 1951), he is for the time being disqualified under any law in force in Azad Jammu and Kashmir from being elected as a member of the Legislative Assembly of Azad Jammu and Kashmir; or

g) he is propagating any opinion, or acting in any manner, prejudicial to the ideology of Pakistan, or the sovereignty, integrity or security of Pakistan, or morality, or the maintenance of public order, or the integrity or independence of the judiciary of Pakistan, or which defames or brings into ridicule the judiciary or the Armed Forces of Pakistan; or

h) he has been, on conviction for any offence which in the opinion of the Chief Election Commissioner involves moral turpitude, sentenced to imprisonment for a term of not less than two years, unless a period of five years has elapsed since his release; or

i) he has been dismissed from the service of Pakistan on the ground of misconduct, unless a period of five years has elapsed since his dismissal; or

j) he has been removed or compulsorily retired from the service of Pakistan on the ground of misconduct unless a period of three years has elapsed since his removal or compulsory retirement; or

k) he has been in the service of Pakistan or of any statutory body or any body which is owned or controlled by the Government or in which the Government has controlling share or interest, unless a period of two years has elapsed since he ceased to be in such service; or

l) he is found guilty of a corrupt or illegal practice under any law for the time being in force, unless a period of five years has elapsed from the date on which that order takes effect; or

m) he has been convicted under section 7 of the Political Parties Act, 1962 (III of 1962), unless a period of five years has elapsed from the date of such conviction; or

n) he, whether by himself or by any person or body of persons in trust for him or for his benefit or on his account or as a member of a Hindu undivided family, has any share or interest in a contract, not being a contract between a cooperative society and Government, for the supply of goods to, or for the execution of any contract or for the performance of any service under taken by, Government: Provided that the disqualification under this paragraph shall not apply to a person--

i) where the share or interest in the contract devolves on him by inheritance or succession or as a legatee, executor or administrator, until the expiration of six months after it has so devolved on him;

ii) where the contract has been entered into by or on behalf of a public company as defined in the Companies Ordinance, 1984 (XLVII of 1984), of which he is a shareholder but is not a director holding an office of profit under the company; or

iii) where he is a member of a Hindu undivided family and the contract has been entered into by any other member of that family in the course of carrying on a separate business in which he has no share or interest; or

Explanation.

In this Article 'goods' does not include agricultural produce or commodity grown or produced by him or such goods as he is, under any directive of Government or any law for the time being in force, under a duty or obligation to supply;

o) he holds any office of profit in the service of Pakistan other than the following offices, namely:-

i)´ an office which is not whole time office remunerated either by salary or by fee;

ii) the office of Lumbardar, whether called by this or any other title;

iii) the Qaumi Razakars;

iv) any office the holder whereof, by virtue of such office, if liable to be called up for military training or military service under any law providing for the constitution or raising of a Force; or

p) he is for the time being disqualified from being elected or chosen as a member of the Majlis-e-Shoora (Parliament) or of a Provincial Assembly under any law for the time being in force.

Appendix C

Conduct of General Elections Order, 2002
C.E.O No. 21 of 2002

Article 8, part D

Qualifications and disqualifications of members of Majlis-e-Shoora (Parliament) and Provincial Assemblies.

Paragraph (1)

In addition to the educational qualification specified in Article 8A, a person shall not be qualified to be elected or chosen as a member of a House of the Majlis-e-Shoora (Parliament) or Provincial Assembly unless-

a) he is a citizen of Pakistan;

b) he is, in the case of National Assembly, not less than twenty-five years and is enrolled as a voter in-

   i) any electoral roll for election to a general seat, or a seat reserved for the non-Muslims; and

   ii) any area in a Province from where he seeks membership for election to a seat reserved for women;

c) he is, in the case of Senate, not less than thirty years of age and is enrolled as a voter in any area in a province or, as the case may be, the federal Capital or the Federally Administered Tribal Areas, from where he seeks membership;

d) he is, in the case of a Provincial Assembly, not less that twenty-five years of age and is enrolled as a voter in any area in a Province from where he seeks membership for that Assembly;

e) he is of good character and is not commonly known as one who violates Islamic injunctions;

f) he has adequate knowledge of Islamic teachings and practices obligatory duties prescribed by Islam as well as abstains from major sins;

g) he is sagacious, righteous and non-profligate and honest and *ameen*;

h) he has not been convicted for a crime involving moral turpitude or for giving false evidence;

i) he has not after the establishment of Pakistan, worked against the integrity if the country or opposed the ideology of Pakistan;

　　Provided that the disqualifications specified in paragraphs (f) and (g) shall not apply to a person who is a non-Muslim, but such a person shall have good moral reputation; and

j) he possesses such other qualifications as may be prescribed by an Act of Majlis-e-Shoora (Parliament)

Paragraph (2)

A person shall be disqualified from being elected or chosen as, and from being, a member of the Majlis-e-Shoora (Parliament) or a Provincial Assembly, if-

a) he is of unsound mind and has been so declared by a competent court; or

b) he is an undischarged insolvent; or

c) he ceases to be a citizen of Pakistan, or acquires the citizenship of a foreign State; or

d) he holds an office of profit in the service of Pakistan other than an office declared be law not to disqualify its holder; or

e) he is in the service of any statutory body or anybody which is owned or controlled by the Government or in which the Government has a controlling share or interests; or

f) he being a citizen of Pakistan by virtue of section 14B of the Pakistan Citizenship Act, 1951 (II of 1951) he is for the time being disqualified under any law in force in Azad Jammu and Kashmir from being elected as a member of the Legislative Assembly of Azad Jammu and Kashmir; or

g) he is propagating any opinion, or in any manner, prejudicial to the Ideology of Pakistan, or the sovereignty, integrity or security of Pakistan, or morality, or the maintenance of the

Judiciary or Pakistan, or which defames or brings into ridicule the judiciary or the Armed Forces of Pakistan; or

h) he has been convicted by a court of competent jurisdiction on a charge of corrupt practice, moral turpitude or misuse of power or authority under any law for the time being in force; or

i) he has been dismissed from the service of Pakistan or service of a corporation or office set up or controlled by the Federal Government, Provincial Government or a local government on the grounds of misconduct involving moral turpitude; or

j) he has been removed or compulsorily retired from the service of Pakistan or service of a corporation of office set up or controlled by the Federal Government, Provincial Government or a local government on the grounds of misconduct involving moral turpitude; or

k) he has been in the service of Pakistan or any statutory body or any body which is owned or controlled by the Government or in which the Government has a controlling share of interest, unless a period of two years has elapsed since he ceased to be in such service; or

l) he, whether by himself, or by any person or body of persons in trust for him or for his benefit or on his account or as a member of a Hindu undivided family, has any share or interest in a contract, not being a contract between a cooperative society and Government, for the supply of goods to, or for the execution of any contract or for the performance of any service undertaken by, Government;

Provided that the disqualification under this paragraph shall not apply to a person-

i) where the share or interest in the contract devolves on him by inheritance or succession or as a legatee, executor or administrator, until the expiration of six months after it has so devolved on him;

ii) where the contract has been entered into by or on behalf of a public company as defined in the Companies Ordinance, 1984 (XLVII of 1984), of which he is a shareholder but is not a director holding an office of profit under the company; or

(iii) where he is a member of a Hindu undivided family and the contract has been entered into by any other member of that family in the course of carrying on a separate business in which he has no chare or interests; or

Explanation: In this Article 'goods' does not include agricultural produce or commodity grown or produced by him or such goods as he is, under any directive of Government or any law for the time being in force: under a duty or obligation to supply

m) he holds any office of profit in the service of Pakistan other than the following offices namely-

   i) an office which is not whole time office remunerated either by salary or by fee;

   ii) the office of Lumbardar, whether called by this or any other title;

   iii) the Qaumi Razakars;

   iv) any office the holder whereof, by virtue of such office, is liable to be called up for any military training or military service under any law providing for the constitution or raising of a Force, or

n) he has been convicted and sentenced to imprisonment for having absconded by a competent court under any law for the time being in force; or

o) he has obtained a loan for an amount of two million rupees or more, from any bank, financial institution, cooperative society or cooperative body in his own name or in the name of his spouse or any of his dependents, which stands unpaid for more than one year from the due date, or has had such loan written off; or

p) he or his spouse or any of his dependents has defaulted in payment of government dues and utility charges including telephone, electricity, gas and water charges of an amount in excess of ten thousand rupees, for over six months; or

q) he is for the time being disqualified from being elected or chosen as a member of the Majlis-e-Shoora (Parliament) or of a Provincial Assembly under any law for the time being in force.

Notes

1. Pakistan Muslim League (Q) v. Chief Executive of Islamic Republic of Pakistan *PLD* 2002 Supreme Court (SC) 994, 1011.
2. PML(Q) case, 1012.
3. PML(Q) case, 1012.
4. PML(Q) case, 1013.
5. PML(Q) case, 1014.
6. PML(Q) case, 1014-1016.
7. PML(Q) case, 1016.
8. PML(Q) case, 1016.
9. PML(Q) case, 1017.
10. PML(Q) case, 1018.
11. PML(Q) case, 1019.
12. PML(Q) case, 1020.
13. PML(Q) case, 1020-1021.
14. PML(Q) case, 1021-1022.
15. PML(Q) case, 1023.
16. PML(Q) case, 1024.
17. PML(Q) case, 1024.
18. PML(Q) case, 1024.
19. Interestingly, it was the Nawaz Sharif sponsored Thirteenth Amendment which took authority away from the President to dissolve government that the Supreme Court said justified Musharraf's taking of power. By taking away the Presidential check on Prime Ministerial power, there were no Constitutional means for overturning the government therefore, extra-Constitutional means were all that were available.
20. See Charles H. Kennedy, 'User's Guide to Guided Democracy' in this volume.
21. This is the Pakistan organization responsible for creating and establishing the Local Government scheme. They are working closely with the United Nations Development Program.
22. Taken from the UNDP Governance Programme: Synopsis: undp.un.org.pk
23. That is, candidates would have passed their Matric examinations. This suggestion was provided to me by consultants to the NRB who wish to remain anonymous.
24. Local Government Ordinance (2001). See Appendix B.
25. NRB web-site: www.nrb.gov.pk (See Model Laws/Rules, Manuals, Reports & Guidelines, Capacity Building Phase I and II. Although the relevant

deliberations of the NRB for instituting educational requirements for local office are not available, the addition of required training courses lends credibility to this explanation. It would likely prove impossible for someone who was illiterate or only nominally educated to successfully complete the NRB's training programme.

26. Executive Order No. 7 of 2002.
27. Signed into law on 24 June 2002, Chief Executive Order No.17 adding Article 8A.
28. Amendment of Article 2 of the Conduct of General Elections Order 2002, Chief Executive's Order No. 21 of 2002.
29. The hearings were held on 9-11 July 2002. Present were Chief Justice Riaz Ahmed and Justices Munir Sheikh, Nazim Siddiqui, Iftikhar Chaudhry and Qazi Farooq.
30. Constitution of Pakistan, Articles 62 and 63.
31. PML(Q) case, 1003.
32. PML(Q) case, 1006.
33. PML(Q) case, 1005.
34. PML(Q) case, 1003.
35. PML(Q) case, 1004.
36. PML(Q) case, 1006.
37. PML(Q) case, 1006.
38. PML(Q) case, 1005.
39. PML(Q) case, 1007.
40. PML(Q) case, 1007.
41. PML(Q) case, 1007-1008.
42. PML(Q) case, 1011.
43. PML(Q) case, 1011.
44. PML(Q) case, 1011.
45. PML(Q) case, 1026-1027.
46. PML(Q) case, 1009.
47. PML(Q) case, 1026.
48. PML(Q) case, 1026.
49. PML(Q) case, 1026.
50. PML(Q) case, 1027.
51. PML(Q) case, 1027-1028.
52. PML(Q) case, 1030-1031.
53. PML(Q) case, 1029.
54. I have no first-hand knowledge that this speculation occurred to Musharraf or any of his party leadership. It is purely Machiavellian logic at work here.
55. Hashmi, Faraz, '101 former legislators face disqualification', *Dawn (Online)*, 12 July 2002.
56. The PML(N) lost their former speaker (Gohar Ayub Khan), deputy chairman of the Senate (Mir Humanyun Khan Mari), Lt. Gen. Majeed Malik, Chaudhry Sher Ali, Secretary General of the PML (N) Saranjam Khan and Ghulam Dastagir Khan. See *Ibid*.

8

Experimenting with Democratic Governance: The Impact of the 2001 Local Government Ordinance on Pakistan's Bureaucracy

Saeed Shafqat and Saeed Wahlah

Introduction

Civil and military regimes in Pakistan have made numerous attempts over the last five decades to reform bureaucracy, expand civil society, and deliver democratic governance but without much success. The Musharraf regime claims that it has changed the philosophy of governance in the country by introducing democracy at the 'grassroots level'. This policy shift, though not explicitly stated in any single document, can be discerned by examining the policy statements of numerous documents, particularly those of the National Reconstruction Bureau (NRB) and the Local Government Ordinance 2001 (LGO).[1] The LGO is particularly important in that it has redefined the role, responsibility, and hierarchy of institutions and actors involved in governance, including those of the civil service and particularly the elite service District Management Group (DMG), which had dominated the management of district administration.

This chapter will compare the past and present philosophical bases of governance and examine to what degree, if any, the Local Government Ordinance 2001 and its subsequent implementation has improved the effectiveness of administration. The study underscores the widely held perception that over the past three decades, the reputation of the Pakistani bureaucracy had been tarnished, being perceived as the 'handmaiden of politicians'. Bureaucrats were seen to run after politicians for attractive postings and district administrators no longer garnered the awe of the public. Most military regimes in the past had generally sought partnership with the bureaucracy, particularly the celebrated and powerful Civil Service of Pakistan (CSP). However, the military regime of General Pervez Musharraf departed from this old pattern. Musharraf's regime decided to uproot the historical lynchpin administrative role of the CSP and its offshoot, the District Management Group (DMG), by abolishing the 'colonial relic of Deputy Commissioner' and moving to empower the elected public official at the grassroots level. We argue in this paper that the abolition of the office of Deputy Commissioner may have permanently weakened the CSP/ DMG but if the goal was to bring about a citizen friendly, participative, efficient and representative local government, then the reform has been a failure.

To understand why the abolition of the office of Deputy Commissioner may have ruined the bureaucracy, we examine how and why the district was and continues to be the lynchpin of administration in Pakistan. Further, we examine to what degree, if any, has the introduction of the LGO redefined the dynamics of relationship between the elected public official and bureaucracy, redefining the relationship between state and civil society. Finally, we take up the question whether these revisions have hindered the fostering of meaningful local governance.

Centrality of the District and the Deputy Commissioner (DC)—Then and Now

Since colonial times, particularly after 1857, the district was the principal unit of administration in India and Pakistan. The colonial rulers instituted the office of the Deputy Commissioner (DC) as the patron—*Mai-Baap* (mother and father)—of the district. The office of the Deputy Commissioner was surrounded by the mystique of a paternal government's idea of justice and citizen welfare. On occasion, the DC was excessive in the use of force and pushing onto a public its rather authoritarian development projects, a legacy which still resonates in popular imagination and among public officials.[2] The DC was the symbol of colonial authority and power, and after independence successive civilian and military governments continued to rely on the office as a means of upholding the writ of government and occasionally to promote development.[3]

The Indian Civil Service (ICS), its successor, the Civil Service of Pakistan (CSP), and its successor, the District Management Group (DMG), the DC, and the district itself, complemented one another. After independence, the role and function of the DC did not change much.[4] The ICS/CSP was the patron who symbolized the authority of the state and controlled sources of reward and punishment; in the district it was the Deputy Commissioner who was the patron. The DC thrived on weaving patron-client relationships more than fostering political participation and representation. Maintaining order, promoting development and revenue collection remained his preoccupation. The local leadership took on the role of petitioners who sought justice, favours, and rewards for themselves and their supporters. The district experience, though short (3-6 years) and potentially very eventful, served as a confidence booster and reputation builder for a young officer, clearly helping to advance his career.[5]

More than a hundred years ago, writing in 1892, W.W. Hunter described the crucial position of the DC for the British Raj in undivided India:

Upon his energy and personal character depends ultimately the efficiency of our Indian government. His own special duties are too numerous and so various as to bewilder the outsider.

He is a fiscal officer, charged with the collection of revenue from the land and other sources; he also is a revenue and criminal judge, both of first instance and appeal. But his title by no means exhausts his multifarious duties. He does in his smaller local sphere all that the Home Secretary Superintendent in England, and a great deal more; for he is the representative of the paternal and not of constitutional government. Police, jails, education, municipalities, roads, sanitation, dispensaries, the local taxation, and the Imperial revenues of his District are to him matters of daily concern. He is expected to make himself acquainted with every phase of the social life of natives, and with each natural aspect of the country. He should be a lawyer, an accountant, a surveyor, and a ready writer of state papers. He ought also to possess no mean knowledge of agriculture, political economy, and engineering.[6]

During the British Raj and early years of Pakistan, the Deputy Commissioner performed all the traditional roles identified by Hunter, i.e. a revenue collector, administrator, magistrate, development planner, and patron of the district. However, as elected public officials began to establish their supremacy, the functions of the district officer underwent a change. The local councillors and the members of the provincial and national assemblies became more assertive about advancing their self-interests and, at times, the interests of their constituents. The district developed into an arena of contest between elected public officials and the DC. What was at stake in the contest was who would govern and rule.

It is important to recognize that after independence, the bureaucracy continued to expend significant amounts of energy on systemizing and expanding the power and authority of the DC, while the political parties and their leadership were unrelenting in their attempts to impose restrictions on the office.[7] In spite of the effort to shift the balance of power at the district level, the Deputy Commissioner continued to perform, more or less, the same main functions that Hunter had drawn our attention to:

Executive Functions. The district officers performed magisterial functions under around 260 different statutes in most of the 105 Districts of Pakistan including crime control, price control, endurance of supply of daily use items, and protocol and security of VIPs. The DCs performed these functions with the assistance of the police, in fact during the early years of Pakistan, following the colonial practice the Deputy Commissioner initiated the Annual Confidential Report (ACR) of police officers—a practice that was resented by the police officers. The Administrative Reforms of 1973 discontinued this practice, giving considerable autonomy to the police officers, thus compromising the effectiveness of the DC in maintaining law and order. After the separation of the judiciary and executive in 1997, the police became nearly completely autonomous and started to resist and defy the directions of the Deputy Commissioners unless such directions were confirmed by its own provincial hierarchy.

Judicial Functions: The Deputy Commissioner used authority given by the Criminal Procedure Code (Cr PC) and other federal and provincial statutes to perform judicial functions and served as a Magistrate in land revenue cases, and after the passage of Family Laws Ordinance (1962), in family law cases as well.

Development functions: The DC originally served as chairman of the District Development Committee, (DDC) and was a member of the Divisional Development Committee, a practice that was gradually discontinued as Pakistan made a transition to electoral democracy between 1985 and 1999. During this transitional period in most districts, an elected public official usually a member of the National or Provincial Assembly (MNA or MPA) acted as the chairman of the DDC or served as a member of the DDC. However, the DC continued to play an important role in development projects and these were usually implemented under the joint supervision of the district officers and elected representatives in practice.

Coordination Functions: The DC also co-ordinated efforts of nation building departments, local councils, NGOs, and others. For example, if the Health Department planned an anti-polio campaign, the DC's office would arrange the provision of vehicles, staff, police protection, and other things required to make the campaign successful.[8]

All this clearly demonstrates that in the post independence period, despite the demands for reform, the district continued to be the primary unit of politics and administration in Pakistan and as a consequence, the office of the DC continued to be a source of envy and awe. Because of this, the elected civilian leaders and the military realized that any redistribution of power and resources would have a direct impact on the concentration of power and authority held by the DC. The military regime under Musharraf concluded that empowering elected governments at the grassroots level required dismantling the office of DC. Whether the military's motive was to promote the public good or to merely serve the corporate interests of the military is unclear. For over three decades successive civil and military governments have been striving to change the character of the DC to make it constitutionally subordinate and accountable to elected public officials.[9]

We now examine the pattern of reform and the resistance of the Pakistani bureaucracy and how this has affected the district.

Pakistani Bureaucracy: Do Purges and Reforms Make a Difference?

In reviewing the fifty-seven years of Pakistan's history, a most revealing pattern emerges; in almost every decade both civil and military regimes have attempted to curtail the power and authority of the CSP. Most of the regimes have used a combination of purges and reforms as tools to approach this goals; each reform effort typically preceded by a purge of the Civil Service of Pakistan. One example discussed in greater detail below, was President Ayub's purge of the CSP in 1962.[10] Because of such repeated efforts to reform the bureaucracy, its institutional will and capacity has been broken and is in disarray.

To save the CSP cadre, CSP officers typically responded adroitly to such challenges. As a first step, they accepted the role of junior partner to the military rulers. Secondly, they conceded the induction of military officers to the CSP, a privilege they had denied to other civil services cadres. They allowed the entry of five military officers to join the batch of 1960. More importantly, between 1960 and 1963, fourteen young officers of the armed forces joined the CSP; out of these, eight had close connections with senior military officers.[11] In return, the military regime allowed the preservation of a 'separate identity' for the CSP. Lastly, the Establishment Division played a crucial role in revitalizing the elite status of the service and adopted a new training policy. After 1959, it was decided to discontinue sending CSP officers for one year training to Oxford or Cambridge. Alternatively, with US intellectual and financial assistance and concurrent support from the military regime, the Pakistan Administrative Staff College, National Institutes of Public Administration (NIPAs) and the Rural Development Academy were created.

The new breed of civil servants enthusiastically supported two new programs created by the military regime: the Basic Democracies and the Rural Development Program. Both programs enormously increased the power, privilege, and prestige of CSP officers, who served in the districts.[12] It also increased their interaction with local politicians. Consequently, although the district officer was able to promote a form of community development and welfare, the CSP as a cadre ran into conflict with the local politicians who saw them as 'political manipulators' and 'instruments' of the military regime.

Thus, by conceding the entry of military officers to the CSP, the reformulation of the training programme, and by enthusiastically supporting the policies of the military regime the CSP was able to protect its elite status. They also proved to be skilful in resisting and subverting the onslaught of the Cornelius Commission report with its set of recommendations, the primary one being that the monopoly of the CSP over top administrative positions, including the district, should be finished once and for all.

However, once the Ayub regime (1958-69) came under criticism from its political opponents and in the aftermath of Ayub's fall, the reputation of the CSP was tarnished, their confidence shaken, and showed signs of a leaderless drift.[13] The publication of the recommendations of the Cornelius Report followed General Yahya's famous purge of 303 civil bureaucrats in 1969. Similarly, Zulfikar Ali Bhutto's 1973 Administrative Reforms were preceded by a massive purge of about 1300 civil servants,[14] which deepened the crisis of confidence among the CSP, weakening its *esprit de corps*. The CSP's response was first one of dismay, followed by policy of self-help, and the adoption of a strategy designed for corporate survival. Discredited and demoralized, the service waited for better times. Bhutto, having served in Ayub's government for eight years (1958–66), was aware of the power and organizational capacity of the bureaucracy and was determined to reduce their power. Bhutto and his party found the CSP in particular, and the bureaucracy in general, potential threats to their power. The PPP and its leadership worked to subordinate the bureaucracy to the will of the political government thus, unleashing a trend in Pakistani politics whereby almost all elected political leaders worked to subordinate the bureaucracy as a means of maintaining power rather than building political consensus or a party system as an institutional alternative. In our estimation a combination of personal motive and the need for reform on the part of the PPP and its leadership provided the context for the 1973 reforms.

Bhutto's 1973 reform struck at the very roots of the civil service structure. In it, the CSP, the lineal descendant of ICS, was abolished. Its members were reorganized into the newly created DMG, Tribal Areas Group (TAG), and the Secretariat Group. Later, in 1981 the DMG and TAG were merged into a single group. The long-standing practice of reservation of posts in the top Secretariat positions for the CSP was discontinued.

The abolition of the cadre system coupled with the establishment of unified pay scales, the introduction of lateral entry, and the provision of greater opportunity for in-service training to all occupational groups, increased the career prospects for other services, while undercutting the privileges and power of the CSP. Because of the 1973 reforms, the elite status of the CSP was considerably diluted. In the eyes of the CSP, Bhutto's reforms were notably anti-CSP. But the reforms were neither structural nor did they aim to change the norms, values and behaviour of the senior bureaucracy. It is clear that the CSP remained the gold standard;[15] as such, structural advantages were devised for the advancement of the CSP with 'reservation of posts' at the federal and provincial level provided for the cadre. In the federal secretariat, the CSP continued its overwhelming dominance at the Deputy Secretary and Joint Secretary Level.[16]

Cognizant of the CSP's alienation and discontent, General Ziaul Haq's regime (1977–88) abandoned and reversed the policy of purges and reforms. Instead, under a former CSP officer and a Supreme Court Justice, Anwar-ul-Haq, it constituted a Commission whose recommendations attempted to rehabilitate and infuse a new sense of confidence among the civil services, particularly the CSP.[17] First, it revived and reactivated the military-CSP collaboration and partnership that had been disrupted and weakened by the 1973 Administrative Reforms. Second, it did what none of the earlier purges and reforms had done—the regime embarked upon a policy meant to redefine the ideological orientation of the civil servant by formally and informally encouraging a uniform dress code, a culture of prayer-break during office hours, and minimal emphasis on professional work ethics. Third, the Ziaul Haq government expanded and institutionalized the induction of armed forces personnel into the civil services. Under this reform, he instituted a 20 per cent quota in the Civil Services for the Armed Forces—10 per cent to be recruited from grade 17 (Captain) and another 10 per cent from ranks of Major and above, including those who may have already retired from the Armed Forces.[18] Most of the captain level inductees were either relatives of senior military officers or their nominees and were recruited to only three groups, —DMG, Police Group and the Foreign Service. Those who were inducted at the Captain level were placed in seniority above those who entered the service through merit and competition (this has been discontinued since 1991), which, understandably, had a demoralizing effect on civilian officers. The cumulative effect of these measures was that modernist, forward looking, and liberal values which had characterized the pre-Zia senior bureaucracy were eroded and the professional competence of the Pakistani bureaucracy was further compromised.

Fourthly, the Zia regime was perhaps most notable in contributing to the revitalization of the importance of the district in Pakistan. As it de-legitimized politics at the national and provincial level and resuscitated the Local Bodies (Local Bodies elections were held in 1979, 1983, 1987), the district became the centre point for governance. Consequently, the DMG and Deputy Commissioner began to re-capture public imagination. Lastly, the Anwar-ul-Haq Commission initiated a Specialized Training Program (STP) for the DMG at the site of the former CSP Academy, thus creating the illusion of succession from the CSP to the DMG. Although late, the move was an effort to inculcate a sense of group identity—an 'esprit de corps' that the CSP had once prided itself on but had lost owing to the Bhutto reforms.

Besides these positive benefits of the Zia reforms, a significant negative effect of the partnership with the Zia regime was that of enforcing Islamization and suppressing popular anti-military protests (1983–84). The district administration arrested and tortured political opponents and DMG officers became a symbol of repression and authoritarianism.[19]

The overall impact of Zia's military regime was that the CSP and the DMG were able to rehabilitate their position both in the policy arena and the districts. However the price of collaboration with the military regime was to prove high; the CSP/DMG was not only perceived as arrogant and authoritarian, but as collaborating with a regime that was both illegitimate and repressive. Thus during Zia years the DC lost its glory, power, privilege, authority and mystique precisely where it had originated—in the district.

To conclude, the purges and reforms shook the confidence of the civil servants, which led to politicization and to a certain degree, encouraged an environment where financial corruption and misuse of authority proportionately increased. It was in this broader context of purge and reform that the government of Nawaz Sharif (1997-99) suspended eighty-seven civil servants in early 1997 and subsequently formed a task force for civil service reform.[20]

Democratization and Politicization of the DMG

Pakistan has a population of 145 million (1998 census), out of which half a million are civil servants, ranked from peon to federal secretary. Ninety per cent of that half a million are in grades 1-16, and 10 per cent are in grades 16-22 (executive grades). Out of these 50, 000 grade 16-22 civil servants, only 5 per cent (around 2, 500) are Central Superior Services (CSS) officers. The DMG officers (numbering around 700) are the elite service, which had a major share in positions running the districts and secretariats before the introduction of the LGO (2001). DMG officers comprise around 28 per cent of the CSS officers, 1.4 per cent of the total number of civil servants in grade 16-22, and 0.14 per cent of the total federal civil service.[21]

Pakistan's transition to democracy in 1985 with the aforementioned purges and reforms of the bureaucracy did not lead to democratic governance, it only revitalized the paternalistic character of governance. Ironically, the civil elected governments that assumed power after the transition (1985–99) led to the politicization of the bureaucracy and particularly the DMG and the Police Group. Each regime change was followed by a large-scale posting and transfer of officers in the district administration and in policy-making positions.[22] This practice compromised what would have been a neutral, upright, citizen friendly and transparent civil service. Instead, electoral politics and democratization created an atmosphere where the corrupt could get away with their schemes— be they politicians, tax evading businessmen, or self-serving civil servants.

Pakistan's decade of electoral democracy (1988–99) intensified the politicization of the bureaucracy. Both the PPP and PML(N) governments chose senior officers who were known for their political affiliation or were in sympathy with one or the other political party, violating the concept of a neutral civil service.[23] A low point was reached when the DC of Sheikhupura declared publicly; 'I am a dog of Nawaz Sharif and am proud of it'.[24] The office of the DC was now increasingly perceived as a tool of the powerful and no longer a patron or protector of the underprivileged. While citizens continued to protest against the politician-bureaucracy collaboration, the military became increasingly indignant toward the collaboration. In the post 1999 phase, the military was determined to break what they regarded as the growing poisonous nexus between politicians and the bureaucracy.

Prior to the LGO 2001, under the local bodies initiative the military regime never challenged the predominance and primacy of the DC in any significant way—at best they sought power-sharing. However, the LGO propounded a dramatically different approach by declaring the office and the institution of the DC superfluous. Ostensibly, the case against the DC was made because of the new commitment to 'empower the people' by enhancing the power of local bodies. In reality the military was skilfully dislodging a potential institutional competitor. The military declared that it would no longer rely on the CSP/DMG to administer policies in the district, nor in the provinces or at the federal level. This struck at the very root of status and merit in the civil services by de-legitimizing the claim of the DMG to rule the district. In the 1999-2000 CSS examination the impact of LGO was visible: the top ranked candidates listed the Police Group as their number one preference. It was clear that a change had begun.

The Changing Global Environment and the Pakistani Bureaucracy

In the 1980s the World Bank started a global campaign for Civil Service Reforms (CSRs). For a nation to receive Structural Adjustment Loans (SALs), they had to privatize state held industry, restructure markets to boost free trade, lower tariffs on imports, and undertake Civil Service Reforms. In the 1980s approximately 44 countries were part of the CSR program, whereas in the 1990s around 146 countries undertook reforms.[25] The World Bank conducted a CSR study in Pakistan in 1998 and one of its recommendations was 'devolution of power'. The CSP/DMG dismissed it contemptuously and their opposition put a temporary hold on its implementation. When General Musharraf assumed power in October 1999, the international community was reluctant to give legitimacy and approval to a military regime. The military regime responded by promising a return to democracy, improvement in governance, and reform in the social and economic sector. Also the Musharraf regime looked at the 1998 World Bank report with an eye to establishing contact and trust with the Bank and other donor agencies. The Local Government Plan was part of this strategy As noted above, most of Pakistan's military rulers had built partnerships with the CSP/DMG; however, this time around the equation changed primarily because donor agencies, the military, and rival services joined together in a concerted effort to cut the DMG down to size. The NRB document clearly targeted the DMG and states:

> The civil service is effectively controlled by the DMG. The group has close relations with international donors...other groups in the public administration chafe under the control of one group and would welcome

a democratisation of civil service structure as a basic element of civil service reform. The end of the domination of the bureaucracy by one group is a necessary pre-condition for the attainment of administrative power by the Army and the creation of conditions for national reconstruction.[26]

Contrary to this assertion, unlike the CSP, the DMG was neither well entrenched in the power structure nor had developed a distinctive group identity. The DMG was weak and relatively more vulnerable compared to their predecessor. Musharraf appointed Tariq Aziz, an Income Tax officer and a close friend, as his civilian Principal Secretary, dismantling the long standing practice of appointing a CSP officer to this powerful position. He also made two additional appointments—men who would be instrumental in reshaping and redefining the policy framework for district governance and the place of the DMG in the Pakistani bureaucracy. He appointed General Tanvir Naqvi as the Chairman of the NRB and General Moinuddin-Haider as Minister of Interior. Both had developed a reputation as efficient and talented administrators, both enjoyed respect and access to Musharraf's policy circles, and both were well known for their anti-CSP/DMG bias. During the Nawaz Sharif government, Moin had emerged as the spokesperson for the Police Commissioner system in Sindh, which the DMG perceived as supporting the Police Group and Naqvi proposed the abolishment of the office of the Deputy Commissioner and an end to the monopoly of the CSP/DMG in district goverment.[27]

Local Government Ordinance 2001

After assuming power in October 1999 the military government established a powerful think tank—the National Reconstruction Bureau (NRB). The task given to the NRB was to suggest ways to improve governance. The military government had earlier announced a far-reaching reform agenda for 'reconstructing the institutions of the state' by establishing democratically elected local government bodies across all four provinces. It was believed that this was necessary in order to deliver 'people centered, rights and responsibilities based on service orientated' local government. It announced the change in philosophy and claimed that the new system was designed to ensure citizen involvement in planning services and to provide mechanisms for citizen oversight of policy implementation. The process began in March 2000 with a NRB discussion paper that called for a series of bold structural changes to be implemented by August 2001—a deadline that was met.[28] The changes included the abolition of the existing three levels of provincial administration (divisions, districts, and *tehsils*) and the creation of a new tier of local government comprising districts (called city districts in the four provincial capitals), *tehsils* (city towns in the four city districts), and union administrations. It also called for the replacement of existing municipal bodies by these new local institutions. These arrangements applied to all provinces, but not to the cantonment (military) areas of towns and cities—which remained under the control of non-elected boards headed by military commanders; nor were they implemented in the Federally Administered Tribal Areas.[29] It is pertinent to note that there are forty-four cantonments in the country.

The NRB asserted that the politicians and bureaucrats were corrupt and were the primary source of bad governance. They claimed that there was no accountability, and little responsiveness to local needs. Therefore effective governance had broken down. The architects of the Devolution Plan further argued that decentralization and the empowerment of local government would lead to efficient administration and effective utilization of resources. This dictated dispersing power and authority, drawing it away from the office of the DC.

Devolution was also seen as a means of providing better 'access to justice'. Falling back on the 1973 Constitution and invoking the separation of executive and judiciary, it propounded that devolution would improve administration, courts, police, and the protection of human rights. It would also improve and protect labour laws and property rights. The salient objectives of the Devolution Plan 2001 are the following:

1. Bureaucracy (that is district administration) should be subordinate to the elected officials in the local councils.

Restructure and decentralize civil service, so that it becomes responsive to public needs.

2. Devolve administrative, financial and developmental powers to the elected officials in the local councils.

3. Ensure grassroots level accountability of the elected and appointed officials through an internal checks and balance system and also through the external system of citizen monitoring committees and the institution of an ombudsman.

4. Enhance public participation at the local level for all segments of the community especially through reserved seats for peasants, workers and women. The 33 per cent reservation of seats for women in local councils aims at bringing women into the mainstream decision making processes at the local level.

5. Reorient the entire administrative system to participatory decision making to make it responsive and efficient for effective service delivery.

6. Introduce new performance evaluation and incentive/reward/ disciplinary procedures for higher performance of the public employees.[30]

The new plan set forth the 'Five D's Strategy': Devolution of political power, Decentralization of administrative authority, Deconcentration of management functions, Diffusion of power-authority nexus, and Distribution of resources. A three-tier local government system evolved: District Government (DG) at the top, Tehsil Municipal Administration (TMA) in the middle, and Union Administration (UA) at the bottom. The DG consists of an indirectly elected mayor (*nazim*). The district administration is comprised of offices at DG, TMA, and UA all coordinated by the District Coordination Officer (DCO) and are responsible or accountable to the nazim. The administrative and financial powers of the now defunct divisional offices were delegated to the DG. Theoretically, the plan makes a strong and persuasive case for the devolution of political power—let us examine the reality.

Prior to 14 August 2001 the four provinces were divided into three administrative levels resulting in twenty-six divisions, 105 districts, and 354 *tehsils*. Other local government bodies existed mainly in urban areas. In decreasing order of size, there were two metropolitan municipal corporations (Lahore and Karachi), twelve municipal corporations, 144 municipal committees, and 303 towns committees. There were also (and still are) forty-one un-elected cantonment boards. In rural areas District (Zila) Councils were responsible for local services. The districts and divisions were distinct legal entities (created by the provinces as envisaged by the 1973 Constitution), but unlike the provinces, they lacked constitutional status. The new administrative changes are presented in Table 1. The District Coordination Officer (DCO) heads the District Coordination Department—the highest-ranking civil servant in the district. An Executive District Officer (EDO) heads each of the remaining departments.

The Politics of Devolution

Direct elections were held in five phases for members of Union Councils including *nazims* and *naib nazims* during 2000-01. On the basis of these direct elections, indirect elections were held in July 2001 for district *nazims, naib nazims, tehsil nazims,* and *tehsil naib nazims.* The new Local Government System was installed on 14 August 2001. Following is the breakup of total constituencies of the Local Government.

Province	Districts	Tehsils	Towns	Total Tehsil/Towns	Unions
Punjab	34	116	6	122	3453
Sind	16	84	18	104	1094
NWFP	24	34	4	38	957
Balochistan	22	71	2	73	518
Total	97	307	30	337	6022

Source: NRB Website

Competing and diverging interpretations have emerged about the outcome of the Local Bodies Elections 2001. The expectation and objective was that once the LGO was implemented, it would induct a new breed of local leaders, empower people, improve governance, enhance women's voice and representation, and streamline provincial and local government relations. The outcome has been mixed and somewhat chaotic.[31]

The political and social landscape at the district level has undergone some change. It is estimated that the system brought in 150,000 new persons into the political arena and led to the creation of more than 6,000 Councils—an astounding socio-political transformation.[32] According to one report, 38 per cent of the newly elected councilors reported that they had never contested an election nor had anyone from their family. However, 62 per cent reported having come from political families with a history of electoral contests.[33] According to another media survey, 30 per cent of the district *nazims* in Punjab were former members of the National and Provincial Assemblies and approximately 90 per cent came from established political families. Interestingly this survey found that the majority of the *nazims* come from landowning political families as well.[34] The LGO has certainly facilitated the rise of new local leadership; however, the land owning class continues to dominate local politics in many districts, which means that for the time being, the promise of democratic governance and empowerment for the people remains unfulfilled.

Part of the difficulty has been that political parties were largely opposed to the LGO and reluctantly allowed party members to participate in the local bodies elections. Those who won were ambivalent about their loyalty to the party, thus weakening the party system. The overall effect is that political parties have now become 'hostage' to a few land-owning political families.

The LGO boldly provided 33 per cent of the seats to women councilors but failed to promote a cultural environment where they could contest and vote. In various parts of the country *jirgas*, tribal leaders, and *biradaries* imposed limits on women's candidature. As a result, a large number of seats reserved for women remain empty. Yet many women contested and won, becoming members of the District Councils but they typically complain, 'We are not recognized as the true representatives of the women folk and hardly allowed to raise our issues in the meetings'.[35] It is obvious that the political parties and civil society NGOs were not vigorous in creating public awareness and mass mobilization to avail the opportunity offered by the LGO.

The feudal and paternalistic mindset was strengthened by another trend. In three districts of Sindh, for example, out of 204 Union Councils the membership of thirty-six Union Councils and sixty-six *nazims* were selected in uncontested 'elections'; thus effectively disenfranchising 300,000 voters by denying them the opportunity to meaningfully vote. This is a clear indicator of feudal/tribal power in the rural areas of Pakistan.[36]

The devolution plan aims to establish a system of local governments without an overt hierarchical relationship between the three component parts; that is, federal, provincial, and local. However, the government seemingly has yet to address the problems inherent in co-ordinating a large number of dispersed governments. Some provinces argue that the devolution design makes it far more difficult to co-ordinate with local government, as the province now has to deal with each local government independently. If the provincial government is subordinate to the federal government in terms of its supervisory role, and the district government is subordinate to the provincial government, then there is no intrinsic reason why this logic cannot be followed at the lower two levels. The difficulties are most evident in the City District governments.[37] Anecdotally, union *nazims* and *naib nazims* report that voters are demanding services from them for which they are not responsible. Also, despite their presence as ex officio members on *tehsil* and district councils, they are not credited with any of the successes of the higher tiers of government.[38] The weak management links between the district, *tehsil*, and union administrations present challenges for inter-governmental relationships and service delivery as well.

The only coordinating mechanism between district and *tehsil* government is the Mushawarat Committee (consultative committee). The District Mushawarat Committee, with the membership of the district and town *nazims* and the DCO, was to be the principal forum for creating district strategic plans and co-ordinating the development plans of local governments. However, it appears this is not happening in practice as the Committees have no leverage over reluctant or recalcitrant parties. The City Districts have similar committees that should serve as the forum for approving capital investments for municipal services but do not. The District Development Committees represent the more formal relationship between districts and union administrations because they are empowered to approve the schemes submitted by the union administrations. Curiously, *tehsil* officers are expected to provide technical advice on them but cannot make a decision on these proposals even though many of the schemes are related to *tehsil* activities; such as drains, water, and sewerage.

Tensions between the Provincial and Local Governments

There are undoubtedly tensions between the levels of government. Given the significance of patronage, it is not surprising that the newly elected provincial governments (after the October 2002 elections) have raised objections to the devolution scheme. Objections to the plan have been most vociferous in the NWFP and Sindh, provinces where the majority of the district *nazims* have political affiliations different from the ruling coalitions in the province.[39] In Sindh, the *nazims* of Khairpur and Karachi, who belong to opposition parties, have complained about transfers of district staff made by the provincial government without their authorization. In NWFP, the provincial Muttihida Majlis-e-Amal (MMA) government (who counts only two districts *nazims* as political supporters) has been accused by *nazims* of interfering in district affairs. *Nazims* have tendered their resignations to the President and asked for the federal government to deal with provincial interference.[40] Tehsil and union council *nazims* have backed the district *nazims* position and offered to resign in sympathy.

One of the first steps of the national elected government (October 2002) was to re-introduce the past practice of providing funds for development schemes identified by the members of the National

Assembly (MNA). As each MNA is allowed to identify schemes up to Rs 5 million (FY02-03 and 10 million thereafter), the maximum expenditure on this program could ultimately be as high as Rs 1.7 billion. Following suit, all the provincial governments have given similar allotments of development funds to the individual MPAs.[41]

Impact of LGO on DMG

The LGO has had a mixed impact on the bureaucracy and on the various levels of government—federal, provincial and local. It is at the local level where the DMG had been most powerful and has been most adversely affected; perhaps even radically dispossessed and disfigured (see Table 2). The office of the DC was abolished and its role and functions were distributed to different offices. Similarly, the offices of Divisional Commissioners were abolished and their responsibilities and powers, by and large, were devolved to the DG under the elected mayor (*nazim*).

The office of the DC was replaced by another office called District Coordination Officer (DCO). Unlike the DC, the DCO has limited autonomy. The DC was a federal/provincial civil servant who worked for and was accountable to the provincial government. The DCO may be a provincial/federal civil servant but now is subordinate to the *nazim*. On important policy matters, before communicating them to the provincial government, the DCO is required to seek permission from the *nazim*. The *nazim* also approves the DCO's posting in and/or out of the district and initiates the DCO's annual confidential report (ACR). To make matters yet more complex, the Chief Secretary (BS Grade 22 civil bureaucrat) writes the technical part of the DCO's ACR. The quandary for the DCO is how to juggle the demands of both the *nazim* and the Chief Secretary.

The LGO envisages DCOs in BS 20 while the DCs used to hold ranks in BS18 or 19. BS 20 officers are equivalent to former Commissioners and current Provincial Secretaries.

The magisterial powers of the DC have been withdrawn and given to the judiciary and police. The role of police oversight formerly held by the DC was abolished; it had been on the decline since 1973. The responsibility of law and order has been entrusted to the *nazims* and the police are accountable to them. In crime control, the police are independent and with more power than before. The relationship between the *nazim* and District Police Officer (DPO) is evolving. The *nazims* continue to complain about the lack of responsiveness of the police; for example, in Balochistan province the district *nazims* have collectively lodged complaints against the police.

Land revenue matters were left with the DMG officers. But, the revenue court, has been made subordinate to the political office of the *nazim*, which has opened the door for new ways of connivance or confrontation between the revenue courts and *nazims*.

The executive role of the DC has been given to the *nazim*, who now acts as the chief executive officer of the district. With the abolition of the DC office, the whole foundation of the DMG has been swept away, deeply affecting its entry point and highest policymaking position. The DMG was the most sought after service because its officers, as young ACs, would be directing subdivisions. Once the positions of AC/DC were abolished, it lost its appeal and splendour. The Establishment Division tried to revive its influence but it was not possible under the new LGO. In the CSS result in July 2002, the DMG fell to sixth place as choice for a posting from its previous perennial number one position.[42] The first preferred service was the Police Group, followed by Customs, Income Tax, Foreign Service, Accounts, and then the DMG. Ultimately fresh induction into the DMG was stopped in July 2002. What the 1973 reforms could not do the LGO has done—buried the elitism and supremacy of CSP/DMG where it originated, in the district.

Response of the DMG to the LGO

Disbelief

When the Musharraf regime announced its Devolution Plan, many DMG officers simply refused to believe that the military could actually implement it. This disbelief was based on two premises widely held among the DMG. First, the false perception that the DMG was the 'best and brightest' and the only service able to manage the districts; and second, that the military government was not serious about devolution and was simply trying to tame the bureaucracy by threatening it with the devolution of power. The DMG was in denial, expecting that like previous military regimes, Musharraf would eventually co-opt them as junior partners.

It came as a rude shock when the military built an alternate coalition with the Police Group, Income Tax Group, and NGOs and then publicly denounced the two main political parties (PPP and PML [N]) for administrative chaos and corruption. They then proceeded to tighten the noose around the bureaucracy, particularly the DMG.[43] The DMG soon discovered that the new coalition was not only unified but had a plan with the political will to weaken the authority of the DMG.

Frustration

The military government constituted Army Monitoring Teams headed by army officers at all levels; including subdivision, district, division, province and federal. Their assigned task was to merely monitor civilian activities, but these teams often effectively ran the districts through the DCs and Superintendent of Police (SP). These Monitoring Teams typically bypassed DMG officers, preferring instead to work with the SPs who were eager to co-operate and comply. To signal that a shift in power relations had indeed occurred, there were many cases in which members of Monitoring Teams intentionally and at times publicly humiliated the DCs (most of whom were DMG officers); for example, the DC Lahore's car was searched at the outer gate of his office; the DC Multan found an army 'Major' occupying his office when he arrived at work, the latter demanded an explanation of why he was late for work; the DC Rawalpindi was called twice a day for several weeks to a District Monitoring Team office for briefing and debriefing; etc.

Flight

The way DMGs have reacted to the LGO is proof that they had not developed into an effective service cadre akin to the CSP. Purging, reform, and democratization broke what little *espirit de corps* existed in the group and the DMG failed to develop a collective response. The erstwhile CSP, whose members continued to dominate the Federal Secretariat, was lukewarm in protecting and supporting the DMG. With their spirit broken and confidence shaken, many of the BS 19 and BS 18 officers began to seek jobs in the private sector. Others have ventured to apply for fellowships to pursue higher studies.

By 2002, about one hundred officers (mostly BS 17-19) had proceeded on Extra Ordinary Leave (EOL). The EOL option was discontinued in July 2002, further alienating the DMG.

According to our estimates, of the officers on EOL about 30 DMG officers have joined NGOs or have found jobs in the private sector or have become employed by local offices of international firms. In most cases such officers draw considerably higher salaries than those provided by government service. They have traded the perquisites, powers, visibility, and above all glory, for better pay.[44] As a cadre, the DMG complains that they have been humiliated by the military though, interestingly, we are aware of only three officers who have submitted their resignations so far. Most of them still want to return to what they call 'public service' but their critics call power hunger and corruption.

Some have begun to recognize the new realities and seem willing to operate under the changed conditions, but a large majority continue to hope and believe that the new system will fail.[45] There is no denying that the new plan is off to a bumpy start; but it is premature and unwise to believe that this means it is destined to fail.

Demotivated and Demoralized

There was no public protest or celebration over the demise of the office of the DC, but the media continued to report the doom and gloom that prevailed among the DMG.[46] Media reports and perhaps the Establishment Division's persuasion led President Musharraf, on 9 August 2001 (five days ahead of the implementation of the LGO) to write a letter of assurance to each DMG officer. He wrote,

> I believe that in our entire life as a nation this is the first genuine attempt at empowering our people. Our government realized that this social engineering would disturb the status quo. However, I was surprised to learn that the officers of the DMG were apprehensive that devolution would involve an abolition of the DMG as a cadre. This does not imply an abolition of the DMG as a cadre. I expect the DMG cadre to be the standard bearer of devolution plan...I can reassure you that your career progression from BS 17 to BS 22 shall be fully protected. You will continue to look forward to working in the highest positions based on your ability and merit. [47]

Ironically, in July 2002, the Establishment Division stopped induction into the DMG. Devolution did, in fact, imply the 'abolition of DMG as a cadre' because of the slow and gradual extinction of power the DMG held over the district has eroded. The DMG is finding ways to resist and redefine its purpose under this changed political and social environment but it is certain that the office of the DC is dead. Right now, the DMG is barely able to hang on by its fingertips.

Adjustment and Conflict

As noted above, the district was and continues to be an arena for struggles over power between elected public officials and the bureaucracy. The Musharraf regime and supporters of the LGO contend that the bureaucracy is now under greater public scrutiny and accountability. However, the *nazims* and councillors continue to complain about bureaucratic inertia, arrogance, and the lack of responsiveness, particularly by the police.

Who the boss is in the district is slowly being established and the change is visible. For example, the *nazims* have higher status and authority than the DCOs; the DC used to unfurl the national flag on Independence Day; this is now the *nazim's* privilege. The *nazim* also resides in what was once the DCs house. In some cases, the district governments, under elected public officials, are pursuing development work with vigour and confidence which augurs well for the new system. However, much is to be overcome as the system is still driven by permits and patronage.

The LGO has made the bureaucrats accountable to the local elected officials, but one of the stated goals of the government is to have a neutral, that is, de-politicized civil service. These goals seem incompatible under the present setup unless a local government civil service, including district cadres of city managers and police chiefs, is created and the provincial and federal civil servants are provided service conditions and protections so they can operate free from fear or favour. Such a local service may be a desirable goal but one would also need to look at the relevance and current structure of the federal civil service. Ultimately, the current recruitment, selection and examination system may require a major overhaul in order to protect the national and federal character of the civil services.

Conclusion

From the foregoing analysis we draw the following conclusions:

First, the LGO has radically altered the foundations of the bureaucracy in Pakistan in the sense that the myth and mystique of CSP/DMG has been dismantled. The District is no longer the monopoly of the DC or CSP/DMG. The LGO has redefined the power relations at the district level where, at least symbolically, a new beginning has been made to establish the supremacy of the elected over the un-elected bureaucrat. The LGO has produced political, social, and administrative turbulence and it will take some time before any modicum of equilibrium is attained.

Second, the LGO has provided an opportunity and challenge to both the DMG and the political leaders. The DMG is challenged to re-think and re-define their role in the bureaucratic and policy structure of Pakistan. They need to make a conscious and collective choice (based on merit and the acquisition of professional skills) either to create a niche in the policy arena or to bemoan the death of the DC and abandon the cadre. An optimistic view holds promise for the DMG. For example, prior to LGO there were only eight BS 20 officers in Punjab holding the position of Divisional Commissioner; the new set up has created thirty-four posts for BS 20 officers as District Coordination Officers (DCOs). Similarly, in the former system there was only one BS 19 officer (Deputy Commissioner) in each district but the new system has created twelve BS 19 Executive District Officers (EDOs) in each district. A similar expansion has also occurred with the BS 18 Deputy District Officers (DDOs) and BS 17 Assistant District Officers (ADOs). Of course, these posts are not exclusively reserved for the DMG and are open to all services but the DMG has an inherent advantage. The challenge for them is to demonstrate that they are professionally competent and better qualified to hold these positions than their civil bureaucratic competitors. For the elected public officials the test is to demonstrate that they can develop and provide an improved framework for governance and development, citizen welfare and participation. The dominance of the landowning/feudal/tribal groups continues to reinforce a paternalistic rule rather than representative government. Empowerment of the people, a declared objective of the LGO, remains far from fulfilled.

A third and worrisome outcome of the LGO has been the growing tension between the provinces and the local government. Conflicts of interest between members of the provincial/national assemblies and the *nazims* could hamper the smooth functioning of district governments and may intensify power struggles that derail the objectives of democratic governance. At this unique moment of social and political transformation in Pakistan, the DMG could weigh in as bridge builders between the local and provincial/national leaders to facilitate conditions for democratic governance by harmonizing diverging interests at the district and provincial level. If the DMG rises to the occasion they may succeed in redefining their role at all three levels of government: the local, provincial and federal.

Finally, the military has been deft in weakening the civil bureaucracy. However, in the process it has become over exposed and could face public rage. Weakened political parties, a demoralized bureaucracy, and NGOs can set in motion movements of social protest from civil society making military hegemony unsustainable. The LGO has opened up new pathways of patronage and domination while its promise of democratic governance, development, and citizen empowerment remains distant and elusive. The LGO offers political parties a window of opportunity to restructure the district politics by embracing the devolution of power and in turn democratizing and reforming themselves as a bedrock for democratic governance.

Table 1
Structure of District Governments

District Coordination: Coordination, Human Resource Management and Civil Defence.

Agriculture: Agriculture (Extension), Livestock, Farm Water Management, Soil Conservation, Soil Fertility, Fisheries, Forests and Wildlife.

Community Development: Community Organization, Labour, Social Welfare, Sports and Culture, Co-operatives, and Registration office.

Education: Boys Schools, Girls Schools, Technical Education, Colleges, (other than professional) Sports (Education) and Special Education.

Finance and Planning: Finance & Budget, Planning & Development, Accounts, Enterprise and Investment Promotion.

Health: Public Health, Basic & Rural Health, Children & Women's Health, Population Welfare, District and Tehsil (Headquarters.) hospitals.

Information Technology: Information Technology Development, Information Technology Promotion, and Database.

Law: Litigation, Legal advice, Legislation, and Environment.

Literacy: Literacy Campaigns, Continuing Education, and Vocational Education.

Revenue: Land Revenue & Estate and Excise and Taxation.

Works and Services, Housing, Urban & Rural Development, District Roads and Buildings, Energy and Transport.

Table 2
Impact of the LGO on each level of government

Federal Government:	• No change • Remains with largely the same structure.
Provinces:	• The de-concentrated units of the major service delivery line departments (staff, assets and budgets) devolved to local government. • Provincial government now has no local representation in the devolved service delivery sectors, except for provincial functions, but head offices and directorates remain unchanged.
Divisional tier of the province:	• Abolished, except for police. • Functions, staff and budgets allocated to districts.
District level:	• Grouped in 11 'Groups of Offices' with creation of new offices of F&P, Law and Literacy. • The 11 Groups, an elected nazim and a Zila Council created to form the new tier of district government; 97 district governments and 4 city district governments created urban and rural, local bodies under LGO 1979. • The earlier jurisdictions redrawn to merge rural and urban areas; in most cases the new precincts remain conterminous with the revenue tehsils, while in case of 'city districts' the municipal areas were divided to form 'towns'; provincial departments of public health engineering devolved to this level (although not in all provinces). • 335 Tehsil/Taluka/Town Municipal Administrations created largely with the municipal service delivery mandates of the local bodies.

Union administrations:
- In some cases larger unions have been divided and in case of urban areas also new unions have been created.
- 6022 Union Administrations have been created with minimal executive functions but, legally, a potential to gain more functions.

Notes

1. *Local Government: Devolution of Power and Responsibility, Establishing the Foundation of Genuine Democracy*, (Islamabad: National Reconstruction Bureau, Government of Pakistan, May 2000). *Local Government Plan 2000*. Final Shape 14 August 2000. *The SBNP Local Government (Model) Ordinance 2000* (Islamabad: National Reconstruction Bureau, 30 June 2001).
2. Philip Mason, *The Men Who Ruled India* (London: J. Cape, 1985) abridged edition, pp. 212-219, 289-305.
3. For an excellent and concise study concerning district administration in Pakistan and the pivotal role of the DC, see, Musharraf, Rasool, *The Imperative of Optimizing the Institutional Framework for Development in Districts in Pakistan* (London: DPU Working Paper No. 94, University College London, September 1999). See also, S.K. Mahmud, 'District Administration' in Jameel Ur Rahman Khan, *Government and Administration in Pakistan*, (Islamabad: Pakistan Public Administration Research Center, Government of Pakistan, 1987), pp. 201-251.
4. Muneer Ahmad *Civil Servant in Pakistan*, (Karachi: Oxford University Press 1964).
5. Many DCs express this view., For an interesting account of the interactions of young Assistant Commissioners, Deputy Commissioners and local political leaders in the early 1950s and 1960s see Roedad Khan, *Pakistan: A Dream Gone Sour* (Karachi: Oxford University Press, 1997), pp. 11-20. For a spirited defence of the office of Deputy Commissioner, see, Humayun Khan, 'Deputy Commissioner deserves an epitaph' *The News*, online edition 24 November 2001. For an entertaining and insightful account on the role of DC in Urdu, also see Qudrat Ullah Shahab, *Shahab Nama*. (Lahore: Sang-e-Meel Publishers. 1987/88), pp. 620-625.
6. W.W. Hunter, *The Indian Empire: Its People, History and Products*, (London: Smith, Elder, 1892), pp. 513-514.
7. S.K. Mahmud, op. cit.
8. W.W. Hunter, op. cit.

9. For an early and wide ranging treatment of the subject see, Ralph Braibanti, *Research on the Bureaucracy of Pakistan: A Critique of Sources and Issues*, (Durham, N.C.: Duke University Press, 1966).

10. A.R. Cornelius, *Report of the Pay and Services Commission*, (Karachi: Manager Publications, Government of Pakistan, 1969).

11. Shahid Javed Burki, 'Twenty Years of the Civil Service of Pakistan: A Re-evaluation', *Asian Survey*, Vol. XI No. 4. (April 1969), pp. 239-254.

12. Saeed Shafqat, *Civil- Military Relations in Pakistan: From Zulfikar Ali Bhutto to Benazir Bhutto.* (Boulder Westview Press/Pak Book Corporation 1997), pp. 39-41.

13. Charles H. Kennedy, *Bureaucracy in Pakistan*, (Karachi: Oxford University Press 1987), pp. 209-226.

14. Z.A. Bhutto, *Address to the Nation August 20, 1973: Implementation of the Administrative Reforms. Islamabad*: Administrative Reforms Cell 1975. For a perceptive analysis of the context of these reforms, see, Muneer Ahmad, 'The Political Context of Civil Service Reorganization in Pakistan' in *Aspects of Pakistan's Politics and Administration* (Lahore: University of Punjab 1974), pp. 133-169.

15. See, Nazim. *Babus, Brahmins, and Bureaucrats: A Critique of the Administrative Systems in Pakistan*, (Lahore: People's Publishing House 1973).

16. Kennedy, pp. 31-49.

17. Anwar-ul-Haq Commission Report, 1979.

18. *Estacode: Civil Establish Code*, (Lahore: Pakistan Service Law Publications 1992) pp. 164-170.

19. For example, in 1982-83, the Human Rights Commission of Pakistan reported that there were over 6, 000 political prisoners in Pakistani jails. In 1983, the Movement of Restoration of Democracy (MRD) an alliance of eight political parties dominated by the Pakistan Peoples Party launched a protest movement against the regime in Sindh. The protesters were harshly dealt with by the district administrations.

20. Saeed Shafqat, 'Pakistani Bureaucracy: Crisis of Governance and Prospects of Reform' in *The Pakistan Development Review*, 38:4 Part II (Winter 1999), pp. 995-1017.

21. Ibid., p. 999

22. For example, extensive postings and transfers of the civil servants, particularly at the district level, followed each regime change in 1990, 1993, 1997 and 1999.

23. To name a few, Ahmad Sadik, Principal Staff Officer to Prime Minister Benazir Bhutto, A.Z.K. Sherdil and Saeed Mehdi held the same position under Prime Minister Nawaz Sharif.

24. Khwaja Sadiq, a DMG officer was the DC.

25. Administrative and Civil Services Reforms. *www.worldbank.org/publicsector/civilservice/subnational.htm*

26. *'Structural Analysis of National Reconstruction'* (National Reconstruction Bureau, 27 May 2000).

27. General Naqvi, while addressing officers undergoing training at the DMG campus, Lahore in April 2000 advocated this point of view.

28. Amir Mateen who was working with the Asian Development Bank as a consultant and was advising the NRB shared this with me. The UNDP was the principal donor providing technical expertise to the NRB.

29. The SBPN Local Government Ordinance 2001

30. Ibid., pp. 11-20.

31. See for example two early assessments of performance of district governments after elections under the LGO. Sajid Mansoor Qaisrani, 'District set- up too slow to deliver', *Dawn,* 16 March 2002 and Farhan Anwar, 'Weaving Social Capital in Local Government —I and II'. *Business Recorder,* 3 and 10 August 2002.

32. Sarwar Bari, 'Devolution and Civil Society'. *The News,* 16 July 2004 online edition.

33. Shahrukh Rafi Khan, *The Devolution Plan.* SDPI Volume 8, No 1. November 2001-February 2002.

34. *Herald*, August 2001.

35. Ghazala Saad, a member of the Lahore District Council. See 'Women Councillors not satisfied under new system'. *The Daily Nation,* 11 March 2002 online edition.

36. See two news reports, 'Majority of Nazims relatives stand victorious'. *The News,* 13 October 2002 online edition. 'New District System fails to come up to people's expectation'. *The News,* 17 August 2002 online edition.

37. For a critique of district governments and its relationship with the provinces and possible impact on political parties, see Syed Zafar Ali Shah, 'Devolution sans Democracy'. *Dawn,* 14 February 2002 online edition.

38. Saeed Wahlah found this in his informal conversations with *nazims* and councillors in District Gujranwala. The *nazims* of Kohat and Bannu have publicly complained of lack of funds and the expectations of the public on the developmental role of local government. They also complain about the overlap of functions between the provincial and local government. For details see news report, 'Peshawar: Nazims complain about lack of power, funds'. *Dawn,* 25 August 2004 online edition.

39. Several newspaper reports note a chronic conflict between the *nazim* and the provincial government concerning postings and transfers of the officers. *Dawn,* February 2003 online edition. For growing tensions between provincial and district governments in Sindh see a report by Hameed Sheikh in *Weekly Takbeer* (Urdu) Karachi, 30 January -5 February 2003, pp. 48-50.

40. On 2 June 2003, all twenty-four *nazims* in the NWFP resigned in protest over the 'interference' of the MMA's provincial government. The provincial government transferred the officers in the district without the consent of Local

Government and threatened 'bad consequences if they did not obey directives about transfers'. *The News*, 2 June 2002 online edition.

41. Since the non-party elections in 1985 and the installation of Prime Minister Mohammad Khan Junejo's government, the civilian governments in Pakistan have embarked on the policy of giving a development grant of rupees 5 million to members of the national and provincial assemblies. Successive governments have found it difficult to discontinue the practice.

42. Ansar Abassi, 'PSP top target of CSS candidates'. *The News* online edition, 20 July 2002.

43. LGO 2000.

44. These are the people who either were expecting posting as DC before August 2001, or were serving as DCs, or recently had served as DCs and were hoping for other similar opportunities.

45. Interviews with DMG officers.

46. Ansar Abbasi, 'DMG doom Nears'. *The News*, 15 March 2002, online edition.

47. For text of the letter see, *Dawn*, 10 August 2001 online edition.

9

Religious Education and Violence in Pakistan

Christopher Candland[1]

For centuries, Islamic schools have preserved and transmitted knowledge, not only knowledge of Islam, but also knowledge of languages, literatures, reasoning, rhetoric, and natural sciences. *Madrasas* were established at about the same time—in the sixth century of the Muslim calendar/eleventh century of the Christian calendar—as the Christian seminaries that grew into modern Western universities. Madrasas have long been vital to Muslim societies as places to transmit religious learning. Pakistani madrasas were once known throughout the Muslim world for their well-preserved Hanafi teachings. Today, they are better known, among ordinary Pakistanis, as places where ones' children may get an ethical education, in a disciplined environment, with low-cost accommodations and meals, and improved employment prospects.

Outside Pakistan, madrasas are known today as breeding grounds for violence. The image is as misleading as it is simple, but is not without cause. In September 1996, Taliban [madrasa students], mainly Afghan refugees from Jamiat-i-Ulema madrasas in Pakistan's North West Frontier Province, marched on Kabul, toppled the government of Afghanistan, and imposed their version of *Shariah* [Islamic law] on the people living under their control. The Taliban used violence to enforce a *Shariah* that banned women's formal education, paid work, and appearance in public without a male relative companion, and mandated a schedule of daily prayer and specific (bearded) appearance for men. The rules of public, and private, life that the Taliban apparently learned in their madrasas were strict and unforgiving.

The Pakistani madrasas has been transformed from a place to preserve Islamic knowledge from Western influence and the colonial politics of the day to a place to mobilize for political influence. Colonial practices fostered suspicions between *ulema* and government as recently as two generations ago. Government mistreatment of. religious activists after Independence—such as arbitrary arrest and detention and prohibitions on political parties and religious associations—has sustained the mutual suspicions between governments and religious boarding schools, but only since the 1980s have madrasas advocated and been involved in organized violence. The transformation of the madrasas is recent.

Questions related to Pakistan's madrasas have been under public consideration in Pakistan for decades. What role do they play in Pakistani society? What role should they play? Should the government recognize their graduation degrees or provide their students with financial support? Are some madrasas involved in organized violence? Will government curricular and registration reform initiatives work? This chapter focuses on these questions. At the same time, related social and political questions arise. Why is the national public education system in Pakistan unable to cover most children? Is there any ready alternative to the public educational (and social welfare) that madrasas provide to more than one million children? Can anti-American sentiment in madrasas be transformed without a change in the foreign policy of the United States? Accordingly, this study also addresses such issues as: (1) US and Pakistan government connections to militant organizations, (2) Pakistani government failure to facilitate human development, and (3) Pakistani religious parties' response to an education vacuum.

Madrasas are vital to the social life of many ordinary Pakistanis. At the same time, some madrasas foster hatred of secular government, of members of other faiths, and of Muslims of different sects. These teachings, quite apart from the activities of specific militant madrasas, do contribute to sectarian violence. Militant sectarianism did not arise organically within the madrasas. Sectarianism found fertile soil in the communities, especially in the refugee communities, that madrasas served. But militancy was not so much the aim of madrasa principals, teachers, and students as much as their environment.

The decade long struggle against the Soviet army beginning in 1979 promoted pervasive militarization, what some call a Kalashnikov culture, throughout Pakistan, and especially in the provinces bordering Afghanistan. The madrasas did not escape this. Many of them took Afghan refugees as students. Additionally, the Pakistani and US governments used the madrasas and influenced their curriculum to intentionally encourage students to engage in sectarian militancy. As a result of these various forces, *jihad* [struggle] is understood by much of a generation of madrasa students not as a personal struggle against the forces that prevent one from living faithfully, but as a violent struggle for the imposition of an Islamic state upon society.

Making matters even more pressing is that more than one and a half million children are studying in madrasas today because the national education system does not reach them or because the education that does reach them is not useful. Former Minister for Religious Affairs Mahmood Ahmed Ghazi estimated recently that as many as 1.7 million students, roughly one tenth of the school-going population, attend madrasas in some capacity.[2] While many parents of these students can afford other schools but prefer an Islamic education, many poor families cannot afford to educate their children in any school other than a low-cost madrasa or a private religiously affiliated school.[3] The central issue in madrasa reform should be that millions of students are headed for education in an institution that is not intended to provide general education.

The Pakistani state has failed to meet one of the most basic requirements of any modern state: national general education. Subsequently, the life opportunities of millions are being forfeited. Today, madrasas are extensively involved in the care and education of the poor because they are more responsive to social need than the government. There are enormous pressures on existing madrasas and various incentives to establish new ones. Consequently, many madrasas do not provide students with adequate general knowledge. Further, the failures of the state threaten to prevent them from performing their intended function: to provide future *ulema* with the interpretative and reasoning skills to understand the Quran and *Ahadith* and *Islamiya* [Islamic studies]. Subsequently, and rather counter-intuitively, the failures of the Pakistani state endanger the social relevance of the *ulema*. The Islamic political parties, whose appeal is largely based on criticism of corrupt Westernized governments, are strengthened, on the other hand, by the failures of the state.

Removing violence from Pakistani society will require multiple efforts, including in the educational curricula. The incitement to religious and sectarian violence in the government curriculum would be an appropriate place for curricular reform and peace education.[4] Madrasas reform may help to reduce but will not eliminate violence in Pakistan.

I begin with a brief description of the origin and evolution of the South Asian madrasas. I then place the madrasas within the larger context of Pakistan's: (1) crisis in public education, (2) ideological and political conflicts (seemingly) related to Islam and (3) promotion of militancy during the war against the Soviets in Afghanistan (1979–1988). Together, these considerations— madrasas' education, public education, and violent sectarianism— help us to assess the viability of the government's present attempts to reform the madrasas.

Education in *Madrasas*

Islam does not recognize a formal clergy. Instead, the authority of religious leaders depends upon attainment of *ilm* [knowledge]. An *alim* [possessor of *ilm*] is respected for his *ilm* in three areas: (1) theology, (2) Islamic jurisprudence [*fiqh*], and (3) Islamic law [*Shariah*]. The *ummah* [community of believers] acknowledge the *alim's* religious education not his birth or office.

The role of madrasas in Pakistani society has changed rapidly and considerably. Madrasas in South Asia began as institutions to preserve Islamic learning. Initially, the state—first the Mughal state, then the British state—needed the kinds of graduates whom madrasas produced; those skilled in reading, writing, mathematics, logic, and Persian. With the change of the official language of government from Persian to English, the British colonial government stopped being the chief employer of madrasa graduates.

For most students in South Asia, to study in a madrasa is a religious commitment to preserve Islamic *ilm* against the intrusions of modern secular education.[5] Their curriculum is broadly similar throughout South Asia. Twenty subjects are covered using about eighty standard textbooks. Twenty books might be used in any given madrasa. Textbooks are written in Arabic and subjects include Logic, Mathematics and Astrology, Philosophy, Theology, Jurisprudence, Quranic exegesis, Rhetoric, and Grammar. Mullah Nasiruddin Tusi is said to have founded the first madrasa in 1067 in Baghdad and madrasas spread quickly, as did Islam itself.

Religious learning in Islam takes place in a variety of institutions. *Jamia* [colleges] and *darul uloom* [universities, literally, abodes of knowledge] which provide higher education. *Darul uloom* often approve of the establishment of affiliated madrasas from which prospective *darul uloom* students might apply for admission. At a local *musholla* [places for daily prayer] and *masjid* [mosques], children learn Arabic, passages of the Quran, and *Ahadith*, very often from madrasa graduates. A madrasa is distinguished from other religious schools in that it is residential.

A madrasa is sometimes characterized as a place where students endlessly and mindlessly recite the Quran. Recitation and memorization is a common pedagogical device. Indeed, to aid in their memorization, many standard madrasa textbooks are written in rhymed couplets. However, the Quran is not typically the principal text and madrasas rely heavily on books of *fiqh* [Islamic jurisprudence].

Often these lessons are not discussed or applied to real life situations. Unlike madrasas before the middle of the nineteenth century, contemporary madrasas in Pakistan do not provide sufficient education in *tafsir* [explanation] for graduates to understand and apply the meaning of the Quran and *Ahadith* [traditions of the Prophet] for the benefit of everyday life. The content of the curriculum and the pedagogy used deserves further study. Much material leaves the impression that madrasa education is based on doctrinal knowledge rather than knowledge to aid reasoning and on dichotomies (e.g., true and false beliefs).

Madrasas can differ significantly in the selection of texts, and of the authority of legal scholars on lawful and forbidden behaviour. Books of *fiqh* are books of ethics. The Prophet Muhammad (PBUH) received the word of Allah (Revelation) for twenty-three years and issued clarifications to fellow Muslims on Allah's path [*Shariah*]. After the Prophet's death, differences arose about the meaning of the Quran and about what was reported and remembered about what the Prophet himself did and said (i.e., *Sunnah*). Books of *fiqh* speculate—using logic, analogies, and precedence—on what would be permissible and forbidden behaviour for Muslims. The four major schools of Islamic jurisprudence—Hanafi, Hanbali, Shafi'i, and Malaki—agreeing to disagree—hold somewhat different beliefs about *fiqh*. Before the tenth century, even the renowned authors of today's orthodox book of *fiqh* did not regard their speculations as authoritative or as opposed in any way to others' speculations. A problem in the pedagogy of many madrasas is that even though the founders of the four schools considered other *fiqh* to be equally authentic and mutually acceptable, *fiqh* is taught as if it were divinely specified.

Parents send their children to madrasas for a variety of reasons. Many madrasas are free and they provide children with a place to sleep, meals as well as books and instruction. The most obvious reason for sending one's child to a madrasa is often overlooked: the opportunity to strengthen one's children's faith. It is important to many parents that their sons are pious Muslims. Parents also often want to teach their children *adab* [manners]. Parents of madrasa students express the hope that their children will learn to obey their elders and to be disciplined in life. Children are instructed in how to greet and converse with people of different ages and status and how to address family members and others respectfully.[6] Madrasas also provide protection from a vagrancy law under which thousands of Pakistani children are in jail.[7] Parents also hope that madrasa education will keep their children protected from gangs, drugs, and the violence of everyday life.[8] Madrasas often serve as care-providing institutions for parents who cannot take care of their children. All madrasas are single-sex institutions and most are for male students. One hundred thousand Pakistani girls and young women are students in female madrasas.[9]

National Education

Pakistan's educational system reflects a deeply divided society. The classes whose educational needs are served by the *ulema* are not the same classes as those who are served by the English-medium government schools. It is possible to identify six forms of education in Pakistan. Elite private English-medium schools serve the upper and upper middle classes. The middle classes send their children to the more affordable elite public English-medium schools or English-medium cadet colleges. Those in lower classes who can afford to pay something for their children's schooling send their children to low cost English-medium or Urdu medium schools. The poor who send their children to school can send their children to very low cost vernacular-medium (e.g., Sindhi or Punjabi) schools or send their boys to free madrasas.[10]

Madrasas largely educate children who are neglected by the national educational system. Nearly half of the country's primary school aged population—nearly 20 million children—does not attend school. Nearly one half of the children who do manage to enrol in first grade will not complete fifth grade. Many children of poor families are prevented from obtaining an education by the cost of uniforms, books, supplies, and transportation expenses. Many children are also driven-out of school by low educational standards and difficult conditions at school. Teacher absenteeism is high. Students report regular beatings at school.[11] Drop-out rates are more accurately thought of as push-out rates as Myron Weiner argued.[12] Pakistan's push-out rates are among the world's highest. Studies of school continuation rates find that the most significant factor leading to drop-out is the absence of teachers and classrooms.[13] Even where there are teachers and classrooms, the quality of education is very poor.

Public school teachers face great disincentives. Working and living conditions are difficult; pay is poor; and status is low.

Teachers typically teach a number of subjects and a number of different classes at the same time in the same classroom and there are few facilities. One-fifth of the country's primary schools have no facilities other than a chair, a mat, and a blackboard. Teachers are ranked at the bottom of the government employee scale[14] and this entails less than a living wage and professional embarrassment. According to Omar Noman, 'teachers salaries are frequently almost at par with domestic servants... a driver can earn more'.[15] Teachers receive no medical or transportation benefits and there are no avenues for promotion. There are no pension plans for most teachers and they are not permitted to form unions. There is a social stigma associated with the profession and many only choose the profession as a last chance at regular employment. Provincial governments have difficulty filling teaching positions with *bona fide* teachers.

The revival of electoral politics and imposition of structural adjustment policies between December 1988 and October 1999 did not have a positive impact on the educational crisis. When the military-appointed government handed over power to a Pakistan People's Party government in December 1988, it also handed over its commitment to International Monetary Fund economic austerity measures. Those measures helped to drag into poverty millions of agricultural labourers, subsistence farmers, low wage manufacturing workers, service sector workers, and their dependents. Although the gross national product (GNP) grew at a respectable 4.5 per cent per annum between 1991 and 1995, an additional 18 million—half the 1991 levels—people were ground into poverty (defined by minimum caloric intake).[16] At the same time, allocations to education by provincial governments, which largely fund social sector programmes, dropped precipitously between 1988 and 1991, both in constant prices and in per capita terms.[17]

A later infusion of funds did not improve government education. Expenditure on human development increased when the World Bank and the Aid to Pakistan Consortium committed major external funding to Pakistan's Social Action Programme in 1992. After 1996, provincial governments began to spend more than half of their budget on social sectors. The increased funds, however, did not improve education. Provincial governments built new schools but failed to staff them.[18] Many fictitious schools, especially primary and middle schools appeared in payrolls. Thinly populated villages may have more than one 'ghost school' which appears complete on paper but, on site, consists of empty, unfinished buildings. As Governor of Sindh, Moinuddin Haider estimated in December 1998, Sindh province alone had 19,000 'ghost teachers'.[19]

The provincial assembly members who were in charge of provincial education ministries are responsible for appointing teachers and principals throughout the country. Typically, a political connection is the chief criterion for appointment. Appointees are not necessarily capable of teaching or intending to teach. Rather, they accept an appointment with salary as a kind of political reward.

Decades of electoral politics and economic reforms since the late 1980s failed to make government more responsive to public educational needs. The assessment of teachers and principals is not made at the local level, and thereby, does not involve the communities where teachers and principals work. Parents are not given influence over the provision of public education. Military governments may do some things better than elected governments, but involving local groups in the management of public good is not one of them.

In the 1990s, the proportion of students in private schools increased nationally even while total enrollment and completion rates declined. Studies conducted by the Social Policy and Development Centre found that the public is both willing and able to pay for educational services.[20] Problems within Pakistani education are overwhelmingly in supply not in demand. It is not surprising that madrasas are most prevalent in the rural North West Frontier Province, Balochistan, rural Punjab and rural Sindh where the national (i.e., public) school system is most inaccessible or unlikely—given the structure of employment in the area—to guarantee against unemployment. Ulema have organized madrasas to fill an educational and a social vacuum, as well as to indoctrinate children in the ideology of the political parties to which they may be allied.

Access to education and the quality of educational opportunities are far worse in Pakistan than in countries with similar per capita income. The government's investment in education compares unfavourably even to countries with much lower real per capita income. Only four of the countries for which the United Nations Development Programme keeps data spent less of their total government expenditure on education.[21]

Like madrasas, private religious educational institutions in Pakistan have educated millions of students and like them these private religious schools are a part of Pakistan's *de facto* national education system. Individuals and groups have established a large number of private schools through trusts and foundations. According to Professor Ghafoor Ahmed, Deputy Chief of the Jamaat-i-Islami, the Nizamat-i-Islami, the Jamaat-i-Islami's education office oversees approximately 2,000 such private schools. These schools are affiliated with the Jamaat-i-Islami. Members of the Jamaat-i-Islami often privately establish trusts and associations that are not formally associated with the Jamaat-i-Islami or the Nizamat-i-Islami's 2,000 madrasas. These independent Jamaat-i-Islami schools solicit and collect funds, build and supply schools, hire and train teachers, and conduct their education on the basis of Jamaat-i-Islami thinking. The Green Crescent Trust operates dozens of such schools in Sindh.[22] The Rural Education and Development Program Trust operates more than 150 such schools in Azad Kashmir.[23] Males and females attend and teach in these schools. Indeed, most teachers are women.

Jamaat-i-Islami members claim that these programmes infuse the government curriculum with Islamic studies to favourably influence young people toward Jamaat-i-Islami ideology.[24] Their students take the national government examinations, unlike most madrasa students, and may go on to higher studies in public and private colleges and universities.

There is an important distinction between *ulema* and educators from Islamist political parties. *Ulema* do not necessarily see it as obligatory to struggle to establish an Islamic state. Many *ulema* are content to operate and educate within a specialized religious sphere that need not suddenly transform the current political system. An Islamist seeks the imposition of Islamic law on society.

Origins of Violent Sectarianism

Suspicion between government and religious authorities was the legacy of British rule in India. It did not, however, engender widespread *ulema* violence, even in response to repression of the Indian Revolt led by Muslim Sepoys in 1857. Violence was, as it is now, the means used by a very small (nevertheless threatening) group of militant utopians, violent 'revivalists'.

Some of the most obvious causes of sectarianism are the treatment of Muslim institutions under British rule; the creation of Pakistan as a 'homeland for Muslims'; the responses of some religious activists to the idea of Pakistan; Pakistani, United States, and Saudi government responses to the Soviet occupation of Afghanistan; and militarism within the national social science curriculum. Each of these forces of violent sectarianism deserves a detailed discussion. For our immediate purposes—to establish that these historical and political dynamics, not the madrasas' curriculum, promoted violent sectarianism—a brief survey must suffice.

After the Indian Revolt of 1857, madrasas became an outpost of learning to protect learned Muslims from Western colonial influences. Francis Robinson states 'Islamic knowledge was uncoupled from power' under the British.[25] When the British re-took Delhi and other cities in July 1857, they arrested the emperor and other rulers, destroyed Muslim institutions, demolished Muslim buildings, and expelled Muslim populations from their homes and major cities. Mosques were turned into army barracks and large swathes of Delhi and Lucknow, centres of Indian Muslim culture and learning, were leveled.[26] 'Do not go into the ruins of Delhi', warned Khwaja Altaf Husain in 1874. 'At every step priceless pearls lie buried beneath the dust'.[27] 'It was at this time, when Islam had lost its hold on power in India', according to Francis Robinson, 'that paradoxically the ulama were best placed to lead their fellow Muslims and to spread knowledge of their faith'.[28] The *ulema* spread this knowledge by establishing the *darul uloom*, the madrasa's predecessor.

A *darul uloom* in Aligarh and another in Deoband, each established in the United Provinces soon after the Mutiny, reflect two distinct responses by Muslims to the inescapable superiority of British military power in India. The Aligarh school was based on acceptance of British sovereignty and a focus on modern subjects, especially those subjects—principally the natural sciences—that had allowed the British to dominate the modern world.[29] Francis Robinson describes the Aligarh school as 'the [Muslim] elite's route to survival under the British'.[30] The *Darul uloom*, established by a group of 'reformist' Muslims in Deoband in 1867, in contrast, attempted to strengthen Islam by purging the *ummah* [Muslim community] of beliefs and practices that it regarded as un-Islamic. Soon, thereafter, a movement lead by Raza Ahmed Khan of Bareli, reaffirmed what the Deoband movement wanted to eliminate. These included visiting the graves of ancestors or revered teachers or offering prayers to ancestors and *pirs* [Muslim saints].[31] Differences between the Barelvi and the Deobandi in matters of worship and social practice demonstrated the opportunism of sectarianism. Inherent in the Deobandi madrasas—the most popular and widespread madrasas in Pakistan—is a deep suspicion of Westernized rulers, British or local, and of interference from the government.

Demographic changes caused by the creation of Pakistan had a powerful impact on Pakistani society. The creation of Pakistan brought about one of the twentieth century's greatest humanitarian disasters. Hundreds of thousands of people were killed, more than twelve million people were displaced, communities and families were torn apart. That division—and the other-worldly legalistic logic behind it—made questions about the appropriate system of government for Pakistan—the hard-won homeland for Muslims—all the more important and all the more difficult to answer. The *ulema* of the Jamaat-i-Islami and Deoband gained ascendance in Pakistan.

The politicization of Islam was inherent in the very notion of Pakistan. The religious violence that precipitated, accompanied, and followed Pakistan's creation raised serious questions about the meaning of Islam in Pakistan. Pakistan was made possible by a political strategy that articulated the need for a homeland for Indian Muslims (on the basis of religion) but did not articulate any parameters for this new community.[32] That the movement for Pakistan centred on Mohammad Ali Jinnah, a modern, Western-educated Muslim attorney, was enough for the Jamaat-i-Islami and others to oppose the creation of Pakistan. Maududi and leaders of other Islamist parties argued that Muslims left behind in a divided India would be vulnerable. They believed that the leadership of Pakistan would be antithetical to Islam. They also held that the *ummah* [community of believers] already constituted a nation that would only be divided by partition.

Abul A'ala Maududi published the *Tarjuman al-Quran* in 1931 to promote his understanding of Islam, which differed both with that of the Deobandi *ulema* and with that of the modern Muslims in the All India Muslim League. Maududi opposed the creation of Pakistan. In 1941, the year after the adoption of the All India Muslim League's resolution (at the Lahore session) in favour of Pakistan, Maududi founded the Jamaat-i-Islami and became its *Amir* [Chief]. Deobandi *ulema* organized the Jamiat-Ulema-Islam in 1945. While otherwise opposed to the Jamaat-i-Islami, Husain Ahmad Madani, the head of the Deoband madrasas, also opposed the creation of a separate state for Muslims because it would leave the Muslims in India even more vulnerable.[33]

With the precipitous creation of this most complex of human products, the state, those *ulema* who were opposed to Pakistan's creation turned their attention to the struggle for a state that was guided by Islamic teaching. After the creation of Pakistan, Maududi and the Jamaat-i-Islami demanded an Islamic Constitution. Maududi persuaded his followers that Muslims suffered economic servitude and political occupation because they were not living properly as Muslims and that the prescription for Islamic revival was control of the state by a *khilafat* [righteous leader].[34] According to Abul A'ala Maududi:

The root of all the evils you find in the world lies in the bad character of government.... The real objective of Islam is to remove the lordship of man over man and to establish the kingdom of God on Earth. To stake one's life and everything else to achieve this purpose is called *jihad* [struggle] while *salah* [prayer], fasting, *hajj* [pilgrimage to Mecca], and *zakat* [charity] are all meant as a preparation for this task.[35]

The Objectives Resolution was the compromise designed to placate the Jamaat-i-Islami and others who demanded that the government adopt *Shariah* as the law of the state. The first paragraph of the Objectives Resolution, adopted by the Constituent Assembly in 1949, declares that sovereignty over the entire universe belongs to Allah Almighty alone and the authority which He has delegated to the State of Pakistan through its people for being exercised within the limits prescribed by Him is a sacred trust.[36] The Objectives Resolution clearly places the authority of the state with Allah, not the people whom the state serves.

Religious political parties continued their campaign to ensure that the State took a commanding role over politics. The Jamaat-i-Islami launched the campaign in 1953 in Punjab against the Ahmadi community, which lead to thousands of deaths in Jamaat-i-Islami clashes with police. The military acted to contain sectarianism and Martial Law was declared in Punjab under Martial Law Administrator, General Azam Khan, to prevent sectarian policies as a response to street violence.

The major religious political parties of today—in a field of sixteen at last count—emerged by the 1960s. The three major Sunni political parties are the Jamaat-i-Islami, the Jamiat-i-Ulema-i-Islam, and the Jamiat-i-Ulema-i-Islam Pakistan. The Jamiat-i-Ulema-i-Islam is now divided into three groups, that of faction leaders Samiul Haq of the Haqqania madrasa, Fazlur Rahman, and Ajmal Qadri.[37]

The political party-based madrasas are a relatively recent phenomenon in South Asia. Militant madrasas were established with the mission of organizing resistance to the Soviets in Afghanistan after the Soviet invasion in December 1979.[38] These madrasas grew, as did the refugee community, which sent their boys for education in madrasas, if they were fortunate enough to find a place, especially as a boarding student, in any school. Generally, it is political party scholars, not the *ulema*, who run these madrasas.

Not only political parties, but also Pakistan's governments (from the 1970s until 1999) have been major catalysts of sectarianism. Zulfikar Ali Bhutto, prime minister from 1972 until July 1977, did not politicize Islam as much as his successor, General Ziaul Haq, who imposed professedly Islamic injunctions on law and society. Bhutto did, however, set a precedent for capitulating to the demands of Islamists. To distinguish itself from Field Marshal Ayub Khan's government (since 1958), Bhutto's Pakistan People's Party managed to articulate a popularly appealing vision of Islamic social justice. Once in office, Bhutto worked to destroy organizations that could rival him. In 1973, Bhutto used the language of the Objectives Resolution to placate his detractors in the religious parties. Bhutto's 1973 constitution begins with the same language as the Resolution:

> Whereas sovereignty over the entire Universe belongs to Almighty Allah alone, and the authority to be exercised by the people of Pakistan within the limits prescribed by him is a sacred trust.[39]

In 1974, Bhutto consented to the Jamaat-i-Islami's long-standing demand that Ahmadis be officially declared non-Muslim and the PPP controlled National Assembly passed an act to that effect. Bhutto managed to sanction the 'Islamization' of law and public policy and unite the religious opposition. At the very end of his rule, after the contested 1977 elections in which the PPP captured 155 of the 173 contested seats with 80 per cent voter turn-out, Bhutto gave concessions to Islamic political parties, including changing the weekly holiday from Sunday to Friday and banning the sale and consumption of alcohol. The Pakistan National Alliance (PNA), which included the major religious political parties, successfully boycotted the March 1977 provincial assembly polls. Bhutto agreed, in negotiations with the PNA that had originally paralyzed the country with protests demanding his resignation, to constitute a body to hold new elections and manage the transition.

However, it was too late to prevent Bhutto's Chief of Army Staff, General Ziaul Haq, from removing him from office.

General Ziaul Haq used Islam to 'disarm' his adversaries.[40] While Bhutto's successor was known to be a devout Muslim, General Zia manipulated Islamic associations in ways that continue to have unwelcome effects on the role of *ulema* in society. The military government promoted violent sectarianism by promulgating ordinances and taking administrative actions that favoured any one school or sect's interpretation of the Quran or *Ahadith* or it's opinion on social policy. The overwhelming benefactor of Zia's sectarian policies' was the Jamaat-i-Islami.[41]

Zia promoted the Shia–Sunni conflict. The Zakat and Ushr Ordinance, promulgated in 1979 and still in effect today, directed banks to make annual withdrawals from personal savings accounts for distribution by government Zakat Boards to select charities and madrasas, the overwhelming majority of which were Sunni-based. The promulgation of the Ordinance displeased the minority Shia community, which demonstrated against it until an exception was made for Shias who then formed an organization to protect the community from future ordinances of a similar kind. The Zia government is alleged to have split that organization, the Tehrik-i-Jafria, by sponsoring a faction within it and by assassinating the popularly recognized leader.[42] The Tehrik-i-Jafria is one of the two political organizations that was identified as a terrorist organization and banned by General Pervez Musharraf, then Chief Executive, in January 2002.

In 1979, Zia began to promote 'Islamization'. He established the Federal Shariat Court to test for repugnancy to Islam. Zia also enhanced the authority of the Islamic Ideology Council to recommend policies and laws in accordance with Islam and to advise on whether any policies or laws were repugnant to Islam. Zia then promulgated a series of ordinances, commonly known as the Hudood Ordinances in 1979. These included the *Zina* [illicit sex] Ordinance, the Prohibition Order [related to alcohol], the Offence Against Property Ordinance [related to theft], the Offence of *Qazf* Order [false accusation of *zina*]. In 1984, Zia held a national referendum in which support for his continued rule was conflated with support for Islam. In addition to fostering militancy in religious political parties and in imposing his government's authority in civil and criminal law as if it were the authority of Islam itself, Zia introduced 'Islamization' in the armed services. Zia promoted distribution among soldiers of passages from the Quran on Islam and the conduct of war and appointed *qazis* to military units.[43]

The US government also conflated military and religious activities. The United States used madrasas and Islamic teachings to promote militancy during the war against the Soviet Union in Afghanistan. With more than $51 million in US Agency for International Development funding, between 1984 and 1994, the Centre for Afghanistan Studies at the University of Nebraska, Omaha, developed textbooks that gave religious sanction to armed struggle in defence of Islam. Thirteen million volumes were distributed.[44] Other agencies of the United States government also promoted a militant version of Islam.

The relationship between the military and the madrasas continues to be complex, combining elements of deep mutual suspicion and of explicit and implicit cooperation.[45] A large part of the violence and intolerance emanating from religious political parties must be ascribed to the use of religious institutions by government agencies within and from outside Pakistan for military ends.

Madrasa Reform Initiatives

Many *ulema* think that madrasa reform is necessary to sustain the true meaning and social relevance of Islam. Many *ulema* and religious educators would like to see curriculum reform in madrasas. Many *ulema* have argued against militant interpretations of the Quran and *Ahadith*.[46] They see radical reformation of madrasas to be essential to the propagation and continued relevance of Islam. To advance Islam without sectarianism, some *ulema* and Islamic educators have introduced reforms in their own madrasas while some have opened new madrasas or *jamia* or *darul uloom*. Similarly, others have established private schools. There is broad support among *ulema* and educators today for more progressive Islamic education in madrasas and in other places of religious instruction.

A number of *ulema* and other educators are attempting to initiate madrasa reformation. They note that madrasas suffer from serious pedagogical problems and these reformers are particularly critical of the narrow and doctrinal way in which *fiqh* [jurisprudence] is taught. Mohammad Farooq Khan, for example, notes that the leading *fiqh* sourcebook used in the madrasas, *Kitab ul Fiqh*, devotes nearly 100 pages of dense text to how to perform *wudu* [ablution], arguing at length over where the face ends and the forehead and neck begin and students may spend two months mastering the passage. Much of what passes for *fiqh* education in the madrasas, progressive Muslims argue, is entirely unrelated to Islamic law, distracts students from their relationship to Allah, and makes a mockery of Islamic teachings.[47] They advocate a focus on the Quran and its relevance for contemporary law and society and many *ulema* have drawn the conclusion that madrasas need to be reformed to ensure the survival of Islam.

The Federal Minister for Religious Affairs in Musharraf's government proposed to create model madrasas in each of Pakistan's four provinces and in the federal area of Islamabad. Model madrasas were established in Islamabad, Karachi, and Sukkur. The Federal Minister for Religious Affairs developed materials for them. An accomplished graduate of one of Pakistan's most progressive madrasas is leading the model madrasas in Karachi. The model madrasas in Islamabad and Sukkur are developing but more slowly.

The model madrasas experiment is a remarkable success but will require decades to grow to substitute for the tens of thousands of existing madrasas. By late August 2004—twenty-six months after the Ordinance's promulgation—forty madrasas had affiliated with the Madrasas Education Board. Students in these schools were eligible for bi-annual tuition and personal expense allowances of Rs 500 (US$8.62). To collect this sum, parents are required to produce a certificate verifying their status as *mustahiqeen* [deserving poor], and thereby, their eligibility for *zakat* funds. Islam cautions against seeking *zakat*; and Muslims, generally, would prefer not to have the status of *mustahiqeen*.

The timing of the Ordinance works against its chances of effective implementation. The Indian Parliament was attacked in December 2001 and the government of India blamed Pakistan for the attack. In the 11 post-September 2001 environment, India demanded that Pakistan close all militant training camps under threat of pre-emptive strikes. In response, Musharraf declared a ban on two sectarian organizations—the anti-Shia Sipah-i-Sahaba Pakistan and the Shia Tehrik-i-Jafria—and placed controls on the madrasas to prevent their use for sectarian purposes.

The Deeni Madrasas (Regulation and Control) Ordinance was one of the ordinances issued by Musharraf in a compromise with the MMA over the Legal Framework Ordinance (LFO). The Madrasas Ordinance gives the choice to all madrasas to register with the Pakistan Madrasas Education Board. Madrasas registered with the Pakistan Madrasas Education Board are given preference in distribution of *zakat* scholarships granted by the Ministry of Religious Affairs. It is ultimately the madrasa teachers who will effect (or prevent) reform not government officials. Pedagogical and curricular improvements need to be designed and implemented by the *ulema*. The instrumental use of madrasas by the United States and Pakistan governments in the 1980s caused many *ulema* to regard government reform initiatives with suspicion.

The government already has the authority to close down madrasas that do not comply with registration requirements. But neither closing them down nor threatening to do so will scare the *ulema* into providing financial, curricular, and enrollment information to the government. The Societies Registration Act of 1860 already requires madrasas to register with and provide financial disclosure to provincial governments; and government aid is contingent upon such registration and disclosure. The threat of an end to public funding will only confirm, again, the *ulema*'s sense that dependence on government funding invites interference. They do not want to be audited and private contributions, given in the Islamic spirit of generosity to the needy, will be seen as the only dependable source of funding.

This is not the first government that attempted such reforms. Ayub Khan and Ziaul Haq constituted committees with government and *ulema* representatives in 1962 and 1979, respectively.[48] Pervez Musharraf's Ordinance was designed and announced without consultation with the *ulema* and they believe that the Ordinance was announced at the behest of the United States. With US armed forces in Afghanistan and Iraq and the perception in Pakistan that the US government is discriminating against Muslims in the US and launching unprovoked military attacks on Muslim countries, mistrust of the US government and its initiatives (real or perceived) is at an all time low.

The conflict between government officials and *ulema* can be transformed by a more mutually respectful relationship. Many religious leaders including Qazi Hussain Ahmad, the Chief of the Jamaat-i-Islami regard many government officials as corrupt, immoral, and stooges of anti-Islamic foreign powers. However, the government's approach to the madrasas and *ulema* is not always well informed and is often unnecessarily heavy-handed.

Some *ulema* argue that the latest reforms will fail, not because the madrasas are not in need of a more socially relevant curriculum, but because the reforms were designed and implemented without consultation with *ulema* and are directed by government officials who do not have a passable understanding of the madrasas' curriculum and atmosphere.[49]

It is still too early—less than three years since the cabinet approved passage of the Madrasas Ordinance—to pronounce the madrasas' reformation initiative successful or unsuccessful. The Model Deeni Madrasa in Karachi is thriving. Realistically, however, ground-up ('green-field') madrasa reformation on a national scale could take generations. Effective reformation will require meaningful participation by *ulema*. To accomplish this, both the *ulema* and the governmental officials responsible for the reforms must find ways to reduce their mutual animosity. In the past, *ulema* have worked with the government to improve education in madrasas.[50] However, today especially, reform or innovation in the curriculum at the insistence of the federal government is unwelcome to many *ulema*. Discussions and cooperation between education officials and *ulema* that can lay a real foundation for broad improvement in the madrasas' curriculum will need to focus on rebuilding trust rather than resolving outstanding questions about religious education. For example, parents in more conservative areas are more likely to send their daughters to madrasa schools to study religious subjects than to a government school. Some *ulema* have established educational programmes for girls with that advantage in mind without having won the argument in an official committee that women have rights to education.

One proposal for reform is to institute a curriculum change that emphasizes science. The thought is to bring about social change by adding science as a means of insulating students from religious radicalism. However, education in the sciences will not necessarily promote a modern, progressive orientation that will insulate students from radical tendencies. Madrasa students are not among the ranks of suicide bombers. Indeed, many of the most enthusiastic militants are university graduates in the natural sciences. There is no evidence that an education in the sciences ensures students will not become militants.

Efforts to reform madrasas in Pakistan might learn from similar efforts in other predominantly Muslim countries. The religious association that has overseen *pesantren*, the counterpart of madrasas in Indonesia, has struggled to maintain independence from state power. The choice of *mazhab*, use of *fiqh*, history of the relationship between colonial rule, independence, and religious associations is widely different. It is significant, however, that in Indonesia the graduates of religious schooling are versed in many topics, literate in Arabic, Javanese (or their native language), Indonesian, and experienced in critical debate. In Indonesia, and other countries, *ulema* have an effective and sometimes critical role in promoting democracy, human rights, and social justice from an Islamic foundation.

Conclusions

Militancy can be reduced. The roots of militancy in Pakistani society, however, do not lie within institutions for Islamic education. Some of the roots of militancy in Pakistani society are as old as the British colonial responses to political movements, Muslim educational institutions, and other sites of social power not controlled by the state. Some of the roots of militancy are as recent as the Soviet invasion of Afghanistan and the Pakistan, United States, and Saudi Arabia arming and funding of self-professed *mujahideen.*

The importance that the madrasa system has obtained is largely a reflection of the government's failure to provide education to its citizens. It is not mandatory for parents to send their children to school. Nor could the government implement such a policy should it wish to do so without massive new investments, new management of schools and teachers, and an overhaul of the present public education system.[51] The greatest threat to personal security and social stability is not the narrow religious curriculum taught in the madrasas but the government's nearly complete neglect of citizen's basic universal rights, including the right to an education.

The madrasas are in need of new reforms, not because they can equip students with justifications for violence but because they are trying to perform a vital role in society—national education of poor and excluded segments of society—with institutions designed to preserve Islamic knowledge rather than to provide general or vocational education. Governments have a moral obligation to provide basic education so that people can lead meaningful and useful lives. Because education is the primary means to a full and gainful life, education is a basic human right.[52]

The consequences of a politically motivated instrumental approach to education are evident in the manner in which the major sponsors of militant teaching are now some of its chief targets. The governments of the United States and Pakistan embraced militant associations and teachings when these could be used to train militants to fight the Soviets and their allies in Afghanistan. Few opposed the policy at the time because their concern was only with using madrasas to defeat the Soviets in Afghanistan. The United States did not address concerns about the long-term security consequences of arming and funding known militant religious revivalists.[53] It is not clear to militant *ulema* why fighting the other superpower should not now be similarly embraced.

Madrasas and private religious schools are addressing a widespread need as poor parents have very limited educational options. Successful madrasa reformation ultimately rests on the successful reformation of the entire system of public education. Schools will not merely need to be free, they will need to provide additional incentives that may off-set the cost of not having one's children work—such as free meals, primary health care, uniforms, and books. A better public education system could reduce the socially and politically destabilizing class inequalities that are promoted by the vast difference in private (especially English medium) and public school quality in Pakistan.

In the present climate of deep suspicion of US government designs for Pakistan, it would be counter-productive for effective educational reform in Pakistan if the US government is perceived to be involved. Anti-Americanism in Pakistan is high but sufficient funding and other support for the construction of a national educational system in Pakistan are, nonetheless, required.

Notes

1. I am grateful to Ghafoor Ahmed, Abdul Baqi Farooqi, Satish Bindra, Shehzad Chishti, Suleiman Gul, Abdul Jalil Jan, Niamatullah Khan, Tahseenullah Khan, Mohammad Farooq Khan, Meera Khan, Siraj Khilji, Niaz Mohammad, Allah Rabani, and Shehzad Saleem for interviews and assistance in the preparation of this chapter, and to each of them and to Roxanne Euben, Charles Kennedy, and Cynthia Botteron for helpful comments on earlier drafts.
2. Estimate of madrasa enrollment by former Minister for Religious Affairs, Mahmood Ahmed Ghazi, in an interview in April 2002 with International Crisis Group. International Crisis Group 'Pakistan: Madrasas, Extremism and the Military', Asia Report No. 36, (Islamabad: International Crisis Group,) p. 2. Proportion of school-going population calculated from Government of Pakistan, *Pakistan Economic Survey 1994-95*, Islamabad: Government of Pakistan, 1995, 212, which puts primary, secondary, and vocational combined male and female enrollment at just over 18 million.
3. This essay largely leaves aside the religiously affiliated private foundations, trust, and charities and their schools, which number in the thousands and have a nation-wide reach. These schools prepare students to pass national matriculation examinations but also infuse their curriculum with an Islamic education, often with beliefs unique to a political party or sect of Islam. This is an important and understudied phenomenon.

4. On education for religious intolerance, see the analysis of government social science curriculum by Khurshid Hasanain and A.H. Nayyar, 'Conflict and Violence in the Educational Process in Pakistan', in Zia Mian and Iftikar Ahmad, eds., *Making Enemies, Creating Conflict: Pakistan's Crises of State and Society*, (Lahore: Mashal: 1997), pp. 129-146.

5. For details on Islamic education in pre-modern South Asia, see Aziz Ahmed, *Islamic Surveys 7* (Edinburgh: Edinburgh University Press, 1969), pp. 52-57.

6. Shaikh Allah Rabani, Jamia Banuria Masjid, Karachi, interview, 3 January 2000.

7. Myron Weiner and Omar Noman, *The Child and the State in India and Pakistan*, (Oxford: Oxford University Press, 1993).

8. Ibid.

9. Qibla Ayaz, Dean and Professor of Seerat Studies, Centre for Islamic and Oriental Studies, University of Peshawar, Peshawar interview, August 13, 2004.

10. Tariq Rahman, 'Worlds Apart: An Opinion Survey', *News* (12 May 2000), p. 4.

11. Donald Warwick and Fernando Reimers, *Hope or Despair? Learning in Pakistan's Primary Schools*, (Westport: London, 1995), pp. 19-22.

12. Myron Weiner and Omar Noman, *The Child and the State in India and Pakistan*, 71.

13. Social Policy and Development Centre, *Review of the Social Action Program*, (Karachi: SPDC, June 1997), vii.

14. Warwick and Reimers, *Hope or Despair?*, pp. 29-41.

15. Omar Noman, 'Primary Education in Pakistan', in Weiner and Noman, *The Child and the State in India and Pakistan*, (Karachi: Oxford University Press, 1995), p. 258.

16. Mahbub ul Haq reported an increase in the poverty rate over the period from 20% to 30% of the total population. Mahbub ul Haq and Khadija Haq, *Human Development in South Asia 1998* (Oxford: Human Development Centre, 1998), p. 17.

17. World Bank, Country Operations Division, South Asia Region, *Pakistan: Poverty Assessment*, (Washington, DC: World Bank, 25 September 1995), pp. 68-69.

18. Aisha Ghaus-Pasha, et al., *Social Development in Pakistan*, p. 40.

19. 'Sindh has 19, 000 ghost teachers', *Dawn*, (December 1, 1998), p. 3.

20. Zafar Ishmail and Asif Iqbal, *User Charges in Education* (Islamabad: Social Policy and Development Center, 1994).

21. United Nations Development Programme, *Human Development Report 2004*, (New York: Oxford University Press, 2004), pp. 172-175. In 1999-2001, the latest year for which figures are available, only Equatorial Guinea (1.6), Greece (7.0), Guinea-Bissau (4.8), and Panama (7.5) spent a smaller percentage of total government expenditure on education than Pakistan (7.8).

22. Siraj Khilji, Central Working Committee, Center for Educational Research and Development, and Shehzad Chishti, Chief, Nizamati Islami, Jamaat-i-Islami, Sindh Province, Karachi, interview, 26 June 1999.
23. See David Lelyveld, *Aligarh's First Generation: Muslim Solidarity in British India* (Princeton: Princeton University Press, 1978).
24. Abrara Ahmed, Director, Shafi Reso-Chem and Treasurer and Member Central Working Committee, Green Crescent Trust, and Zahid Saeed, Managing Director, Indus Pharma and Chairman, Central Working Committee, Green Crescent Trust, Karachi, interview, 29 June 1999.
25. Francis Robinson, 'Knowledge, Its Transmission, and the Making of Muslim Societies', in Francis Robinson, ed., *Cambridge Illustrated History of the Islamic World*, (London: Cambridge University Press, 1996) p. 242.
26. On the impact on Muslims of the suppression of Indian Mutiny, see Francis Robinson, 'The Muslims of Upper India and the Shock of the Mutiny', in Francis Robinson, *Islam and Muslim History in South Asia*, (New Delhi: Oxford University Press, 2000), pp. 138-155.
27. Ibid, p. 149.
28. Ibid.
29. See David Lelyveld, *Aligarh's First Generation: Muslim Solidarity in British India*, (Princeton: Princeton University Press, 1978).
30. Francis Robinson, 'Nineteenth-Century Indian Islam', in Francis Robinson, *Islam and Muslim History in South Asia*, p. 240.
31. See Barbara Metcalf, *Islamic Revival in British India: Deoband 1860-1900*, (Princeton: Princeton University Press, 1982).
32. Ayesha Jalal, *The Sole Spokesman: Jinnah, the Muslim League and the Demand for Pakistan*, (Cambridge: Cambridge University Press, 1985).
33. Faruqi, *Pakistan: A Crisis in the Renaissance of Islam*, p. 179.
34. See Zafaryab Ahmed, 'Maudoodi's Islamic State', in Asghar Khan, ed., *Islam, Politics and the State, The Pakistan Experience*, (London: Zed Books, 1985).
35. Syed Abul A'la Maududi, *Fundamentals of Islam* (Lahore: Islamic Publications, 1975), p. 243.
36. Government of Pakistan, Federal Judicial Academy, *The Constitution of the Islamic Republic of Pakistan*, (Islamabad: Government of Pakistan, 1989), p. 211.
37. International Crisis Group, 'Pakistan: Madrasas, Extremism and the Military', p. 6.
38. See Mumtaz Ahmad, 'Continuity and Change in the Traditional System of Islamic Education: The Case of Pakistan', in Charles Kennedy and Craig Baxter, eds., *Pakistan 2000* (Karachi: Oxford University Press, 2000), pp. 182-194 and Husain Haqqani, 'Islam's Medieval Outposts', *Foreign Policy*, (November-December 2002), pp. 68-64.
39. Government of Pakistan, *The Constitution of the Islamic Republic of Pakistan*, p. 1.

40. Abbas Rashidi, 'Pakistan: The Ideological Dimension', in Asghar Khan, ed., *Islam, Politics and the State, The Pakistan Experience*, (London: Zed Books, 1985).

41. Mumtaz Ahmad, 'Islamic Fundamentalism in South Asia', in Martin Marty and Scott Appleby, eds., *Fundamentalisms Observed* (Chicago: The University of Chicago Press), 1991).

42. For details see Azhat Abbas, 'Sectarianism: The Players and the Game', (Islamabad: South Asia Partnership, February 2002), pp. 7-9.

43. Owen Bennett Jones, *Pakistan: Eye of the Storm*, (Lahore: Vanguard, 2002), p. 253.

44. Joe Stephens and David Ottaway, 'The ABCs of Jihad in Afghanistan: Violent Soviet-Era Textbooks Complicate Afghan Education Efforts', *The Washington Post*, (23 March 2002), A01. Cited in International Crisis Group, 'Pakistan: Madrasas, Extremism, and the Military', p. 13.

45. International Crisis Group, 'Pakistan: Madrasas, Extremism and the Military', p. 3

46. See, for example, Nazir Sadiq, 'Jehad vs. Terrorism: In perspective of Kashmir issue', n.p, n.d. Sadiq argues, against Maulana Fazal Mohammad, that the private Muslim armies are un-Islamic.

47. Mohammad Farooq Khan, President Dainish Sara, Mardan, interview, 1 January 2003.

48. See Muhammad Qasim Zaman, 'Religious Education and the Rhetoric of Reform: The Madrasas in British India and Pakistan', *Comparative Studies in Society and History*, 41: 2, (April 1999) and Muhammad Qasim Zaman, *The Ulama in Contemporary Islam: Custodians of Change* (Princeton: Princeton University Press, 2002).

49. Abdul Jalil Jan, Secretary of Information, Jamiat-Ulema-i-Islam, Northwest Frontier Province, Peshawar, interview, 31 December 2002, Niaz Mohammad, Principal, Karachi Model Deeni Madrasas, Karachi, interview, 4 January 2003, and Abdul Baqi Farooqi, Madrasas Talimul, Karachi, interview, 4 January 2003.

50. For details on some of the policies and programs since 1953 to establish government madrasas see R.A. Farooq, *Education System in Pakistan: Issues and Problems* (Islamabad: Asia Society for Promotion of Innovation and Reform in Education, 1994), pp. 57-69.

51. See further Christopher Candland, 'Institutional Impediments to Human Development in Pakistan', in Amita Shastri and A. Jeyaratnam Wilson, eds., *The Post-Colonial States of South Asia: Democracy, Development, and Identity* (London: Curzon Press, 2001).

52. See further Jean Dréze and Amartya Sen, 'Education as a Basic Right' in *India: Economic Development and Social Opportunity* revised edition (New York: Oxford University Press, 2002).

53. Christopher Candland, *The Afghan Crisis* (New York: Church World Service, 1988).

CHRONOLOGY OF EVENTS: 12 OCTOBER 1999–SEPTEMBER 2004

Kathleen Mcneil

12 October 1999 Military commanders oust the Nawaz Sharif government, installing General Pervez Musharraf as the country's chief executive. The coup is achieved without bloodshed and receives only mild condemnation from domestic or international political actors. As a consequence the British Commonwealth suspends Pakistan's membership in the organization.

12–17 October 1999 Ministers of the Sharif government are put under house arrest and Nawaz Sharif, along with his brother and son, are incarcerated. Most are released after 17 October, but Sharif remains in government custody.

17 October 1999 Musharraf addresses the nation and claims that the objectives of the new military government are to reduce provincial disharmony, revive the economy, ensure law and order, and reduce corruption through accountability measures.

10 November 1999 Nawaz Sharif and others are charged with conspiracy for alleged efforts to murder General Musharraf through a plane hijacking. Evidence is heard against the accused in an anti-terrorism court set up by the new Musharraf regime. A verdict is not reached until 6 April 2000.

17 November 1999 The newly created National Accountability Bureau (NAB) indicts forty-seven individuals on charges of corruption and wilful loan default. Many members of both the Sharif and Bhutto families are among those indicted.

24–31 December 1999 Five Kashmiri separatists hijack an Indian airliner and take the 189 passengers on board hostage. The Airbus A-300, which was scheduled to travel from Kathmandu to New Delhi, lands in Lahore and then continues to Dubai where twenty-seven passengers are released and the rest remain aboard to travel to Kandahar. The Indian government agrees to release three Kashmiris in their custody in exchange for the release of the hostages, and the hijackers escape arrest. In response to the hijacking, India reinforces troops in Kashmir and tensions mount in the region.

17 January 2000 A bombing in Karachi kills twelve people and injures twenty-two others.

25 January 2000 The Chief Justice of Pakistan, Saiduzzaman Siddique, along with five other Supreme Court justices, resigns in protest after the Musharraf regime requires them to affirm (through a new oath of office) the legality of the regime's constitutional abeyance or step down.

January 2000 The Human Rights Commission of Pakistan releases a report entitled 'The Dimensions of Violence' that catalogues the increasing violence perpetrated against women in the Lahore area. 'Between January and November 1999, 675 women were murdered, 272 died or suffered from burn injuries, 597 were raped, and 713 were kidnapped'.

February 2000 Tensions heighten between Pakistan and India. After India announces that it will be testing a submarine launched nuclear-capable missile, Pakistan tests a short range ballistic missile on 7 February. After three Indian security men are killed by militants, remaining Indian forces riot in the streets of Srinagar; civilians suffer beatings and arson and thousands flee the area. On

18 February, India expels Pakistani diplomats. Violence continues along the LoC.

1 March 2000 India increases defence budget by 28 percent citing 'security situation'.

9 March 2000 The Musharraf government announces that it is forming a permanent commission on the status of women to make policy recommendations concerning women's rights.

10 March 2000 Iqbal Raad, Nawaz Sharif's defence lawyer is killed by an unknown assailant.

13 March 2000 Amid continued violence in Kashmir, both Indian Prime Minister Vajpayee and Pakistani leader Pervez Musharraf assure the international community that the two countries are not on the brink of a nuclear conflict.

25 March 2000 Bill Clinton, President of the United States, visits Pakistan at the end of a six-day tour of South Asia. During his five- day stay in India' he praises the country and offers his friendship. In contrast, his visit to Pakistan lasts only a few hours and sends a firm warning that Pakistan may find itself isolated if it fails to stem terrorist activities within and around its borders.

March 2000 Extreme drought continues in areas of Sindh and Balochistan. Large numbers of villagers suffer from dehydration and other health problems related to hunger and a lack of water for drinking and hygiene. Many die.

6 April 2000 Nawaz Sharif, the recently deposed Prime Minister of Pakistan, is found guilty of conspiracy to commit murder by an anti-terrorism court; he is sentenced to life imprisonment.

17 April 2000 Zafran Bibi is sentenced to death by stoning by a local court under the Hudood Ordinance. She had been raped but was accused of *zina* (illicit sexual relations) after it had became apparent that she had become pregnant while her husband was in jail.

30 April 2000 The United States Department of State releases a report on international terrorism that identifies Pakistan and Afghanistan as areas of significant terrorist activity. The report argues that the struggle in Kashmir is promoting terrorist activity.

3 May 2000 Seven Christian girls are attacked and gang-raped on their way home from factory work in a rural area north of Lahore. The perpetrators are charged with 'petty dacoity'.

27 May 2000 The government initiates a survey by which it plans to document business and residential properties for tax purposes. Nation-wide strikes are staged in protest of the survey.

9 June 2000 Several trade groups reach an agreement with tax authorities. Strikes dissipate over the next week. However, sporadic clashes between merchants and police continue into July.

17 June 2000 India successfully tests a short-range surface to surface missile. Pakistan says it will not reciprocate in order to avoid escalating hostilities.

22 July 2000 The National Accountability Court sentences Nawaz Sharif to a fourteen year prison sentence and bans him from holding political office for twenty-one years.

25 July 2000 Hizbul Mujahideen (a dominant Kashmiri separatist group) announces a unilateral cease-fire in Kashmir in order to revive the peace process.

3 August 2000 General Musharraf invites India to have a dialogue with Pakistan about Kashmir 'anywhere, at any place, at any level'.

10 August 2000 The cease-fire breaks down in Kashmir after India refuses to allow Pakistan to attend planned talks and 100 people are killed in a bombing blamed on the Lashkar-i-Tayyaba.

August 2000 The government establishes a National Commission on the Status of Women to examine violence against women, yet fails to intervene as a violent campaign against women's NGOs continues in the North West Frontier Province.

7 September 2000 In a press conference, Pervez Musharraf reiterates that there can be no peace without a solution to the Kashmir crisis which he says has been 'denied resolution since 1948'.

4 October 2000 Dr Younas Sheikh is arrested on charges of blasphemy after allegedly making derogatory comments about the Prophet Mohammad (PBUH) during a lecture given at the Homeopathic College in Islamabad where he (Dr Sheikh) was a teacher.

12 October 2000 The Supreme Court gives a decision that justifies the Musharraf regime's military coup on the grounds that the military had acted out of state necessity. The decision gives the regime three years to restore order and return power to a democratic civilian government.

30 October 2000 An Ahmadi mosque in Ghatalian Village is attacked by Sunni extremists. Five worshippers are killed and ten others are seriously injured.

26 November 2000 India announces a ceasefire in Kashmir for the Muslim fasting month of Ramadan. Pakistan replies by ordering its troops to 'exercise maximum restraint on the Line of Control'.

9 December 2000 The Sharif family is exiled from Pakistan in exchange for their promising not to participate in politics for the next ten years. The exile, and the accompanying pardon for the remainder of their sentences, was granted after Nawaz Sharif filed a petition for mercy.

31 December 2000 The first phase of the local bodies elections takes place. Elected officials will take office in August after all the local bodies elections have taken place.

December 2000 The Indian ceasefire in disputed Kashmir is extended for an additional month after Ramadan and is again extended at the end of December. Pakistan responds by withdrawing some of its troops from the line of control.

12 January 2001 The UN High Commissioner for Refugees reports that the drought and increased numbers of refugees travelling from Afghanistan into Pakistan are creating famine conditions and a humanitarian crisis.

25 January 2001 A major earthquake devastates India and Pakistan's Thar Desert regions. Thousands of homes, schools, and wells are damaged.

28 January 2001 Six men are shot dead and fourteen wounded when they are attacked by unidentified assailants in Karachi. Mourners riot, setting vehicles on fire, beating police, and damaging property.

9 February 2001 As 80,000 Afghan refugees wait at the border in wretched conditions, Pakistan turns down the UNHCR request to open an additional camp and keeps its borders closed claiming that it cannot support more than the two million refugees already in the country.

12 February 2001 The Supreme Court starts hearings of petitions against the National Accountability Bureau (NAB) and the laws that brought it into being. The petitions allege that the NAB is being used strategically by the Musharraf government to target enemies and sanction human rights abuses.

23 February 2001 Retired Indian Army officers visit Lahore as part of an event planned by the India-Pakistan Soldiers Initiative for Peace.

1 March 2001 United Nations Secretary General Kofi Annan offers to mediate the Kashmir dispute. Pakistan says that it would welcome third-party mediation while India remains committed to a bilateral solution.

23 March 2001 The ruling military regime arrests members of the Alliance for the Restoration of Democracy (ARD). The arrests prevent the group from proceeding with their planned rally, which would have defied a national ban on political activity.

24–28 March 2001 The Institute of Women's Studies at Lahore holds a women's studies conference and drafts an unconditional apology to the Bangladeshis who suffered at the hands of the West Pakistan army in the 1971 war.

20 March–10 April 2001 Awami Tehrik and Sindhi Tehrik stage a march to protest government neglect and mismanagement of the Sindh region that had worsened the severity of a drought and its damages. Police arrest marchers throughout the entire protest. When the marchers reach Karachi, they are joined by MQM and JSQM activists.

16–19 April 2001 Four thousand demonstrators become violent in Karachi as they prepare for a general strike ordered by the MQM and JSQM to protest both national water policies and their treatment in previous protests. On April 19, the massive strikes throughout Sindh bring the region to a halt. The strike is to protest the extreme water shortage situation in Sindh as the drought continues and severely hinders agricultural activity. Police use tear gas, arrests, and beatings to quell the protests and the associated violence.

18 April 2001 The Supreme Court gives a judgment that overturns an earlier ruling against former Prime Minister Benazir Bhutto and her husband. The judgment accused Justice Malik Muhammad Qayyum of the Lahore High Court of deliberately miscarrying justice in the earlier ruling.

24 April 2001 The Supreme Court rules that the National Accountability Bureau Ordinance is legal, therefore lending legitimacy to the military government's accountability campaign.

12 May 2001 Zhou Rongji, China's Prime Minister, holds a ceremony with Pervez Musharraf during his trip to Pakistan to discuss Chinese/Pakistan relations. China supports Pakistan's demand for a resolution of the Kashmir conflict but maintains that Pakistan's defence issues are an internal matter. During the visit India stages massive war games near the Pakistani border.

18–19 May 2001 Sunni Tehrik leader Saleem Qadri and several of his companions are killed by gunmen in Karachi as they travel to Friday prayers. Some 500 mourners gather outside the hospital where the victims are taken. The crowd becomes violent and clashes with police.

22 May 2001 Lahore Joint Action Committee members stage a protest against the IMF and World Bank.

23 May 2001 India calls off its cease-fire in Kashmir but 'remains committed to exercising maximum restraint'.

25 May 2001 Indian Prime Minister Vajpayee formally invites Pervez Musharraf to travel to India to discuss outstanding issues between the two countries, including Kashmir. Musharraf accepts the invitation.

3 June 2001 Fourteen militants are killed in a gun battle with Indian police in disputed Kashmir.

13 June 2001 The MQM and JSQM jointly stage a sit-in along a major route to the Punjab in order both to pressure Punjabi authorities to share water resources and to protest police brutality during previous protests. Gunfire and bombs kill one policeman and injure fourteen other people when the protest turns violent.

June 2001 The Afghan refugee situation worsens at camps in Jalozai and in Kabul. Temperatures rise to 110 degrees. Dozens of deaths from malnutrition, disease, and lack of sanitation are reported.

20 June 2001 General Musharraf declares himself President of Pakistan, and replaces Rafiq Tarar. The new president pledges to hold elections in October 2002.

26 June 2001 Justice Malik Mohammad Qayyum resigns from the Lahore High Court after accusations by the Supreme Court that he miscarried justice in his conviction of former Prime Minister Benazir Bhutto and her husband Asif Zardari.

14–16 July 2001 General Pervez Musharaf meets with Indian Prime Minister Atal Behari Vajpayee at the Agra Summit. Talks end in a deadlock over Kashmir issues.

14 August 2001 A new system of local government is installed after direct elections had taken place during 2000 and 2001. Indirect elections for *nazims* had been held immediately prior in July and August.

15 August 2001 Musharraf outlines his plan for democracy and orders general elections for October 2002.

18 August 2001 An Additional Session Judge finds Dr Sheikh, an allopathic physician and teacher at a homeopathic medical college in Islamabad, guilty of the crime of blasphemy and sentences him to death.

19 August 2001 The government announces that the elections scheduled for October 2002 will be held on a party basis and existing bans on political rallies will be lifted ninety days prior to the elections.

6 September 2001 Indian Prime Minister Vajpayee announces that he and Musharraf plan to meet in New York where they both plan to travel for a UN General Assembly meeting in late September.

11 September 2001 (and immediate aftermath) Attacks on the United States lead to pressure on Pakistan to support US military operations in neighbouring Afghanistan. Pakistani authorities implore the Taliban to avert US military attacks by releasing Osama bin Laden into third-party custody. When the Taliban refuse to do so and the US rejects Taliban offers to discuss the issue, the military regime has little choice but to accept the United States' plans to attack Afghanistan.

21 September 2001 Strikes and protests against planned US attacks in neighbouring Afghanistan occur across the country. Karachi is brought to a standstill, and many protesters clash with police and become violent; four people are killed.

22 September 2001 In response to Pakistan's help during the current situation, the US ends nuclear non-proliferation related sanctions against Pakistan.

24 September 2001 The Afghan ambassador to Pakistan makes a statement at the Afghan embassy in which he says that the Taliban are still hoping to find a negotiated resolution to the current conflict so as to avoid further blood-shed in the war-torn country. Pakistan removes its diplomatic staff from Afghanistan, citing security concerns. Diplomatic ties nevertheless remain intact.

1 October 2001 Militants attack the state assembly complex in disputed Kashmir. Thirty-eight people are killed and seventy-five injured, including Indian security forces, employees of the legislature, and civilians. Tensions mount between Pakistan and India in the aftermath of the attack.

7–11 October 2001 As the US-led attacks begin against Afghanistan, reports are made of wide-spread devastation in Kabul. Anti-US protests continue and tribal groups pledge to support the Taliban. Approximately 2, 000 new Afghan refugees are entering Pakistan each day.

16 October 2001 During a trip to Pakistan, US Secretary of State Colin Powell meets with Musharraf to discuss plans for a broad-based democratic government (that would include moderate elements of the Taliban) in post-war Afghanistan.

17–18 October 2001 The US lifts remaining sanctions against Pakistan. The UK announces that $84 million of Pakistani debt will be forgiven as part of a debt relief package.

18–22 October 2001 Twenty-five people are killed in disputed Kashmir as Indian and Pakistani troops exchange fire across the LoC. As violence continues, Pakistan accuses India of escalating military activity in hopes of capitalizing on the Afghan crisis.

30 October 2001 Pakistan officially opens its borders to refugees fleeing from Afghanistan. UN agencies plan to open fifteen new camps.

8 November 2001 Maulana Abdul Sattar Edhi visits Afghanistan to assess the relief work being done by the Edhi Foundation there. He warns that four million Afghans have been dislocated by the US-led bombing and that these people face possible starvation and exposure to severe weather in the upcoming winter months.

10 November 2001 Musharraf addresses the UN General Assembly, assuring the world that Pakistan's nuclear weapons are in safe hands, requesting that the unsettled political disputes at the root of terrorist activity be addressed, and calling for the American-led bombing of Afghanistan to be stopped as soon as possible.

12 November 2001 Indian forces attack Pakistani positions along the LoC and the All Parties Hurriyat Conference calls for a ceasefire among all parties, including militants and Indian forces.

22 November 2001 Pakistan closes the Taliban embassy. The Foreign Office spokesperson states that Pakistan will reopen the embassy when a broad-based government is in place in Afghanistan.

13 December 2001 Islamist insurgents attack the Indian Parliament. Twelve people are killed and twenty-two others injured after five men attack the building with guns and grenades. All the gunmen are killed in the ensuing shootout with authorities. No ministers or members of parliament are injured in the attack. In the aftermath of the attack, India accuses Pakistan of harbouring terrorists and demands that twenty suspected militants be handed over to Indian authorities. As tensions mount, both nations deploy additional troops to their shared borders, and villagers flee from these areas.

19 December 2001 After arresting approximately 155 suspected Al-Qaeda operatives who had been caught fleeing into Pakistan, Pakistani security forces face a prisoner revolt in which seven Al-Qaeda suspects and six Pakistani security officers are killed. Twenty-one additional prisoners escape during the revolt, which occurred *en route* to a security facility in Kohar.

28 December–5 January 2001 After being postponed due to tensions between India and Pakistan, the South Asia Association for Regional Cooperation (SAARC) goes forward in Nepal. Both Musharraf and Vajpayee attended, but the two leaders failed to ease tensions between the two regional powers. Pakistan withdraws an undisclosed number of troops from the LoC in efforts to reduce tensions.

30 December 2001 Pakistani authorities arrest Masood Azhar, leader of the militant group Jaish-e-Mohammad, along with approximately fifty other members of two Kashmiri separatist groups accused of participating in terrorist activities.

12 January 2002 Musharraf pledges to crackdown on extremists and bans two Kashmiri separatist groups (Lashkar-e-Tayyaba and Jaish-e-Mohammed) as well as three other militant groups. He also calls for a negotiated settlement between India and Pakistan concerning Kashmir. Shortly after the groups are outlawed, approximately 1100 suspected militants are detained.

15 January 2002 US secretary of State, Colin Powell, travels to India and Pakistan where he urges leaders of both states to ease tensions along their borders and cooperate with international efforts to prevent terrorist activities.

27 January 2002 US journalist, Daniel Pearl, is captured by militants in Karachi.

5–8 February 2002 Three suspects are arrested and later charged with the abduction of US journalist Daniel Pearl.

13 February 2002 Musharraf is welcomed by US President George Bush in Washington, DC. The two hold a joint press conference where they pledge to support each other in ongoing anti-terrorist operations. Bush supports Musharraf's efforts to ease tensions between Pakistan and India by suggesting that the US could act as a third-party facilitator in talks between the two.

21 Februarys 2002 US journalist Daniel Pearl is confirmed to be dead after abductors release a video tape of his execution.

16 March 2002 Five are dead and forty-five are injured after militants bomb a Protestant church in Islamabad.

21 March 2002 British militant, Ahmed Omar Saeed Sheikh, is charged with kidnapping and murdering US journalist Daniel Pearl.

27 March–4 April 2002 Over several days, Pakistani authorities arrest and interrogate approximately 100 suspected Al-Qaeda operatives. These interrogations lead to the arrest of Abu Zubaydah, an allegedly high-ranking Al-Qaeda operative.

17 April 2002 Zafran Bibi is convicted of *Zina* and sentenced to be stoned to death by a judge in Kohat. This sentence is later suspended. (7 May 2002)

25 April 2002 Twelve people die and twenty-five others are injured when a bomb goes off during worship at a Shia mosque in Bhakkar. The bombing follows several violent attacks on prominent Shia individuals in Karachi. Sunni extremists are suspected of perpetrating the violence.

26 April 2002 Labour Party Pakistan (LPP) members are arrested while protesting the upcoming presidential referendum. They are later released following the referendum (on 30 April).

30 April 2002 Musharraf wins a controversial referendum endorsing his presidency. This victory will allow him to remain in power for five more years.

7 May 2002 A car bomb explodes next to a bus outside a Karachi hotel, leaving fourteen people dead, including eleven French citizens, and twenty or more wounded. While no one claims responsibility, anti-government militants are suspected.

14 May 2002 Kashmiri separatists attack an Indian army encampment in Kaluchak, killing nineteen people and injuring twenty-five. The gunmen were subsequently killed in a shoot-out with Indian soldiers.

May 2002 India and Pakistan both send additional troops to the line of control in Kashmir and place them on 'high alert'. For several days at the end of the month gunfire is exchanged between Indian and Pakistani troops. As tensions mount, Pakistan successfully tests medium range ballistic missiles in a show of strength intended to deter India from initiating a pre-emptive strike on Pakistan.

3 June 2002 While the heads of state of Pakistan and India attend an Asian summit in Kazakhstan, efforts to bring the leaders together to discuss peace fail.

7 June 2002 Amid great concern about a possible war between India and Pakistan, US Deputy Secretary of State, Richard Armitage, visits the region. After a cordial meeting with Musharraf, Mr Armitage relayed to Indian Prime Minister Vajpayee that Pakistan was acting in good faith in efforts both to disband militant groups in general and to prevent militants from entering Kashmir. While Armitage is in India an unmanned Indian spy plane is shot down near Lahore.

10 June 2002 As a gesture of non-aggression, India announces that it will lift the ban on Pakistani airliners flying over its territory. In addition, India moves several naval vessels from their placements near Pakistani waters.

12–18 June 2002 In ongoing efforts to prevent war in South Asia, US Secretary of Defence, Donald Rumsfeld, visits the region and meets with top officials in both countries. On 16 June, India announces that it will withdraw some of its troops from the LoC in disputed Kashmir. On 18 June, Pakistan announces that it will reciprocate.

13 June 2002 Ten people are killed and fifty-one other injured when a car bomb goes off at the US Consulate Office in Karachi. All of the victims are Pakistanis. The previously unknown group, 'Al-Qanoon', claims responsibility.

22 June 2002 A tribal council in Meerwala, a small village, sentences a thirty year old woman (Mukhtar Mai) to gang rape to avenge an alleged illicit affair between the victim's 12 year-old brother and a Mastoi tribal woman. The victim is raped by four men acting on the council's behalf.

26 June–3 July 2002 Ten Pakistani soldiers and several Al-Qaeda suspects are killed in fighting along the Afghan border.

7–10 July 2002 Anti-Pakistani demonstrations lead to a mob attacking and damaging the Pakistan embassy in Kabul (July 7). President Pervez Musharraf and Prime Minister Mir Zafarullah Khan Jamali meet on 8 July to discuss the situation while protests continue.

9 July Two gang rape suspects are held by Pakistani authorities in the Meerwala case.

10 July 2002 Musharraf issues a presidential order scheduling parliamentary elections for 10 October.

12 July 2002 The Pakistan Supreme Court upholds the validity of new laws requiring candidates running for Parliament to hold a university degree. Many who oppose the new laws feel the laws are too elitist because so few Pakistanis meet this requirement.

13 July 2002 Twenty-seven people are killed and many more injured in a grenade and gun attack on a residential area in Jammu. India blames Pakistan and claims that Pakistan is supporting insurgents in the area. The Pakistan government denounces the attack and urges India to promote a peaceful solution in the region. No militant groups claim responsibility.

14 July 2002 Ahmed Omar Saeed is sentenced to death and three others are sentenced to life imprisonment for their involvement in the kidnapping and murder of US journalist Daniel Pearl.

18–21 July 2002 British Foreign Secretary Jack Straw visits both Islamabad and New Delhi to discuss the violence in Kashmir with ministers on both sides.

26–28 July 2002 US secretary of State Colin Powel travels to India and Pakistan to meet with Musharraf and Vajpayee as well as with other senior officials from both governments.

5, 9 August 2002 Unidentified militants attack a Christian school in Murree (5 August) killing six and wounding several others. On 9 August, militants attack a Christian missionary hospital near Islamabad and kill six people (including one assailant) and injure twenty others. While no one claims responsibility for the attacks, the government names members of the militant group Lashkar-i-Jhangvi as suspects. Due to fears of additional violence, the American Cultural Center is closed.

23–25 August 2002 While US deputy secretary of state Richard Armitage is visiting South Asia to promote peace, India wages air strikes against Pakistani forces at the LoC. Armitage credits Pakistan with stemming the tide of militants crossing into Kashmir.

31 August 2002 Six men are sentenced to hanging by the anti-terrorism court after being found guilty of either raping or ordering the rape of Mukhtar Mai. Eight others were acquitted from charges that they also participated in the Meerwala gang-rape.

1 September 2002 Election officials in Pakistan ban former Prime Minister Benazir Bhutto from running in October's elections. Her supporters demonstrate in the streets and Musharraf receives international criticism for thwarting democracy.

13 September 2002 Pakistani security forces arrest Ramzi Binalshibh, an Al-Qaeda operative suspected of planning the World Trade Center bombings of 11 September 2001. On 16 September, he is put in US custody.

13–16 September 2002 As Indian authorities plan the upcoming elections in disputed Kashmir (16 September–8 October), violence leads to the death of several political activists and civilians. After two boys are killed by Indian troops, mourners protest in the streets. Indian authorities tear gas the crowds to break up the demonstration.

19 September 2002 Seven militants from the group Harkatul Mujahideen Al-Alami are arrested and their arms seized by Pakistani police. The militants are accused of carrying out an attack on the US consulate as well as attempting to assassinate the President on 26 April.

24 September 2002 Pakistan condemns the attack on a Hindu temple in Gujarat which killed thirty people. India blames Pakistan for the violence.

25 September 2002 Two gunmen kill seven workers at a Karachi Christian welfare agency.

4–8 October 2002 Pakistan successfully test fires a medium range ballistic missile and India successfully test fires a surface to air Akash missile (4 October). Pakistan again successfully test fires a medium range ballistic missile (8 October).

8 October 2002 Controversial elections finish in Kashmir. There is a very low turn out at the polls. From the time that elections had been announced in August until 8 October, 600 people have been killed.

10 October 2002 Pakistan holds elections for the National Assembly. Voter turn-out is low. Observers have differing claims as to the transparency and fairness of the polling. Of the 272 seats, seventy-six were won by the pro-military Pakistan Muslim League (Q); sixty-two were won by the People's Party Parliamentarians; fifty-one were won by the Muttahida Majlis-i-Amal party; twenty-six were won by independents; fourteen were won by the Pakistan

Muslim League (N); thirteen were won by the Muttahida Qaumi Movement; eleven were won by the National Alliance; and the rest were won by smaller parties.

16–24 October 2002 India and Pakistan pull back troops from their border regions.

3 November 2002 An earthquake in the Northern Areas of Pakistan kills ten, injures thirty, and leaves 1,500 homeless.

6 November 2002 Upcoming Senate elections (scheduled for November 12) are postponed by the government on the grounds that the provincial and national assemblies that form the Electoral College have yet to convene.

21 November 2002 Zafarullah Khan Jamali of the Muslim League (Q) party is elected Prime Minister by the newly elected parliament by winning 172 out of 329 votes.

14 December 2002 Violence continues in Kashmir: seven Kashmiris and one Indian soldier die.

25 December 2002 Three young girls are killed and sixteen injured during a grenade attack on a Presbyterian Church in Daska.

January 2003 After US President, George Bush makes statements (29 December) encouraging India to take note of Pakistan's efforts to stem militant activity, US State Department official Richard Haas attends a meeting in Hyderabad, India and urges India to seek a peaceful solution to its conflict with Pakistan. India threatens to annihilate Pakistan if it uses nuclear weapons in retaliation for Indian military attacks (7 January).

9 January 2003 Three Al-Qaeda suspects are arrested after a shootout between suspects and US FBI agents acting with Pakistani police in Karachi.

16 January 2003 By-elections are held in Pakistan to fill ten seats in the National Assembly and eighteen seats in the four provincial assemblies. While the pro-military PML-Q wins three of the national seats and ten of the provincial seats, many observers are surprised by how well the MMA party does; they win three national seats and two provincial seats.

22–24 January 2003 India accuses four Pakistani diplomatic officials of carrying out activities incompatible with their mission and sends them back to Pakistan. Pakistan responds by expelling three members of the Indian diplomatic staff.

9 February 2003 After India expels five more diplomatic officials, Pakistan responds in kind. The expulsions signal yet further deterioration in relations between the two countries.

20 February 2003 Pakistan's Air Chief Marshal Mushaf Ali Mir and sixteen other passengers die when their plane crashes near Kohat. Musharraf makes a public statement honouring the lost air force leader.

22 February 2003 A Shia mosque in Karachi is attacked, leaving nine dead and seven others wounded.

1 March 2003 Khalid Shaikh Mohammed, the alleged third ranking officer of the Al-Qaeda network and planner of the 9/11 attacks in New York, is arrested in Pakistan.

2–23 March 2003 On 2 March, thousands protest in Karachi and in Rawalpindi, and on 9 March nearly 100,000 people march in a protest condemning US plans to attack Iraq. The marches had been planned by the MMA (Muttahida Majlis-i-Amal) party. Protests continue throughout the month as the US plans and carries out its invasion of Iraq. The Pakistani government expresses concern over US plans.

24 March 2003 Twenty-four people are killed when militants attack Hindu-minority civilians in Nandimarg Village in Kashmir. India blames Pakistan for the massacre. Pakistan condemns the violence.

18 April 2003 Indian Prime Minister Vajpayee gives a talk in Srinagar in which he offers to participate in talks with both Pakistan and Kashmiri groups. The overture is greeted enthusiastically by Pakistani Prime Minister Jamali who states that Pakistan has long wished to settle the issue of Kashmir and bring peace to the region.

28 April 2003 Pakistan's Prime Minister Zafarullah Khan Jamali has a 'positive' exchange with Indian Prime Minister Atal Bihari Vajpayee over the telephone. The discussion is hailed as a move forward in reducing hostilities between the two countries.

29 April 2003 Continued violence leaves six Indian soldiers and thirteen separatists dead in the Doda district of disputed Kashmir.

2 May 2003 Two rockets target a women's development NGO in Dir. No one is killed in the attack, but women express their concern over the rising level of violence directed at NGOs since the US-led bombing of Afghanistan began in the fall of 2001.

2 May 2003 India and Pakistan take steps to normalize relations by pledging to restore diplomatic relations and holding talks concerning the disputed territory of Kashmir. India offers to open rail and air transportation links between the two countries.

5 May 2003 Pakistan offers to destroy its nuclear weapons on the condition that India does so as well. On 8 May, India officially refuses the offer.

6 May 2003 In further efforts to bring peace to South Asia, Pakistan announces that it too will reopen ground and air transportation between India and Pakistan.

8–10 May 2003 US Deputy Secretary of State Richard Armitage visits both Islamabad and New Delhi on his trip to Asia. He encourages both sides to continue peace efforts.

29 May 2003 Pakistani authorities arrest suspected militant Qari Abdul Hayee of the banned militant group Lashkar-e-Jhangvi. He is suspected of participating in the kidnapping and murder of US journalist Daniel Pearl.

2 June 2003 The NWFP provincial assembly, led by the MMA, unanimously votes to adopt the North West Frontier Province Shariat Bill, 2003. The 15-point law will go into effect immediately. Among other provisions, the law requires universities to be segregated by sex and bans male doctors from seeing female patients.

15 June 2003 Musharraf makes a rare appearance on television to discuss his upcoming travels to Britain, France, Germany, and the US. He states that he will ask the US to recognize Pakistan's cooperation in the 'war on terror' by offering concrete economic help and bringing pressure to bear on India to resolve the Kashmir conflict.

17 June 2003 Pakistani forces arrest alleged Al-Qaeda operative Adil Al-Jazeeri, an Algerian national, and hand him over to American officials who move him to an 'undisclosed location' for interrogation.

24 June 2003 US President George Bush welcomes Musharraf to Camp David and praises his efforts to stem terrorist activity both in Pakistan and Afghanistan. The two leaders reportedly discuss economic incentives that Pakistan may receive.

27 June 2003 Pakistani security forces arrest alleged Al-Qaeda operative and Egyptian national Haris bin Asim in Peshawar. The suspect has in his possession a video tape that purportedly contains footage of Osama bin Laden warning of attacks on US interests in Saudi Arabia.

30 June 2003 An anti-terrorism court sentences three men to death who had been found guilty of planting a car bomb that killed eleven French engineers in Karachi the previous year.

1 July 2003 Human rights activists in the North West Frontier Province vigorously campaign against the new Sharia Implementation Act of 2003 and the Hisba Act. Activists fear that these pieces of legislation, which were unanimously supported by the ruling six party religious alliance (Muttahida Majlis-e-Amal) in the NWFP general assembly, will result in not only serious curbs on women's mobility and freedom, but also sanction vigilantism in other provinces.

4 July 2003 Three gunmen kill fifty worshippers and injure over sixty more at a Shiite mosque in Quetta during Friday prayers. After police shoot one of the attackers, the other two blow themselves up. Many citizens come out to protest the violence and sympathize with the mourners.

8 July 2003 Munawwar Mohsin, a journalist from the *Frontier Post*, is sentenced to life imprisonment after being arrested on 29 January, 2001 for allowing a sacrilegious letter to the editor to be printed under his watch.

9 July 2003 Hundreds of Afghans break into and loot the Pakistan embassy in Kabul to protest clashes that had been occurring along the Pakistan/Afghanistan border. Afghan President Hamid Karzai makes a public statement condemning the attack; Pakistan closes down its embassy.

27 July–31 August 2003 The Greek oil tanker, the *Tasman Spirit*, is grounded on a Karachi beach. When the ship breaks apart, almost 30,000 tons of oil spill into the water causing an environmental disaster and creating a health crisis for both the wildlife and human residents of the area.

5 August 2003 Benazir Bhutto (former Prime Minister of Pakistan) and her husband are convicted of money laundering by a Swiss court. The two, are ordered to pay $11 million to the Pakistani government as well as to each serve a six-month suspended jail term. At this time, Benazir is living in self-imposed exile and her husband, Asif Ali Zardari is already in jail on various charges.

24 August 2003 Naseem Bibi, a forty-five year old widow accused of blasphemy, dies in custody at Lahore's Kot Lakhpat Jail after over a year of detention. Her two co-accused teenage sons await trial in this case, which critics claim is motivated by a personal vendetta.

26 August 2003 A bomb kills fifty-two people and injures another 150 in Bombay, India. The Indian government blames Kashmiri separatists. Pakistan condemns the blasts, reaffirming its opposition to violence directed at civilians.

19 September 2003 A large bomb blast in a Karachi business district leaves several buildings damaged but no one is injured.

23 September 2003 Fourteen students from Malaysia and Indonesia, including the brother of alleged Indonesian Al-Qaeda leader Riduan Ismauddin, are arrested in Karachi and held as terrorist suspects.

27 September 2003 Nawabzada Nasrullah Khan, chief of the opposition group, the Alliance for the Restoration of Democracy, dies. People from all levels of government publicly express their condolences.

1 October 2003 Prime Minister Mir Zafarullah Khan Jamali meets with US president George Bush. The two agree to continue joint efforts to combat terrorism.

2 October 2003 In an intense, all day gun battle in Waziristan near the Afghan border, eight suspected terrorists and two Pakistani soldiers are killed. Eighteen suspects are taken into custody.

6 October 2003 Maulana Azam Tariq, MNA and leader of a banned sectarian Sunni group, and his body guards are killed by unidentified gunmen in Islamabad. Anti-Shia violence breaks out across the country as he is mourned by his followers.

23 October 2003 India's foreign minister proposes several possible steps toward normalizing relations between the two countries. Pakistan welcomes these efforts, but expresses regret that India did not include an offer to resume substantive dialogue concerning Kashmir.

30 October 2003 Pakistan agrees to several parts of the twelve-point proposal offered by India and commits to further discussing such critical issues as Kashmir.

15 November 2003 Three Islamist groups are banned by the Pakistan government in efforts to curb extremist violence and other terrorist activities. The three groups are: Islami Tehrik Pakistan (formerly Tehrik-i-Jafria Pakistan), Millat-i-Islamia Pakistan (formerly Sipah-i-Sahaba Pakistan), and Khuddam-ul-Islam (formerly Jaish-i-Mohammad).

22 November 2003 Prime Minister Mir Zafarullah Jamali announces a unilateral ceasefire along the Line of Control in Kashmir. In the same speech, he announces his desire to open bus, ferry, and air services between India and Pakistan. On 26 November, the cease-fire goes into effect.

11 December 2003 Six Indonesian students who had been arrested in September on charges of terrorism are released to Indonesia.

14 December 2003 Pervez Musharraf survives an assassination attempt in which a large bomb exploded under a bridge just seconds after he and his entourage had passed over it. No one is injured.

18 December 2003 Pakistan authorities arrest two French journalists on charges of violating visa restrictions by traveling to Quetta.

25 December 2003 Pervez Musharraf survives a second assassination attempt. Two suicide bombers target his convoy, but the president escapes unharmed.

31 December 2003 Pakistan's parliament passes the Seventeenth Amendment retroactively validating General Pervez Musharraf's rule and legalizing several of his policy initiatives. The amendment requires that he win a vote of confidence by the Electoral College (the parliament and provincial assemblies) in order to secure the five year term as president that he won in a highly controversial referendum on 30 April, 2002.

1 January 2004 General Pervez Musharraf wins an Electoral College vote of confidence, enabling him to serve as president with constitutional legitimacy until 2007.

1 January 2004 Air travel is opened between Pakistan and India.

3–5 January 2004 India's Prime Minister Atal Bihari Vajpayee visits Pakistan for the first time in four years to attend the 12th SAARC Summit Conference. Vajpayee and Musharraf meet on state-run television, and in a highly symbolic gesture of goodwill, shake hands while agreeing to hold future talks in order to resolve the dispute in Kashmir.

6–24 January 2004 Pakistan is accused of proliferating nuclear weapons technologies illegally, particularly to Libya, Iran, and North Korea. As Pakistan questions officials, scientists involved in the nuclear programme are barred from leaving the country until the investigation is complete. On the 23rd, General Pervez

Musharraf announces that the investigation has turned up evidence suggesting that some scientists from Pakistan's nuclear programme have been selling weapons designs. Musharraf assures the international community that these activities have not been condoned either by the state or the military. Abdul Qadeer Khan, the father of Pakistan's nuclear programme, is suspected of participating.

11 January 2004 Two French journalists who had been arrested for violating visa restrictions are each sentenced to six months imprisonment and deported.

13 January 2004 Pakistan's Prime Minister, Zafarullah Khan Jamali, visits Afghanistan and pledges Pakistan's cooperation to the Afghan government.

18 January 2004 Many lawmakers protest by either walking out or booing when President Pervez Musharraf gives his first address to parliament since taking control of the government in October 1999.

28 January 2004 Khawar Mehdi Rizvi, a Pakistani journalist, is charged with sedition and conspiracy for allegedly assisting two French journalists in their illegal travel to Quetta.

31 January 2004 Due to mounting evidence that he may have been involved in the illegal sale of nuclear weapon's technologies, Abdul Qadeer Khan is dismissed from his position as a high-level advisor to the Pakistan government.

4–5 February 2004 Abdul Qadeer Khan confesses to having illegally sold nuclear weapons technologies; he apologizes to the nation and takes full responsibility for his actions, absolving the state of any complicity. General Pervez Musharraf pardons this highly respected national hero for his crimes.

17 February 2004 Representatives from India and Pakistan meet to discuss up-coming peace talks. They agree on a 'road map for peace' and schedule talks concerning Kashmir, terrorism, and economic issues that will take place over the following six months.

2 March 2004 As Shiite worshippers participate in a holy day procession in Quetta, gunmen open fire on them, killing forty people and wounding 150 others before killing themselves.

11 March 2004 Pakistan hosts India's cricket team for the first time in fifteen years. The welcome received by the Indian players and thousands of their fans signals an important step toward friendlier relations between the two frequently warring countries.

14 March 2004 Khan Research Laboratories is further implicated in illegal activities, including illegal cooperation with North Korea's nuclear programme.

15 March 2004 Musharraf makes his first public statements concerning the investigation of two attempts to assassinate him. He reveals that authorities suspect a Libyan national with links to Al-Qaeda.

16–28 March 2004 Heavy fighting on 16 March between troops and suspected militants in South Waziristan (a tribal region near the Afghan border) leaves twenty-four suspected militants and fourteen soldiers dead. The massive military initiative continues until March 20 when 100 suspected foreign militants and their local supporters are arrested. On 25 March, 140 more suspected militants and their protectors are arrested. After militants release eleven hostages, the Pakistani army ends its operations, allowing the NWFP governor to restore law and order to the devastated tribal area.

4 April 2004 Gunmen attack the Gulistan-i-Jauhar police station in Karachi, killing five police officers.

5 April 2004 Pakistan proposes talks with India concerning nuclear confidence building measures.

6 April 2004 Nine suspects are arrested on charges related to Karachi suicide bombings.

7 May 2004 Twenty-three people are killed and eighty-seven wounded when a suicide bomber attacks the Sindh Madrasatul Islam Mosque in Karachi during Friday prayers.

13 May 2004 Congress Party wins elections in India. This change of ruling party raises concerns in Pakistan that recent gains made in the relations between Pakistan and India may be lost.

22 May 2004 Pakistan is reinstated by the British Commonwealth after having been suspended after the military take-over of General Pervez Musharraf in October 1999. The committee, announcing the reinstatement, expressed a strong desire for Pakistan to continue to work towards restoring full democracy.

29 May 2004 Prime Minister Mir Zafarullah Khan Jamali talks with the new Indian Prime Ministser, Dr Manmohan Singh over the phone. Mr Jamali reiterates Pakistan's resolve concerning bringing about a lasting peace between the two countries. Dr Singh assures Mr Jamali that his government plans to build on the progress made thus far between the two countries.

31 May 2004 The Imambargah Ali Raza in Karachi is attacked by a suicide bomber. Twenty-four people are killed during the attack and violence immediately follows. The city is brought to a stop the next day as mourners' protests erupt into violence.

8 June 2004 Thousands attend the funeral of slain moderate Kashmiri leader Maulvi Mushtaq Ahmed. He had been shot on 29 May, and died of his wounds on 6 June.

9 June 2004 Tensions erupt into large scale clashes between suspected militants and military personnel in South Waziristan after local efforts to end militant activity in the area fail. Fifteen soldiers and twenty suspected militants are killed. Fighting continues as the military attacks tribal areas where the residents are accused of supporting militants.

10 June 2004 An assassination attempt on the Corps Commander of Karachi kills eleven and injures twelve more. The commander escapes unharmed.

13 June 2004 Eight Al-Qaeda suspects are detained. The suspects are accused of being involved in multiple attacks in Karachi and Quetta, including the 10 June attack on a Corps Commander in Karachi.

17 June 2004 PPP activist and close associate of Benazir Bhutto, Munawwar Suhrawardy, is killed by unknown assailants.

18 June 2004 A delegation of six travels to New Delhi to discuss nuclear confidence building measures between Pakistan and India. The two countries agree to several measures to prevent nuclear conflict including a high-level hotline between the two powers and a continued ban on nuclear testing.

26 June 2004 Prime Minister Zafarullah Jamali resigns from office, dissolves the cabinet, and nominates Chaudhry Shujaat Hussain (the president of the Pakistan Muslim League) as his successor. Former Finance Minister and General Prevez Musharraf's ally, Shaukat Aziz is slated to become the next prime minister after Chaudhry Shujaat Hussain has finished his interim term in office.

13 July 2004 Ashraf Jehangir Qazi is chosen to be the UN's top envoy to Iraq. Mr Qazi has forty years of experience in the Foreign Service of Pakistan and most recently served as Pakistan's ambassador to the United States.

21 July 2004 Joint US/Pakistan military operations against Al-Qaeda in South Waziristan force thousands of Afghan refugees to flee the area. UN refugee workers report a looming humanitarian crisis.

23–26 July 2004 Two Pakistani men from villages in Azad Kashmir, Raja Azad Khan (an engineer) and Sajid Naeem (a driver), are abducted (23 July) and executed (27 July) in Iraq by a militant group calling itself the 'Islamic Army of Iraq'. The two had no political connections in Iraq; they had each taken jobs there to provide for their families.

30 July 2004 In an apparent attempt to assassinate Pakistan's prime minister-designate, Shaukat Aziz, extremists calling themselves the 'Islambouli Brigade of Al-Qaeda' kill eight people in a suicide attack after an election meeting.

9 August 2004 Pakistan registers its protest with the United States after an FBI operation used a fictitious plot involving a plan to kill Pakistan's ambassador to the United Nations, Mr Muneer Akram, as a means to trap the alleged terrorist Mohammed Hossain. Pakistan accused the United States of unnecessarily endangering Mr Akram's life.

18 August 2004 Shaukat Aziz wins a seat in Parliament, qualifying him to replace Zafarullah Khan Jamali, who resigned as prime minister in June. General Pervez Musharraf had already designated Mr Aziz, his colleague and finance minister, to be the preferred replacement.

23–24 August 2004 President Hamid Karzai of Afghanistan visits Islamabad. He and Musharraf pledge to work together to prevent Islamist militants from interfering with the upcoming elections in Afghanistan.

8 September–30 September 2004 The military and militants continue to clash in South Waziristan. On 14 September the government reiterates its offer of amnesty to foreign militants who are willing to register with the authorities and live peacefully in the region. Opposition party members continue to question the purpose and ethical legitimacy of military operations in the area.

12 September 2004 After three years in custody, 368 Pakistani prisoners of war who were fighting alongside the Taliban against US coalition forces are released to Pakistani authorities in Peshawar where they are to be screened and then sent home.

10–18 September 2004 Senior members of the Pakistani government, including the newly elected Prime Minister, Shaukat Aziz, publicly request that Pervez Musharraf remain the head of the military. On 18 September, Pakistan Muslim League President Chaudhry Shujaat Hussain announces that parliament will decide whether or not to overturn Article 63-1(d) of the constitution that requires Musharraf to step down as Chief of the Army Staff by December 2004.

Index